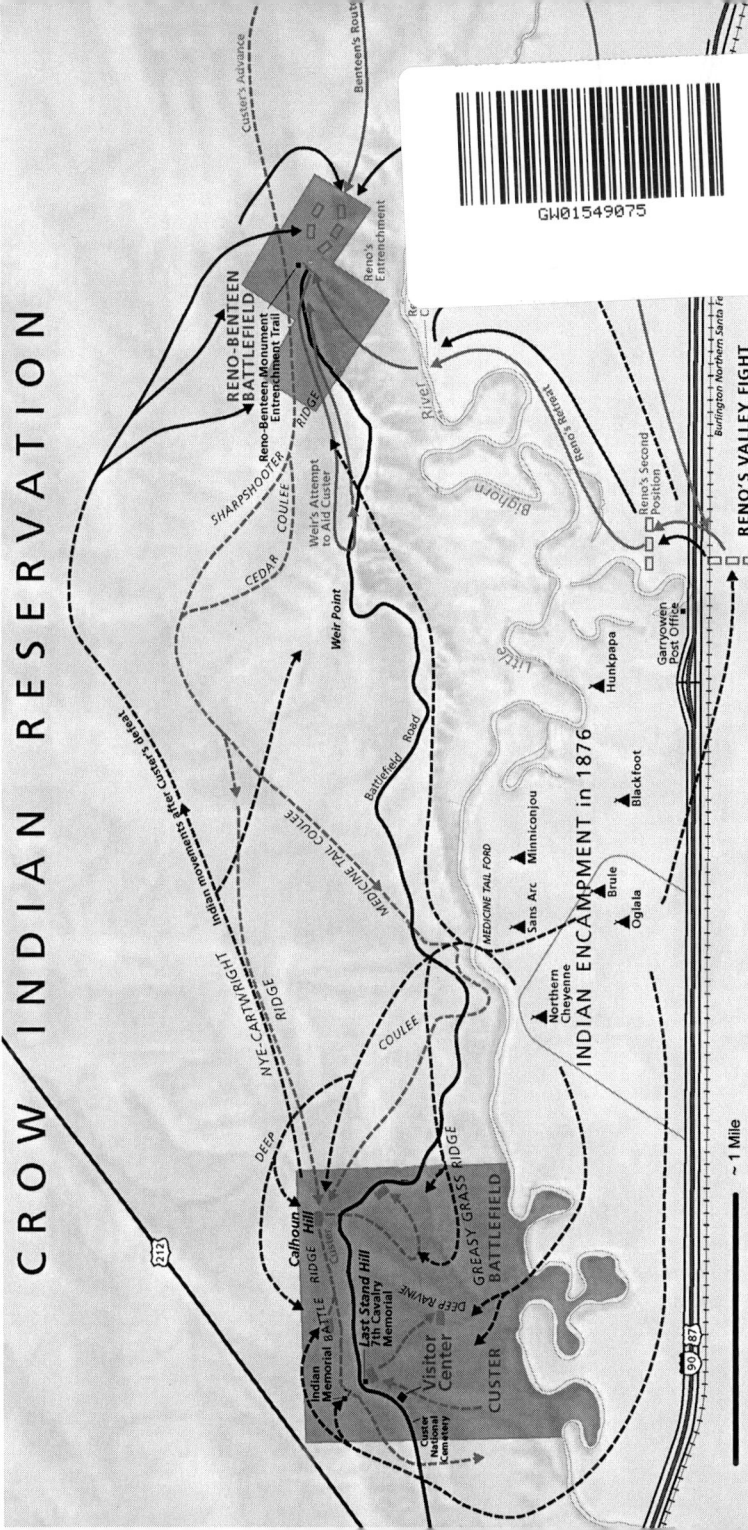

FREDERICK W. BENTEEN

BRAZEN TRUMPET

FREDERICK BENTEEN AND THE BATTLE OF THE LITTLE BIG HORN

BY TERRENCE J. DONOVAN

Copyright ©2007 Terrence J. Donovan
All Rights Reserved
First Edition: corrected, updated and reprinted, 2009

Maps designed by Shawn Coyle and Alan Radecki. Graphic data from National Park Service, U.S. Geological Survey. Topographic contouring licensed from Topozone.com, composite rendering by Alan Radecki

Inside front cover: Map showing the known and surmised movements and disposition of combatants at the Battle of the Little Big Horn. Black solid line: known Indian movements. Black dashed lines: inferred Indian movements. Gray solid lines: known troop movements. Gray dashed lines: inferred troop movements. North is approximately along the diagonal from lower right to upper left.

ISBN 978-0-615-22077-2

CONTENTS

Preface i

1 - None So Cursed 1
2 - Epiphany 27
3 - The Fighting Seventh 55
4 - Plenty of Indians for Us All 95
5 - Across the River . . . and Into the Trees 129
6 - High Ground 157
7 - Diligence or Dalliance 193
8 - End of the Line 235
Appendix A - Benteen's Anonymous Letter to the *Missouri Democrat* 245
Appendix B - Benteen's Official Report 253
Appendix C - Benteen's Letter to the *Kansas City Times* 257
Appendix D - Benteen's Medical Examination Report 265
Appendix E - Numerical Precision and Uncertainty 271
Bibliography 275

All stories are still alive, all stories have colors in them... The past - all stories...all colored. So we chose our colors... We chose what colors we see.
-Tu Shu, in *Antarctica* by Kim Stanley Robinson.

PREFACE

First, a word about what this book is not. This is not a biography of Frederick Benteen. It is an analysis of Benteen's actions up to and during the Battle of the Little Big Horn set in the context of his relationship with George Armstrong Custer and the 7th Cavalry. Stephen Pyne, biographer of the great geologist G.K. Gilbert, referred to Gilbert's approach to science as a process of converting a problem of geography and history into one of geometry and physics. I have attempted to apply that same methodology to some of the events associated with what is commonly known as Custer's Last Stand. I have drawn from what I consider to be the most reliable historical sources and recent archeological discoveries. But in the end, what is presented here is my interpretation and any shortcomings therein must rest on my shoulders alone.

I am indebted to a number of people for lively discussion on military matters and history, especially my present and former colleagues at the National Test Pilot School: Tom Benson, John

TERRENCE J. DONOVAN

Bush, Steve Cherry, Ken Clarke, George Cusimano, John Hagen, Greg Lewis, Sean Roberts, Russ Stewart and Fred Watts. Louise Arnold-Friend, Chief Librarian, U.S. Army Military History Institute, Carlisle Barracks, was particularly helpful in tracking down old Army regulations. Myron F. Steves provided information about the Benteen family history. Jerry Keenan and the late Don Rickey virtually overwhelmed me with their knowledge of the Frontier Army and the Indian Wars. Long conversations with John Doyle helped round out my insights into Benteen's soldierly character. John Doerner of the U.S. Park Service at the Battlefield was of great assistance in sharing some of his thoughts on the Benteen scout with me. Sherry Cappa edited an early draft of the manuscript and Karol Asay critically and insightfully edited and reviewed the final version.

I am grateful to Ed Harris for his careful review of the mathematical treatment in Chapter 7. Doug O'Brien contributed the digitized cross sections of the Custer and Benteen routes. A special tip of the hat goes to my publisher, Alan Radecki, of Mojave-West Books. Many thanks to Jan Duggan and Putt Thompson. Charles and Shawn Real Bird, of the Crow Reservation, my horse wranglers, rode Benteen's route with me, sustained by Ramona Real Bird's amazing hot lunch on the trail, followed by a scrumptious dinner at the Real Bird Ranch at Garry Owen. I thank my sweat lodge comrades, Charles and Floyd Real Bird and Wayne Moccasin, for sharing their spirituality with me along the banks of the Little Big Horn on a dark, starry night under Montana's big sky.

Finally, I want to dedicate this meager work not only to my loving wife and greatest supporter, Sharon, but also to my friends, colleagues and former students, who, in the eloquent words of Earnest Gann, now "rest with wings forever folded."

Fred Daniloff, U.S. Army, 1974
John Bishop, US Army, Retired; National Test Pilot School, 1991
John Rattenborg, Royal Danish Air Force, 1994
Rick Culpan, South African Air Force, Retired; Denel Corporation; 1997
Erwin Danuwinata, Industri Pesawat Terbang Nusantara, 1997
Stanley Halim, Industri Pesawat Terbang Nusantara,1997
Didik Permadi, Industri Pesawat Terbang Nusantara,1997
Steve Gallinetti, South African Air Force, Retired, 1998
Hans Oesch, Flight Test Consultants, Inc., 1998
Benoit Nicklaus, French Navy, Retired; International Test Pilot School, 1998
Eric Fiore, Bombardier, 2000
Judson Brohmer, National Test Pilot School and Lockheed Martin, 2001
Affandi Malik, Indonesian Air Force, 2003
Carroll Beeler, U.S. Navy, Retired; Sino Swearingen, 2003
Rick Weinberg, University of Illinois, 2003
Ron Bradley, U.S. Air Force, Retired; National Test Pilot School, 2003
Cheongon Kim, Republic of Korea Air Force, 2003
Dick Lawyer, U.S. Air Force, Retired; National Test Pilot School, 2005
Marta Bohn-Meyer, NASA, 2005
A. Scott Crossfield, World Aerospace Community, 2006
Ed Lewis, NASA, 2007
Greg Jaspers, U.S. Air Force, Retired, 2008
Dave Stock, South African Air Force (Retired), South African Airways 2009

TERRENCE J. DONOVAN

CHAPTER 1

NONE SO CURSED

Despite the dramatic and startling victory by the Sioux and Cheyenne over the 7th Cavalry at the Little Big Horn River in 1876, the U. S. Army was successful in the last quarter of the century in methodically corralling wayward warring tribes and in destroying the Indian way of life. Indian resistance to settlement and railroads faded but did not disappear entirely until near the end of the century.

The Army dealt harshly with the Indians, and when and where they could, the Indians retaliated. General William Tecumseh Sherman, Commander in Chief of the U.S. Army, and General Phillip Sheridan, commanding the Army's Department of the Missouri, were charged with the subjugation of the Indians, and they pursued their task forcefully even though President Grant had initiated an Indian "Peace-Policy" in 1869-1870. But like his own administration, the "Peace Policy" was fraught with corruption and fraud; it did not result in any peace, and in fact the policy resulted in "some of the bitterest warfare in the history of Indian relations."[1]

In 1868, at Fort Laramie, the United States and the main northern plains bands of Cheyenne and Sioux Indians had concluded the Laramie Treaty. The treaty ended Red Cloud's War, a bloody conflict between the Lakota Sioux, under Chief Red Cloud, and the U. S. Army. Red Cloud and his warriors had gone on the warpath to halt the westward flood of white men and close the migratory route known as the Bozeman trail.

The highlight of the resistance for the Indians came on 21 December 1866, when they annihilated Captain William J. Fetterman and his command of 80 troopers.[2] The provisions of the treaty were by and large favorable to the Sioux and the Great Sioux Reservation, encompassing all of what is now South Dakota west of the Missouri River, was created.

The accord called for abandonment of Forts Phil Kearny, Reno, and C. F. Smith, which had been established to protect the Bozeman Trail, and closure of the trail itself.[3] There was also established, as unceded Indian Territory, an enormous parcel of land loosely defined as "that country north of the North Platte River and east of the summits of the Big Horn Mountains" for the benefit of the Indians.[4]

A number of the Indians settled near the Bureau of Indian Affairs agencies to partake of the white man's "generosity." Others, under the Hunkpapa Sioux medicine man Sitting Bull, elected to roam the unceded territory despite entreaties by the government to settle down. It was an agreeable impasse soon made

---

1. Utley, *Indian Frontier,* 155.
2. Jerry Keenan, *Indian Wars,* 187.
3. Ibid, 24-25.
4. Utley, *Controversy,* 18.

untenable by the continued westward flood of settlers and explorers.[5]

As the expansion of the United States began to accelerate in the late 1800s, the Central Rocky Mountain region loomed big in the immigrant's eyes with its vast reaches of land, mineral resources, abundant game and timber. Portions of this area envied by the whites were occupied by various bands of Ute Indians, mainly central and western Colorado, northwestern New Mexico and eastern Utah. Primarily hunters, the Utes traded with Mexicans, the Navajo and Paiutes for necessities but were not averse to raiding other tribes or settlers for horses and cattle.

The Utes entered into their first treaty with the U.S. Government in 1850. But by the summer of 1886 they were riled to the point of war. Having been forcibly removed to the Uintah reservation in eastern Utah from their native lands in Colorado six years earlier, they were in no mood for the shenanigans they perceived were going on at the Indian agency. In late 1879, they had taken to the warpath against a self-righteous and overbearing reservation agent and then thumped a cavalry column dispatched to help him.[6] Only brilliant peacemaking by Chief Ouray had averted a full-scale Indian war. But now Ouray was dead, and the pot simmered.

In early August 1886, Brigadier General George Crook, commanding general of the Department of the Platte, had dispatched three companies of the 21st Infantry Regiment from Fort Sidney into Utah Territory to ward off with a show of force any potential trouble with the Utes. Crook's plan was to maintain a presence by building a fort on the reservation. A grizzled, irascible, 52 year old Civil War hero, veteran Indian fighter, and sometime tippler,

---
5. Ibid, 19.
6. Miller, *Milk Creek*, 1997.

Major Frederick W. Benteen now serving with the 9th Cavalry, was selected to be commander of the new fort. A squadron of two companies from the 9th (B and E) at Fort McKinney, Wyoming Territory, under the command of Benteen, was to join Crook at Fort Bridger, in southwestern Wyoming, for the trek south to Utah. Crook was impatient, stung by lingering criticism of his actions ten years previous at the Battle of the Rosebud, where he was soundly whipped by the Sioux in a prelude to the Battle of the Little Big Horn a week later. His ineffective campaign against Geronimo had resulted in his being relieved of his command of the Department of Arizona, in April 1886.[7] Clearly his reputation and career could not bear his letting the Utes gain an upper hand. An agitated and peeved Crook awaited Benteen's squadron.

Benteen, a surviving officer of Custer's 7th Cavalry's fateful encounter with the Sioux Nation at the Little Big Horn in 1876, had a busy summer.[8] He had been feuding for some time with his commanding officer at Fort McKinney, Colonel Edward Hatch, and now, in the summer of 1886, they were barely speaking. Benteen was chronically ill, many of his ailments no doubt arising from more than twenty hard years in a cavalry saddle, mostly on the frontier. His ill health had not prevented him from performing his duties, but with difficulty. Nonetheless, Colonel Hatch relieved him of his assignment as post range officer and had him carried

---

7. Mills, *Harvest,* 343. Crook had quarreled with his superior, General Phil Sheridan, over his conduct of the Apache campaign and had asked to be relieved. Sheridan promptly agreed, replacing Crook with General Nelson A. Miles. O'Connor, *Sheridan,* 350-51. Sheridan insisted that his orders be carried out to the letter. Crook negotiated surrender with Geronimo with an unauthorized proviso that the Apaches could return to Arizona after their incarceration, which infuriated Sheridan. When the Apaches learned that part of the bargain would not be honored by the War Department, they bolted, further enraging Sheridan. Sheridan quickly accepted Crook's request for relief of his command.
8. Mills, *Harvest,* 340-42.

on post and regimental reports as "sick in quarters," much to Benteen's chagrin.[9] But on 23 June 1886, he was detached from Fort McKinney to Fort Custer to partake in the 10th Anniversary of the Battle of the Little Big Horn. Lieutenant Herbert J. Slocum, who joined the 7th Cavalry, fresh from West Point, in July 1876 after Custer's defeat, organized the fete. At the battlefield, the participants apparently had a rollicking good time; liquor flowed freely and Benteen and another survivor of the disaster, Captain Tom McDougall, as well as other comrades, new and old, got riproaring drunk. Benteen met with other veterans of the battle, including Captains Edgerly and Godfrey, Dr. Porter, and White Swan, the Crow Scout. Also there was Gall, the Sioux war chief who played a major role in the Indian victory. According to Slocum, Gall could not recall where Custer fell, and at the time of the fight, was under the impression the Indians were not battling Custer but Crook, whom they had soundly whipped the week before. There is no evidence that Gall was ill-treated or made unwelcome by the Army participants.[10] In fact, just the opposite was true. Unhappy with the way the interpreter was handling his translation, Gall motioned Godfrey aside and they rode, along with Godfrey's orderly, to Calhoun hill. There, Gall, with sign language, pidgin English and Sioux, graphically told his story of the Custer battle.[11]

In the intervening years since Custer's defeat, Benteen fared well in the Army. He distinguished himself in the 1877 Battle of Canyon Creek against the Nez Perce, for which (along with his

---

9. Post Returns, Fort McKinney, March-April-May 1886, in Mills, *Harvest,* 341.
10. Hammer, *Camp.* Lieutenant Slocum, who organized the celebration, recalled years later that the participants "camped there a week and had a royal time."
11. Godfrey, in Graham, *Myth,* 93.

actions at the Little Big Horn) he would receive his fourth and last brevet, that of Brigadier General. He was considered a capable and reliable officer. Reasonable and comfortable assignments followed: garrison duty; Army Board evaluating weapons at the Springfield Arsenal in Massachusetts; cavalry recruiting officer in New York; special training course in veterinary science; Post Commander, Fort Sill, Oklahoma. While in New York, on 23 January 1883, he received word of his promotion to Major, and was assigned to a vacancy in the 9th Cavalry, what the Army referred to as a "colored regiment." Now, in 1886, the Army called on this veteran with a proven track record in commanding cavalry and dealing with hostile Indians to command a fort and maintain order in Utah Territory.

He returned to Fort McKinney from the Little Big Horn anniversary celebration on 30 June and shortly after, on 5 July, he moved up in seniority on the Regimental roster upon the death of Major Thomas B. DeWees, who had served with Crook at the Rosebud defeat. He received his orders to prepare two troops for a forced march to join Crook on 2 August 1886. It would be a permanent change of station for him and he had but two days to prepare his family and his troops for the move.[12]

The journey south from Fort McKinney near Buffalo, northeastern Wyoming, to join the Union Pacific Railroad in southern Wyoming, with wives, children, troops, gear and all, was arduous, taking until mid-August. The anxious and impatient Crook, waiting at Fort Bridger, was eager to get on with building his fort. Orders to proceed immediately to Fort Bridger by special train met Benteen when he arrived at the railroad. Unable to establish a camp and better organize their gear as intended, Benteen's officers, troops, and wives were stuffed into three boxcars and rushed

---
12. Mills, *Harvest*.

westward. The cars were small and dingy and had to be cleaned before boarding. The companies' and headquarters' equipment were jumbled and intermixed and there wasn't room for it all on the train; some had to remain behind until other transport could be arranged. They finally arrived at Fort Bridger only to find that the restive Crook had moved on with the infantry three days earlier, leaving orders for Benteen and his cavalry to follow.

But his infirmities were to plague him on the trek south to join Crook; his eyes smarted, his back ached, and he suffered all over from the acute pain of neuralgia. In addition, he had developed a bladder problem which demanded that he dismount and urinate, or try to urinate, every fifteen minutes or so. Progress on the trail was painfully slow, too slow for Crook, who by courier had ordered Benteen to overtake the infantry. Unable to make adequate progress, Benteen was then instructed to divide his men and send a troop ahead as fast as their horses could be driven, "as trouble was expected."[13] Benteen was not thrilled with dividing his squadron, complaining that, "...Had there been trouble with the Indians, there would not have been a man left to tell the story."[14]

---

13. Kansas City *Times,* 3 January 1887, Ibid., 352-58. An anonymous article published by the *Times* was purported to have been submitted by an unnamed enlisted man. It was highly critical of Crook and subjected him to considerable embarrassment. Mills, *Harvest,* 359-60, postulates that Benteen probably wrote someone at Fort Leavenworth who passed the letter on to a third party, possibly a newspaper reporter, who then incorporated it in the article. Mills' most likely candidate for Benteen's correspondent was Captain Francis Moore of L Troop, 9th Cavalry, a colleague from New York (1882-1883), Fort Riley (1883), and Fort McKinney (1885-1886). Benteen was known for blowing off steam and exposing the malfeasance of his superiors in this indirect way that would cause them public embarrassment while leaving Benteen himself relatively unscathed. An anonymous newspaper contribution was a common method of sarcastic criticism and ridicule of the day; Benteen had used it before.

14. Ibid., 353.

Only a fool would risk incurring the ire of Little Phil Sheridan, Commanding General of the Army, by letting the Utes gain the upper hand. And General Crook was no fool. The pace of the forced march set by Crook, riding in his ambulance, spent the infantry, "making them march fifty miles the last day into DuChesne, thirty-two of it without water. These troops were so exhausted when camp was reached that had there been an attack the Indians would have killed every man of them without firing a shot."[15] Crook and his foot soldiers camped about three miles above the confluence of the DuChesne and Uintah rivers on 20 August. On 21 August he designated the campsite as Fort DuChesne. The next day Benteen, his soldiers, and wagon train stumbled into camp. Crook, on his way out, designated Benteen the commanding officer and on 23 August he formally assumed command of the tent camp called Fort DuChesne.[16]

At the site, a band of about 700 Utes "in full war dress and paint, and as hostile as can be" immediately confronted Benteen and his troops. Benteen and his officers, the Indian agent, and the Ute chiefs powwowed while soldiers hurriedly built breastworks, anticipating the worst. The promise was made that if the Utes stayed peacefully on the reservation, they would have no trouble with the Army. Satisfied, the Utes consented to the building of the fort.[17]

Benteen immediately set about in the first days of his command to quell any further difficulties with the Utes by deploying a detachment of infantry, under the command of Lieutenant Henry D. Styer, to guard the Indian agency headquarters. His next soldierly task was to construct the fort. Through Benteen's stern

---
15. Ibid.
16. The itinerary from Fort McKinney and its travails were adapted from Mills, *Harvest,* 343-45.
17. Hart, *Forts.*

diplomacy, the Indian War was put to rest for the time being, but a bureaucratic battle was about to erupt.

Happy times were not to visit Fort DuChesne. There was inevitable friction between free roaming white civilians and the reservation-bound Indians and to compound that problem, initially there was hostility between the black cavalry troops and the white infantrymen. Benteen was successful in mitigating these potential morale-defeating conflicts; an anonymous reporter wrote "the white infantrymen and the black cavalrymen at the fort fraternize without any discrimination as to color."[18] He managed to keep relations with the Indians harmonious as well. But it all took time and effort.

Benteen was incensed with Crook's rushed and inconsiderate adoption of the location for the post. The site of the fort was Godforsaken, and the construction schedule met with interminable delays in critical supplies due to incompetence and indifference in the Army supply system, resulting in the garrison remaining tent-bound through December. His complaints anonymously, but with characteristic sarcasm, appeared in a Kansas City *Times* article, noting that the post was located in "the most dreary spot" in the region, just short miles from a more suitable and beautiful site.

The Unitah River was so warm in summer "that fish are not found in it during that season." Incessant autumn winds entrained the fine-as-flour alkali dust, driving it through the tent canvas, grinding it into the troop's skin and they had "to eat no small amount of it with their meals." Benteen railed at the ineptness of the Fort Bridger quartermaster and Crook's broken "rosy promises" to insure adequate and timely supply. Hot days and cold nights made life miserable, "ninety-six in the shade, while nights

---

18. Ibid.

were so cool that ice formed in our tents in the water buckets. . ." Inadequate bedding added to the discomfort and hard work of fort building wore out the single suit of clothes the troops had brought, giving them the appearance of "ragamuffins." Supplies that did arrive were useless or extraneous; shelter tent poles, street lamps, doors and window frames, but no tools or nails. No shoes were available for the mules and "the blacksmiths were at work cutting up wagon tires and iron bunks to get iron to make shoes and save the mules. [The] horses are barefoot and unable to take to the field...." And with classic bureaucratic logic and cost-saving, "After months of delay, contracts were let. All the stoves at the post are coal burners, so the only fuel contracted for is wood, and rotten cottonwood at that to save $2 a cord. . ."[19] In mid-September, Mr. George Jewett, the newly appointed Post Trader arrived at Fort DuChesne and set up shop. The store immediately became a popular watering hole for the post officers, and there was much carousing and carrying on day and night.[20] Benteen was among those who spent considerable time wetting his whistle at Jewett's, probably unaware that Jewett was a close friend of Major Thaddeus H. Stanton, General Crook's paymaster.

    A wagon train carrying some of the equipment and supplies that were left at Fort Bridger on the march to Fort DuChesne arrived on 25 September, under the command of Lieutenant Harry L. Bailey, 21st Infantry. Accompanying Bailey and the train were Bailey's wife and Lieutenant Harry G. Trout who was posted to one of the Cavalry companies. Benteen and the post officers fell out to greet the newcomers. Benteen ordered a tent erected for the Baileys and proceeded to tease and joke with Trout, who

---

19. Kansas City *Times*. The complete text of the article is reproduced in Appendix C.
20. Mills, *Harvest*, 345-46.

was spanking new out of West Point. He good-naturedly commented something to the effect that Trout had the look of a cavalryman about him. Then at Benteen's tent he began to tease Mrs. Bailey with, "Your husband must have a hell of a time with you." Mrs. Bailey, apparently pleased with the attention, laughed and coyly asked whatever did he mean by that. Witness accounts vary as to Benteen's response. One version was that a woman with eyes like hers "would make it lively for any man." Another thought that Benteen had said any woman "having eyes such as yours must be a holy terror." All, except for Captain Jerrauld A. Olmsted, seemed to enjoy the *tete-a-tete*, including Mrs. Bailey, thinking it quite witty. Olmsted thought it was insulting.[21]

At some point, with his urinary affliction in apparent remission, Benteen walked outside and proceeded to piss heartily on the side of the tent, well within earshot of the seated ladies and others. In an oblique testament to his ability to hold his liquor, the officers present could not agree as to whether or not Benteen was drunk, although it was generally conceded that he had been drinking. Considering that he prided himself on being a gentleman, it was probably not an act he would perform sober. The ladies' reaction is unknown but given the proprieties of the times, even in a frontier fort, they probably pretended not to notice and may have attempted small talk. But Captain Olmsted was mortified and "got up and left, not knowing what might happen next,"[22] perhaps fearing that the good Major might next piss on his leg.

Benteen was increasingly frustrated at the lack of construction progress, as was Crook. However, Crook, mindful that his career could bear little more criticism from his superiors, held Benteen responsible for the delays. The frustration, pressure from

---

21. Ibid.
22. Ibid.

the Commanding General, and his physical maladies probably all played key roles in his continued and frequent forays to Jewett's. His good drinking buddy on many of these occasions was Lieutenant George R. Burnett. The Lieutenant was an 1880 graduate of West Point who had distinguished himself in 1881 by winning the Medal of Honor under heavy fire in New Mexico Territory.[23] Burnett's thirst apparently was a fair match for Benteen's but evidently he didn't share his commander's obnoxious and belligerent behavior when drunk. On several occasions he intervened to spare Benteen the embarrassment of brawling with civilians who ignored, objected to, or tried to laugh off his caustic, albeit slurred tongue, while conducting business of one kind or another at the post trader's.

In addition to the tent-pissing escapade, several other episodes would come to cause him grief. On the night of 9 October, Benteen was drinking at Jewett's when Kate (Mrs.) Benteen and her niece, Violet Norman, whom the Benteens had taken in upon the death of her parents and regarded as a daughter, unexpectedly showed up and offered to escort him home. He insisted they join him in a drink of ginger ale, which at first they declined to do, wanting him to come with them to their tent immediately. Benteen was insistent, and they reluctantly joined him. Eventually, the ladies prevailed and they all left together. Given the subsequent episodes at Jewett's there is little doubt that Kate and Violet were summoned to intercede before things got out of hand.[24]

---

23. Ibid, 347.
24. Ibid. According to Mills, Vanderhoef, Jewett's storekeeper later could not remember the precise date, thinking perhaps it was the 10th. However, events on the night of the 10th are well documented. Mills concludes that the incident must have occurred on the 9th and that given the events surrounding Benteen's subsequent behavior on the night of the 10th, it is reasonable to conclude that they were probably sent for in order to get the Major home and preclude possible trouble. See also R. A. Huetter, *Duchene*.

Sure enough, on the next night, 10 October, the good Major was not so lucky. According to witnesses, Benteen and Burnett were drunk at Jewett's. They had been drinking since afternoon and Benteen was harassing civilians who were trading at the store, telling them that the store was closed and to "get lost" with a variety of colorful colloquialisms. A citizen jokingly hid behind the stove, peering at Benteen with feigned fright. The Major was not amused. Not one for mincing words, he bellowed, "Boys, there stands the Mormon son of a bitch behind the stove! Give me a revolver and I'll make that Mormon son of a bitch pull his freight." Ned Vanderhoef, who was the son of Jewett's storekeeper, successfully urged the two cavalry officers to leave the trader's at about 9:00 p.m. With Ned in tow, they made a mock inspection of the guards. Benteen ignored the challenges of an infantry sentry, requiring the Corporal of the Guard to be called out and then made disparaging comments about the differences "between the cavalry and the infantry." Ned, having enough of this jocularity, sent a Jewett employee to fetch Lieutenant Styer. Styer, a teetotaling young West Pointer, came to the rescue with the post surgeon, Dr. Robert Benham. Benham and Ned Vanderhoef proceeded to haul Burnett off to his tent. Returning to assist Styer, they found him standing over an inert Benteen, pitched stark still in the mud. They were unsuccessful in trying to haul their limp commander home. While cogitating as to what next to try, the old warrior arose from the mire like some Phoenix bird, stood erect encased in mud, and said, "Styer, I thank you for your guardianship," then stumbled off to his tent without help.[25]

November was also tough. Around noon on 11 November, while drinking with Lieutenant Burnett and Julius Robertson, a civilian physician at the post, the sutler's store began to fill with

---
25. Ibid, 348.

various civilian contractors and tradesmen. A Mr. Lycurgus Johnson joined Benteen's party uninvited, prompting Benteen to rail, eventually calling him a "Mormon son of a bitch." Johnson tried to be a good sport and buy a round of drinks. Benteen refused to accept, saying that he drank only with Army officers. Johnson and a companion, a local sheriff named Cotton, then left but there were still too many contractors to suit Benteen. He ordered John Vanderhoef to serve his party their midday meal privately in a back room, which Vanderhoef did.[26]

Benteen's disdain, to put it mildly, for contractors and associates of Jewett undoubtedly stemmed from his strong suspicion that Jewett was up to no good. He had somehow obtained the contract for building construction at the fort, in addition to position of post trader. While not unheard of, it was nonetheless unusual in the frontier army for the post trader to also serve as building contractor. Whether or not Jewett was involved in some sort of shady dealings at Fort DuChesne is unknown, but the fact remained that now in November, and through December, the post was and would remain in tents.[27]

During the meal service, Benteen began to harp to Vanderhoef about his boss Jewett's business dealings, much to Vanderhoef's aggravation. But he initially declined to debate the issue with the post commander, who growing irate called him "a regular old fart." Angered, Vanderhoef claimed that Benteen was not a gentleman, rubbing a sore spot with the commander. "I was born a gentleman. I was raised a gentleman, and I am a gentleman still," he retorted. The two proceeded to argue with Benteen ultimately asserting that Jewett had needed to borrow money from him in

---

26. Ibid.
27. Ibid, 350.

order to "... run this little one-horse store of his." On that note, Vanderhoef left the room.[28]

Lieutenant Burnett took his commanding officer to task for his bad manners. Admonished, Benteen sent for Sheriff Cotton, who upon his arrival heard Benteen's apology for the ill treatment he and Johnson had received earlier. Later the sheriff testified that a drunken Benteen rambled on about Mormons at the end of his apology, and inquired if he was a Mormon. Cotton stated in effect that he wasn't a particularly devout practitioner, Benteen then called Cotton and the absent Johnson "God damned Mormons." Cotton, also drunk, responded that Benteen was "a God damned liar" and removing his coat, asserted that he was no gentleman in speaking as he did. The crusty old Major, a strapping near six-footer in his younger years, honed in a cavalry saddle, but now a tad portly due to the creeping effects of age and the relative physical inactivity of garrison duty, leaped up from his chair, flung off his uniform jacket, shed his suspenders from his shoulders (causing his trousers to droop about his hips), and rolled up his shirt sleeves. "Come on," he challenged, "and I'll let you know whether I am a gentleman or not." Fortunately, Medal of Honor winner Burnett interceded once again above and beyond the call of duty, and the sheriff was persuaded to leave, with Benteen shouting as Cotton staggered out that Mormons were "a set of God damned sons of bitches" and that he was going to whip him. A sober and contrite Benteen encountered Cotton the next day and apologized, attributing it all to "wine talk." Not unexpectedly, all the civilians involved later stated uniformly that Benteen was drunk. But the ever-protective post officers could not recall any specifics about drunkenness or "brawling". Lieutenant Willis Wittich, post adjutant, stated that he and Major Benteen dealt daily with post

---
28. Ibid, 349.

matters and he did not observe him to be drunk on 11 November.[29]

Benteen was frustrated at the lack of construction progress at the fort, but General Crook, now at the Department of the Platte headquarters in Omaha and under the gun of General Sheridan, was livid about it. Major Robert H. Hall, Crook's Inspector General, arrived at Fort DuChesne late on 29 November, informing Benteen by telegram that he was there under "special instructions" but was tired and would report to Benteen the next morning. Ignoring protocol, he did not, but instead began an inspection of the post, which took all morning. As he left he told Benteen that he couldn't see how any more could be done towards construction than was done. But that was not what Hall reported to Crook on 7 December 1886.[30]

Hall pinned the blame for lack of progress at the fort squarely on Benteen, reporting that the fort commander was frequently so drunk that he could not perform his duties, was obstinate, quarrelsome and abusive to all around him; consequently fort business could not get done. On 18 December, Colonel Edward Hatch, Benteen's regimental commander and "an avowed and bitter enemy", arrived at the fort to conduct an investigation into Hall's allegations.[31] His first step was to relieve Benteen of command. After interviewing officers and civilians alike, Hatch prepared six specifications to the charge of being drunk on duty and forwarded them on the General Crook. Although the details are unknown, Benteen then received, presumably from Crook through the paymaster Major Stanton, a "semiofficial" offer of a six months leave of absence.[32] But then, on 3 January 1887, the infamous Kansas

---
29. Ibid.
30. Ibid.
31. Ibid, 352.
32. Ibid.

City *Times* article appeared criticizing and ridiculing Crook's oversight of Fort DuChesne construction. Crook, furious over this sarcastic piece whose authorship he correctly attributed directly to Benteen, then added the charge of "conduct unbecoming an officer and a gentleman" including as its specification the "brawl" of 11 November. The semiofficial offer of a leave of absence was withdrawn. On 7 January, Crook appointed a court-martial to convene at Fort DuChesne on 7 February 1887 to try Major Frederick W. Benteen on the charge of being drunk on six specific occasions and of conduct unbecoming an officer and gentleman on one occasion. Benteen had the charges read to him and was placed under arrest on 16 January by Colonel Hatch.[33] The career of Major Frederick W. Benteen, U. S. Army, hero of the Civil War battles of Little Osage Crossing, Big Blue River, and the charge on Columbus, hero of the Indian fights at Saline River, Little Big Horn, and Canyon Creek, was about to come to an ignoble end. Such tragic conclusions to Frontier Army officer's careers deriving from drink, dysfunction, and disgrace were somewhat common-place, even though the Army was slow to condemn and often quick to forgive. Those who were cashiered fell into obscurity. Benteen would not be so lucky. Controversy would follow this burned out old war-horse into the next century and beyond.

Benteen's journey into the history books began ten years earlier, with events that cast this beleaguered officer into the limelight that couldn't have been contrived with any more intrigue and subplots by a screenwriter. On the hot, fateful day of 25 June 1876, in what is now southern Montana, Lieutenant Colonel (Brevet Major General) George Armstrong Custer led five companies of the U. S. Army's 7th Cavalry, approximately one-half of the regiment,

---

33. Ibid, 358.

along with kin-folk, assorted Indian scouts and civilian wranglers, indelibly into history in the Battle of the Little Big Horn. The unbelievable defeat of a bigger-than-life hero was a shock to the nation.

Custer's meteoric rise at age twenty-three to Major General commanding the Michigan Volunteers in the Civil War had earned him the sobriquet "Boy-General". His subsequent victory over the southern Cheyenne at the Battle of the Washita brought him public fame and notoriety as an Indian fighter, although it tarnished somewhat his reputation within the Army. He was a legend in life and in death, he was to become a myth.

But not all who served under or over him were in awe. President Ulysses S. Grant distrusted him. Both General Philip H. Sheridan, who commanded the frontier, and General William T. Sherman, who commanded the Army, admired his audacity and fearlessness in the field, but were skeptical of his judgment. This skepticism permeated down the chain of command. The 7th's officer corps was beset with factionalism. Among the officers he played favorites, and he was an unabashed nepotist who would lead to their deaths four members of his own family: two brothers, Captain Tom and civilian Boston; a brother-in-law, 1st Lieutenant James Calhoun; and a nephew, civilian Harry Armstrong Reed. Unquestionably brave in battle, he was a harsh and uneven disciplinarian who on occasion ordered his men whipped as punishment and appeared at times to care less for them than for his hunting hounds; he had survived a potentially career-ending court-martial in 1867 for absence without leave from his command, conduct to the prejudice of good order and military discipline, and summarily ordering the shooting of deserters.

After contriving a war in 1875 against the Sioux Indians to force them onto reservations under government control, the government in Washington issued an ultimatum for the Sioux and their allied tribes who continued to wander their hunting grounds to report to the agencies by the end of January 1876. The Indians essentially ignored the order and the Army was ordered to enforce it. The Army suspected the Sioux were likely to be encamped somewhere in their ancestral summer grounds near the Yellowstone River. Three offensive columns, led by Brigadier General George Crook from the south, Colonel John Gibbon from the west, and General Alfred H. Terry from the east, converged on the area south of the Yellowstone and north of the Big Horn Mountains. Custer with the 7th Cavalry, under Terry's command, was dispatched from Fort Lincoln, Dakota Territory. Although Colonel Gibbon's Crow scouts had earlier spotted the main combined Sioux and Cheyenne camp on the Tongue River and the Indians had decisively whipped General Crook and his column in the Battle of the Rosebud only days before, the whereabouts and numbers of the Indians were unknown to Terry and Custer.

From their bivouac on the Yellowstone, Major Marcus A. Reno was sent with a scouting party on a long reconnaissance of the country to the south. He returned days later without sighting hostiles, but he had discovered a large Indian trail that turned west from Rosebud Creek, a Yellowstone tributary. That intelligence meant only one thing: the Indians were headed for the Little Big Horn Valley. On 22 June, at the confluence of Rosebud Creek and the Yellowstone, Terry ordered Custer up the Rosebud, in a reconnaissance-in-force to pick up the trail and find the Indians. The scouts were certain that the Indians would in fact be found somewhere in the Little Big Horn Valley.

About noon on 25 June 1876, the 7th crossed the divide from the Rosebud drainage into what is now known as Reno Creek, a tributary of the north-flowing Little Big Horn River, with the intent of enclosing the Indians between Custer's cavalry and Gibbon's column. But they were discovered. At the divide, the regiment was separated into battalions. Captain Frederick W. Benteen, with a battalion of three companies, was sent by Custer on an oblique scout to the south with orders to ensure that no Indians escaped upriver, a mission which Benteen regarded as senseless because in his opinion the formidable terrain did not present a likely escape route. The main column, consisting of Reno's battalion of three companies and Custer's two battalions of five companies under the command of Captains George W. M. Yates and Myles W. Keogh, advanced down Reno Creek toward the Little Big Horn. Captain Thomas M. McDougall and one company followed the main column with the mule pack train. Satisfying himself from a high vantage point that there were no Indians upriver, Benteen rejoined the main trail. After watering his horses along Reno Creek, he was summoned by a written note from Custer, hurriedly scribbled by the regimental adjutant and delivered by Custer's trumpeter, admonishing him to "Come on. Be quick" and to bring the pack mules. But the pack train could not maintain the pace of mounted cavalry. How was he to hurry *and* bring the packs?

Confident that there were no Indians to his rear, Benteen advanced at a trot along the trail of the regiment. Behind was the plodding pack train carrying supplies and ammunition, reckoned by Benteen to be amply guarded under the circumstances. He was unaware that a few miles ahead, near the bluffs of the Little Big Horn, Custer had further divided his force and ordered Reno's battalion to cross the River and attack the Indians encamped in a large village on the west bank. Custer turned right and after gaining a full view of the large Indian encampment and Reno's attack on its south edge, he continued downstream along the bluffs. But fierce resistance had met Reno's charge; he halted his advance and formed a skirmish line, which was soon flanked. He then withdrew temporarily to the cover of cottonwoods along the river before being put into full retreat back across the Little Big Horn and up the bluffs. Benteen, meanwhile, proceeded along the trail after Custer. He came upon Reno and the remnants of his battalion essentially in full rout. With the threat to the village by Reno removed, the Indians abandoned for the moment their counterattack on his battalion and turned to Custer and his five companies who were now some miles downstream. By this time Custer was probably also engaged by Indians from the north part of the village.

Although Custer's plans went to his grave with him, he perhaps had been positioning for an attempt to place the Indian village in a pincer with Reno. Or perhaps he planned to round up the non-combatants, the women, children, and elderly, and thereby destroy the warriors' will to fight. Benteen and his men, seeing the remnants of Reno's battalion scurrying up the bluffs, many afoot, joined Reno's troopers with pistols drawn. Reno, with his ammunition spent, ordered reinforcement and a share of Benteen's battalion's ammunition. Seeing that the hatless Reno was clearly flustered, Benteen effectively took command for some indeterminate period of time, and organized and led the defense. Lieutenant Luther Hare was sent back to speed up the pack train and to separate out some ammunition-bearing mules and bring them to the defensive line quickly. Debate ensued among some of the officers as to the feasibility of hurrying to the sound of the guns to the north, but it was deemed impractical. Stragglers from Reno's fight in the valley were still crossing the river and the battalions could not advance at a rapid pace carrying the wounded and without jeopardizing the pack train.

Against the consensus and without authorization, Captain Thomas B. Weir, taking Lieutenant Winfield S. Edgerly with him, advanced with their two companies. After some delay during which stragglers continued to rejoin the troopers on the bluffs and the wounded and the pack mules were gathered up, the main body of troops slowly began to wend its way toward Custer. But by now Custer and his entire command had been destroyed. With Custer out of the way, the Indians returned with a vengeance and drove back Weir, Edgerly and the combined battalions of Reno and Benteen whose advance was slowed by the wounded and pack train. They reached their starting point on the bluffs above the river and were surrounded. The tattered survivors held on through vicious fighting until the Indians withdrew a day later as they became aware of Terry and Gibbon's advance.

In the face of such a disastrous defeat, it was tempting to look for scapegoats and given the makeup of the 7th, one didn't have to look far to find them; the search began and ended with Custer's lieutenants, battalion commanders Reno and Benteen. Reno was an unpopular officer and Benteen's dislike for Custer and his leadership role in the anti-Custer faction of the regiment were well known. Rumors flew regarding Reno's actions in the fight, when he halted his charge on the large Indian encampment on the flood plain and withdrew his force under great duress to high ground across the river. These moves took him out of the fight, which released the Indians to vent their rage on Custer. The rumors amounted to accusations of cowardice and lack of leadership. Reno demanded a Court of Inquiry; he would be exonerated but the finger pointing continues today. His fellow officers testified in his defense, if somewhat tepidly. A number of historians have charged that the proceedings amounted to a whitewash and cover-up. His fellow officers essentially ostracized him until he was eventually cashiered for a variety of unseemly incidents, mostly under the influence of alcohol. He died friendless in Washington, D.C., in 1889.

The over-abundant historical literature on the Custer defeat is swollen with theories as to the reasons that range from the proven, to the probable, and on to the preposterous. It has been proven that Custer disregarded or disbelieved the intelligence from his scouts and divided his force in the face of an enemy without an assessment of their superior numbers through further reconnaissance. It is probable that Reno, demoralized, panicked in the timber to which he was driven after his charge on the Indian village. And it is highly preposterous that General Terry's poor planning was the root cause of Custer's demise.

As for Benteen, he allegedly tarried on the trail as he conducted the scout to the south of the regiment's main route to the battle, an allegation made by non-participants of the battle. His presumed lackadaisical ramble and failure to "Come on…Be quick" in response to Custer's written order had sealed Custer's fate. The question remains to this day: did Benteen so hate Custer that he dallied on the trail and consciously or unconsciously sacrificed half his regiment in order to "do in" his commanding officer? A focused review of the abundant published historical literature and other documents about the battle sheds no new light on the subject. In the absence of a yet-to-be discovered smoking-gun document written by a reliable participant, buried in some archive, the answer has pretty much depended on the investigators' own reading of the largely anecdotal evidence and on their own biases.

The frontier Army of the late 1800s was a motley assortment of veteran noncommissioned officers overseeing ranks of new immigrants, adventurers, the occasional fugitive, wayward youths seeking a new start in life, and even a few veteran Confederates. Commanding these regulars were field officers battle-hardened by the campaigns of the Civil and Indian Wars, assisted by a junior officer cadre posted to the frontier from the graduating classes at West Point. Hard riding and hard drinking, this officer corps was itself contradiction on horseback: collegial and quarrelsome, honorable and dastardly, astute and foolish. Rowdy intemperance broke the difficult and tedious routine of frontier garrison life, and with few exceptions (most notably Custer), to borrow from the poet Robert Service, there was "... none so cursed with a lime-kiln thirst..." as the typical regimental officer.

Life on a frontier Army post was tough. Benteen and his wife Catherine were to lose four children on the prairie to disease and it is impossible to say what effect this may have had on his personality and therefore his relations with his fellow officers. Like Custer, he was incredibly cool under fire and had an exceptional Civil War record. He was an admired and highly competent veteran. His men looked him up to him, and junior officers modeled their own military comportment and leadership style after him. But he and Custer did not get along. Their shaky relationship contributed to dissension among the officers of the regiment and lead to them taking sides. And Benteen's dislike of this commanding officer extended to the clique of officers with whom Custer socialized and by whom he surrounded himself. Benteen was an officer and gentleman of the frontier army and in many ways a caricature of it. He was irascible, a man not to be trifled with, who on occasion could put away the devil's brew with the best of them.

During binges his bachelor comrades often looked him after until he was fit to return to his wife in their quarters.

But what of the question? Did Benteen dally on the trail? There may be no real way to know. The Army didn't think so. Fourteen years after the Battle of the Little Big Horn, the Army awarded him a brevet of Brigadier General for heroism at the Little Big Horn and the Battle of Canyon Creek a year later against Chief Joseph and the Nez Perce. Nonetheless, many of his modern-day critics have used various time/distance estimates to justify the charge of dalliance on the trail, but these studies are highly subjective. However, the data are amenable to a more rigorous treatment. Statistical analysis of the relative rates of the Custer and Benteen columns on their march to the Little Big Horn indicates that there is, mathematically, a high probability that Benteen proceeded at a rate comparable to Custer's. Amid the controversy that still exists, this analysis may be fat on the fire, but that is where the numbers fall.

In retirement, Benteen grew increasingly bitter with time. Custer partisans had pinned responsibility for their hero's demise on Reno, and to a painful extent, on him. This especially galled because Benteen believed, as did Generals Sherman, Sheridan and Terry, that Custer had rashly brought his fate upon himself, and that in fact it was he, Benteen, who was responsible for saving the remnant of the regiment at Reno Hill. It was almost too much for the proud, vain old soldier to bear. It was his correspondence during this embittered retirement that vented most vociferously his hateful feelings about Custer. But he also turned on his Army colleagues, whom he believed did not press hard or publicly enough in his defense. Some of this bitterness was directed at the Army itself. Well into retirement, he would write to Theodore Goldin, a fellow survivor of Reno Hill, "It cost me $10,000 more than my pay came to, to follow the trumpet calls of the United States...I lost four children in following that brazen trumpet around." That is a bitter man.

CHAPTER 2

EPIPHANY

Frederick William Benteen was born to Theodore Charles (Charley) and Caroline Hargrove Benteen in Petersburg, Virginia, on August 24, 1834. The elder Benteen, of Dutch and English stock, hailed from Baltimore, Maryland, where the Benteen family had lived continuously since they immigrated prior to the American Revolutionary war. Family lore maintained that the Old World forbearers were originally of German extraction.[1] Presumably the newborn was named after his uncle, Frederick Damish Benteen, Charley's younger brother. His sister, Henrietta Elizabeth, preceded him in 1831

---

1. Graham, *Myth,* 157. Mills, *Harvest.* Julian, *General Benteen.* Benteen's early life and his Army service apart from events surrounding the Custer fight are drawn largely from these sources. Graham, an Army legal officer and a student of the Little Big Horn battle, greatly admired Benteen and had interviewed and corresponded with members of his family, notably, Benteen's son Fred and his granddaughter Anita Benteen Mitchell. Mills, a historian and Benteen's biographer, was thorough and fair, but less enamored.

and Frederick William was followed in 1837 by Theodore Charles, Jr.

Charley was proprietor of a paint and painting supply business, and by the time Fred reached school age, the business had flourished sufficiently to enable him to own slaves and to send Fred to a private academy. This school most likely was the Petersburg Classical Institute, which offered military training.[2]

Tragedy befell the Benteen family when, in October 1841, Caroline Benteen died. How this influenced young Fred's development is unknown, but it must have had some traumatic effect. Widower Charley continued to raise his brood in Petersburg until early 1849 when he relocated the family to St. Louis, Missouri, after marrying off Henrietta. St. Louis, booming in the midst of the westward expansion and California gold rush, was quickly becoming a major trade, manufacturing, and transportation center. Charley entered into a partnership with Alexander and Hugh Carswell selling paint and supplies to the riverboats trading along the Mississippi. In the midst of this activity, Charley found time to remarry. Beulah Kane brought to the Benteen family three small children from a previous marriage.[3]

The move to St. Louis effectively ended Fred's formal education. He worked in his late teens for his father, then struck out on his own as an independent sign painter, awaiting a higher calling. Conspiring events would indeed orchestrate a clarion call.

Benteen arrived at manhood as a controlled, soft-spoken, independent thinker. At five feet ten and one half inches, he was broad shouldered, lanky, clean-cut, blue eyed, and younger looking

---

2. Mills, *Harvest,* 12. According to Mills, Benteen later referred to the academy as the Petersburg Military Institute, but such an institute did not exist by that name until 1910. It may have been known locally by that name, however.
3. Ibid.

than his years. His tendency when provoked was not to explode with anger at others, but to counter with sarcasm, a trait he would carry throughout his lifetime. He could make friends easily but his demeanor impressed others as one who was aloof, even "courtly"[4]. He was a free thinker but he could be influenced, and no one had greater influence in his life than Catherine Louise Norman (Kate).[5] In 1856 the large Norman family moved to St. Louis from Philadelphia following the death of the family patriarch, Henry Norman. Charley Benteen had wooed Anita Norman, Kate's older sister, for a time and it was through this connection that Fred was introduced to the Normans and to Kate.

These were troubling times for the country and for young Benteen. By 1860, four decades of sectional conflict arising from stark social, political, and economic differences between North and South were coming to a head. Increasing opposition in the North to organization of pro-slavery territories in the West had led to the Missouri Compromise of 1820, which established a line separating free and slave territory in the Louisiana Purchase. In order to maintain party unity and political support in the Democratic and Whig parties, political leaders essentially strove to ignore the slavery issue, but it was becoming increasingly difficult to do so. The Compromise Measures of 1850 among other things gave territories the right to choose their status as free or slave states upon application for statehood.

During the presidential election campaign of 1860, Southern and Northern wings split the Democrats and the rift resulted in Abraham Lincoln's election. Lincoln, a Republican, was elected

---

4. Asay, *Gray Head*, 6.
5. The name on the Benteens' headstone at Arlington National Cemetery is Catherine Louise. Mills refers to her as Catherine Louisa Mills, *Harvest*, 28.

on a platform that included opposition to any expansion of slavery.

In March 1861, Alabama, Florida, Georgia, Louisiana, South Carolina, and Texas seceded from the Union and formed the Confederate States of America, and Jefferson Davis was chosen president. In his inaugural address, Lincoln declared the secession illegal. Confederate strategy called for seizing Federal installations in the South and when, on April 21, 1861, Fort Sumpter in Charleston Bay, South Carolina was fired upon by Southern artillery during a Union re-supply attempt, Lincoln requested troops to squash the rebels. Arkansas, North Carolina, Tennessee, and Virginia immediately pulled out of the Union and joined the Confederacy. The Union succeeded in securing the Border States Delaware, Kentucky, Maryland, and Missouri.

In early August, George B. McClellan was appointed commander-in-chief of the Union Army under Lincoln. McClellan immediately set about reorganizing the Army's Department of the West after firing General John C. Fremont, with whom he had differences. At McClellan's suggestion, and with Lincoln's approval, the Department of the West was reorganized in November 1861, into three distinct departments: New Mexico, Kansas, including Colorado, Dakota, Nebraska, and part of the Indian Territory, and the Department of Missouri, under General Henry W. Halleck, which also included Arkansas, Illinois, Iowa, Minnesota, Wisconsin, and Kentucky west of the Cumberland River.[6]

The Normans were Unionists and as war clouds gathered prior to and after the election of Abraham Lincoln, and with the shelling by the Confederates of Fort Sumpter, they urged Fred to support the Union. Kate in particular imposed this view on Ben-

---

6. Guernsey, *Civil War*, 177.

teen.[7] The majority of the citizens of Missouri supported the Union but most of its politicians did not, and only deft moves by Missouri Unionists prevented the Federal military installations from falling into the hands of the pro-Confederates, as had other Army facilities in the South. St. Louis would remain under Union Army control. Kentucky and Missouri were especially important to Federal war strategy because the Cumberland, Tennessee, and Mississippi Rivers could be used as routes for the North to bring the war to the South.

Benteen did in fact support the Union, but initially somewhat indirectly, by offering his services as a volunteer to train Union troops, probably relying on his own military training at the Petersburg Institute.[8] His official capacity, if any, is unknown. And it was in this vague, "volunteer" status that Benteen came under hostile fire for the first time in the battle of Wilson's Creek on 10 August 1861.

Captain Nathaniel Lyons, commander of the St. Louis Arsenal, led several victorious forays against armed Confederates in the summer of 1861, with the unplanned and unhappy result of forcing disparate small bands of Rebels to join together in a large force. Lyons, who had just received a startling promotion, rocketing from Captain to Brigadier General, discovered on 9 August that the Confederates were encamped southwest of Springfield in a wooded area traversed by Wilson's Creek.

Lyons, with his senior officers, devised a plan to attack the numerically superior Confederates (he was outnumbered by about

---

7. Steves, in Mills, *Harvest*, 19. Mills quotes from unpublished notes of Myron F. Steves, Jr., Benteen's great-great grandson, who transcribed recollections of conversations in the early 1950's with Stephen Mitchell, husband of Anita Benteen Mitchell, had with her father, Benteen's son Frederick Wilson Benteen.
8. Mills, *Harvest*, 14.

22,000 to 5,000) in a pincer movement, relying heavily on the element of surprise.[9] Early on the morning of 10 August 1861, Lyons struck from the northwest. But the attack was botched. The southwest force under the command of Colonel Franz Sigel, a former German Army officer and architect of the overall plan, was late getting into place (his men were occupied with looting overrun outlying rebel tents) and when positioned, did not aggressively pursue the fight. The rebels counterattacked with withering fire, and Sigel's men panicked. With Sigel's force in retreat, the Confederates concentrated on Lyons with a vengeance. The fighting was ferocious with even a regimental surgeon abandoning his scalpel to pick up a rifle. Lyons was killed and a veteran cavalry officer, Major Samuel D. Sturgis, took command of Lyons's forces. Deciding that discretion was the better part of valor, Sturgis immediately ordered a retreat in face of the all-out Confederate assault.

When the smoke cleared just before noon, the Union troops had withdrawn and about one fourth of the force was killed, wounded, or missing. It may not have been a complete rout, but they were thoroughly whipped. Surprisingly, the Confederates suffered even higher casualties. Staggering back to Springfield throughout the day, the Union soldiers then marched on to Rolla, arriving there on 19 August. Most were immediately sent to St. Louis to lick their wounds and regroup, but Benteen remained in Rolla with a small cadre. Significantly, several members of Lyons's brigades would greatly impact Benteen's future.

Benteen's part in the battle is unknown. He stated later that he was just an observer. But given the intensity of the fighting, it is

---

9. Interestingly, Lyons's chief of staff, Major John M. Schofield, who would go on to become Commanding General of the Army, objected to the plan, but in vain.

more than likely he did participate in the combat even though he was not officially in the Army.[10] Regardless of his role at Wilson's Creek, the clarion call was heard: Benteen would join the Union Army. Appalled by the debacle, he now firmly believed that he could make a difference. Holding strong convictions about right and wrong, he was determined to see them through, no matter what the consequences:[11] "A man with my views could no longer withhold offering his services, and life, if necessary, for the preservation of this country."[12]

At Rolla, a cavalry battalion was formed and an election of officers was held. William D. Bowen, who fought at Wilson's Creek, was elected Captain and commanding officer and Benteen was elected First Lieutenant. Since it was common practice in that day for the men of volunteer units to elect those who would lead them into battle, this election implies that Benteen, whatever his status at Wilson's Creek, acquitted himself well enough to earn the respect of the battalion's voters. Daniel W. Ballou was elected Second Lieutenant. Benteen was commissioned a First Lieutenant on 1 September 1861, and "...then commenced my services in the cavalry."[13]

Benteen had just a month to accomplish the daunting task of training his cavalrymen. By 1 October the battalion reached full

---

10. Steves, in Mills, *Harvest* 14. Again quoting from the Steves notes, Mills reports that Benteen stated his role as "sight-seer". But the fighting at Wilson's Creek was too vicious for anyone to remain uninvolved.
11. Graham, *Myth,* 158.
12. Mills, *Harvest,* 14.
13. Ibid, 22. Election of officers by state volunteer units was the norm early in the war. These elections were supervised by the U.S. Mustering Officer for the state. The Mustering Officer at that time was Major Schofield. Mills also notes (p. 14) that when Benteen was mustered in as an officer on 1 September, a notation was made on his record to date his service from mid-July. This clearly predates the 10 August Battle of Wilson's Creek and implies a more formal role than Benteen himself alluded to.

strength, and a second election was held. Captain Bowen was elected Major and battalion commander, 1st Battalion, Missouri Cavalry, and Benteen was elected Captain and commander of Company C. Ballou was moved up to First Lieutenant and Edwin M. Emerson was elected Second Lieutenant.[14]

Back at home in St. Louis, Fred's father Charley, an avowed secessionist, was not impressed. Benteen's consorting as a volunteer with the Union troops enraged him. "I hope the first God damned bullet gets you", he bellowed, and promptly disowned his son.[15] Fred's subsequent acceptance of a Union commission must have made old Charley apoplectic. Thus Benteen began his military career with the knowledge that "the prayers of my nearest kin were being offered up that I might get so badly wounded that I could render no service."[16]

Benteen first tasted battle as an officer against Confederate guerrillas at Dutch Hollow in Central Missouri, on 13 October 1861. Major Bowen's 1st Battalion, Missouri Cavalry was attached to the 13th Illinois Volunteers, under the command of Colonel John B. Wyman. Major Bowen's battalion was riding point on a column followed by another cavalry battalion, the Fremont Hussars, with Colonel Wyman's 13th Illinois infantry in trail, when they learned of a large number of guerrilla cavalry a few miles ahead. Deploying Company B to his right and Benteen's Company C to his left, Bowen led the cavalry line to meet the rebels. The Confederates withdrew about three miles and then fell into position to meet the attack. Bowen charged and the enemy was

---

14. Ibid, 28.
15. Bentley, in Mills, *Harvest,* 19. Mills quotes from unpublished notes of Bentley who interviewed Stephen and Anita Benteen Mitchell in 1974 and 1975. Charley Benteen held slaves in Virginia and may have done so in Missouri as well.
16. Mills, *Harvest,* 19.

forced to retreat for a bit until reinforced by a unit of approximately 600 men. The combined force then counterattacked and Bowen fell back. They then attacked Bowen's left flank, where they were repulsed by volley fire from Benteen's dismounted Company C. The Fremont Hussars rode up in support, followed by Wyman's infantry and in short order the tide was turned with the Confederates in full retreat. The Union cavalry pursued until nightfall and inflicting additional casualties. This skirmish was followed by another victory the next day at Linn Creek.[17]

In the predawn of the morning of 3 December while camped outside Salem, Missouri, Confederate infiltrators opened fire on the cavalry camp from inside the camp perimeter. Benteen, sleeping a few hundred yards from the shooting, leapt from his tent, rallied his men and some of those from Company B and immediately counterattacked on foot. The firefight was intense. Benteen and his men were slowly driving the guerrillas back when Bowen arrived in support with Company D, who charged on horseback, forcing the Southerners from the camp. Benteen survived unscathed, but the battalion suffered four killed and eight wounded. The 1st Battalion, with support of a company of Fremont Hussars, pursued the guerrillas for four days, returning only after running out of supplies, but with 20 prisoners. Benteen saw no more action in 1861.[18]

A new problem arose for Benteen. His sister Henrietta's husband took to abusing her and in late December, 1861, Benteen petitioned Major Bowen in writing for a ten day leave to fetch her from New York and relocate her in St. Louis, "...where I can be in more direct communication with her." Benteen wanted to handle the delicate personal matter himself, closing his written petition

---

17. War Department, "Rebellion.", Ibid, 22.
18. Ibid, 24.

with, "If it is impolitic or impossible to grant my request, I shall be compelled to resign, as the greatest measure of my happiness is constituted in the well doing of my sister."[19]

Major Bowen signed off on the request and forwarded it to Colonel Wyman who did likewise, sending it up the chain of command. General Halleck approved the request on New Year's Day, 1862, and Benteen shortly thereafter safely ensconced Henrietta and her three daughters in St. Louis. While home, Frederick Benteen married Catherine Norman in St. Louis on 7 January 1862, in an Episcopal ceremony. Kate was twenty-six. The honeymoon was short; Benteen was back in Rolla on 10 January 1862.[20] That month, General Halleck gave General Samuel R. Curtis command of the Department of Missouri army in the field.[21] Curtis reorganized the Union forces in Missouri and the 1st Missouri Cavalry, under Bowen, was kept at his headquarters for guard and escort duty.

The war initially did not go well for the Union in the East, but gains were made quickly on the western front under General Ulysses S. Grant. The Federal objective was to divide the Confederacy, control the Mississippi valley, and stem reinforcements of men and materiel from Arkansas, Louisiana, and Texas. General Halleck, who was not noted as a military strategist, planned this western campaign, so Grant's execution of the plan probably played a considerable part in its success.[22]

On 10 February 1862, General Curtis began a campaign to drive the Confederates under Brigadier General Sterling Price from Missouri. In early March, Curtis was advancing into south-

---

19. Ibid, 27.
20. Ibid.
21. Guernsey, *Civil War*, 282.
22. In July 1862, Halleck was appointed general in chief of the Union armies, a post he held until Lincoln replaced him with Grant in 1864.

western Missouri but this forced him to stretch his lines by leaving detachments to guard his communications and supply lines. Retreating under the Union's superior numbers, the Confederates under Price joined with Brigadier General Ben McCulloch to concentrate a large force near Fayetteville, Arkansas. This force also included Cherokee allies, commanded by Brigadier General Albert Pike. These Indians, mainly from the Indian Territory, opposed the Union and its westward expansion. Major General Earl Van Dorn then assumed command of this combined force. In mid February, advance scouts from Benteen's Company C, under the command of Lieutenant Ballou, located rear echelons of the Confederates along Sugar Creek, in northwestern Arkansas. Rushing forward, the 1st Battalion engaged in a running fight with the southerners, ultimately sending them into retreat with intense howitzer bombardment. The next day, in pursuit of the rebels along Sugar Creek, Bowen was wounded in the wrist.[23]

While encamped at Sugar Creek, Benteen was ordered to provide escort for Curtis' staff subsistence officer for an indefinite period. This was none other than feisty Captain Philip H. Sheridan, U.S. 13th Infantry. His job was to scour the countryside for provisions and grain for the Army, a task fraught with danger as the woods were harboring untold numbers of Rebel guerrillas. Normally, a commander would use such an opportunity to unload his undesirables, but in a departure from tradition, Benteen detailed 28 of his best men, under command of highly regarded 2nd Lieutenant Edwin M. Emerson, to the subsistence officer. Captain Sheridan would not forget this gracious gesture.

By early March, General Curtis was amassing his troops for battle. He received intelligence that Van Dorn was taking the ini-

---

23. Wert, in Faust, *Civil War,* 566-67. Guernsey, *Civil War,* 284-85. Mills, *Harvest.*

tiative, sending Price and McCulloch back northward. Sugar Creek flows westward along the south flank of an east-west trending escarpment called Pea Ridge before turning north. Drawing his line in the sand at Sugar Creek, Curtis awaited the Confederate attack from the bluffs south of Pea Ridge, overlooking the creek. He ordered his advance unit under General Sigel,[24] now near Bentonville, to retire to Sugar Creek where they would join to meet the enemy. Sigel's men came under attack during the withdrawal on 6 March, but he was able to successfully disengage and join Curtis.

As the day passed into night, Curtis became convinced that the rebels were not only attempting to flank him but to get to his rear west of Pea Ridge. Curtis repositioned his divisions North-South, with Colonel Eugene E. Carr's infantry division and another division under a Colonel from Indiana with the unfortunate name of Jefferson C. Davis[25] on his left flank; General Sigel's cavalry was placed on his right. Carr's position was near Elkhorn Tavern, a crossroads stage stop at the base of Pea Ridge's north slope. Price faced Carr and Davis, and Pike opposed Curtis and Sigel while McCulloch was positioned somewhat against Sigel's right flank.

The Southerners began to feel out the Union troops early on the morning of 7 March. The Confederates had determined to break the Union line through Carr's Division and in short order Northern pickets were being driven back before a thundering charge of Rebels on Elkhorn Tavern from the high ground of Pea Ridge. As Carr was positioning his division to meet the onslaught, Davis waded in on his left with a ferocious assault that killed sev-

---

24. This is the same Sigel whose men forced his removal after the battle at Wilson's Creek.
25. No kin to the Confederate President.

eral high ranking Confederates, including General McCulloch. Demoralized by this turn of events, the Rebels were unable to regain the upper hand.

But Carr was under heavy pressure. Unable to receive reinforcements from General Curtis and ordered to "persevere," Carr himself was wounded several times and his Division was receiving heavy losses.[26] He held but persisted in his request for reinforcements and around noon, Curtis released the only reserves he had at the time, Major Bowen and the 1st Missouri Cavalry. Bowen placed his troops on the eastern slope of Pea Ridge. Benteen and Company C expended all their ammunition firing on a Confederate gun. They regrouped, resupplied, and relocated with Bowen to a position about 300 yards south of Elkhorn Tavern and proceeded to lay down withering shrapnel from their howitzers on the closed ranks of advancing Rebels. Carr was given time to reform but could not halt the numerically superior Confederates from advancing. Carr's Division retreated under fire and the Rebels gained Elkhorn Tavern and the crossroads. The Confederate guns found the range, and Bowen was forced to withdraw from his position but encountered reinforcements moving up. Benteen had held under three fierce charges of General McIntosh's Indian Brigade, giving Carr the time he needed to regroup.[27]

The battle raged throughout the day and into the night. On the morning of 8 March, Curtis counterattacked and when he got his artillery into place and began to bombard the Confederates, that was it. The Rebels went into retreat and the largest Civil War

---

26. War Department, in Mills, *Harvest*, 33. Mills states that Curtis was unable or unwilling to send Carr the reinforcements.
27. Mills, *Harvest*, 33-34.

battle fought west of the Mississippi River, the Battle of Pea Ridge, was over.[28]

By the spring of 1862, Union troops had gone on to capture Forts Henry and Donelson in Tennessee, clearing the way down the Tennessee and Cumberland Rivers to the Mississippi. The Confederate troops in central and western Tennessee were forced to retreat southward toward Mississippi. Grant pursued, halting at Shiloh, Tennessee, to await reinforcement from General Don Carlos Buell's army. On 6 April Generals Pierre G. T. Beauregard and Albert S. Johnson launched a surprise attack, hoping to engage Grant before he could be reinforced. But Buell arrived in time for the combined armies to repel the Confederates, forcing them to retreat into Mississippi. An important Southern railhead at Corinth, Mississippi fell to the Union Army on 30 May leaving Union troops in control of the Mississippi River as far south as Memphis.

Benteen participated in a number of minor skirmishes throughout the spring and summer of 1862. On 3 July 1862, Bowen was promoted to Lieutenant Colonel and in December 1862, a reorganization of volunteer cavalry units resulted in the formation of the 10th Missouri Cavalry Regiment from elements of fragmented regiments. The reorganization was accompanied by considerable political infighting and tension within the merged units. Benteen was promoted to second Major of the regiment, and in early 1863, the 10th was transferred to Major General U. S. Grant's Army of the Tennessee. Colonel F. M. Cornyn commanded the regiment, and Benteen's former commander, Lieuten-

---

28. Bankes, *Hickok*, 52. Varga, *Showdown*, 24. As an aside, also purported to have participated in the fighting for the Union at Wilson's Creek and Pea Ridge was one James Butler Hickok, aka Wild Bill. Wild Bill would scout for General Custer, an admirer, and for the 7th Cavalry after the Civil War. See also Quaife, *Life,* 67-71.

ant Colonel Bowen, was named second-in-command.[29] On 7 February Benteen and the regiment found themselves at Corinth, Mississippi. There Colonel Cornyn was promoted to brigade commander, which elevated Bowen to acting commander of the 10th Missouri Cavalry.[30]

In April 1863, Grant struck for Vicksburg. Crossing the Mississippi he attacked toward the fortress from the south, surprising the Rebels. By mid-May, he laid siege to the city which held for awhile but finally surrendered on 4 July 1863. The Union objective of splitting the Confederacy in two had been accomplished.

Fate now intervened. Bowen, an undisciplined hothead, brought charges against the regiment's senior Major, Thomas Hynes, with whom he had been feuding. The upshot was that Hynes was removed from the chain of command and Benteen effectively became the second-in-command of the 10th Missouri Cavalry Regiment.[31] In this capacity, Benteen saw considerable action in Mississippi and Alabama.

Infighting in the regiment persisted to the point of silliness. Bowen and Cornyn repeatedly placed each other under arrest. On 7 July at Iuka, Mississippi, "it was Bowen's turn to be arrested," placing Benteen as acting commander of the 10th. He led a ferocious charge against a rebel held hill north of Iuka for which he received written commendation. Cornyn wrote, "Major F. W. Benteen commanding the Tenth Missouri Cavalry was where a leader should be, in the front, and, by his coolness and great tact and skill, did much toward gaining the day."[32]

The festering animosities between the officers of the 10th came to a head on 10 August 1863, when at Cornyn's court-mar-

---

29. Mills, *Harvest,* 53-54.
30. Ibid, 54.
31. Ibid, 55.
32. Graham, *Myth,* 158.

tial, he punched Bowen. Bowen drew his revolver, Cornyn attempted to follow suit but was slow on the draw; Bowen cut loose with several rounds and Cronyn fell dead. Bowen was arrested, court-martialed for murder, and dismissed from the Army. Benteen was now acting commander of the 10th Missouri Cavalry Regiment.

In mid-October, the brigade was assigned a new commander, Colonel Edward F. Winslow, of the 4th Iowa Cavalry. The brigade, placed under command of Major General James B. McPherson's XVII Corps, consisted of the 10th Missouri and 4th Iowa along with the 4th, 5th, and 11th Illinois Cavalry Regiments.[33] In late October, Benteen took leave to go home to St. Louis to his wife and daughter of three months, whom he had yet to see. But he was back with his regiment and brigade by mid-November. Throughout the fall and winter into 1864, Benteen saw considerable action in Mississippi.

Benteen's name became increasingly mentioned in dispatches and correspondence. On 16 October, while in temporary command of the brigade and under heavy cannon fire, Winslow reported Benteen, among others, "as being a valuable and gallant officer." Again on 3 February 1864 Benteen led a dismounted attack near Bolton, Mississippi, and the enemy was "driven immediately from his positions with some loss," and on 5 February at Jackson, the 10th led by Benteen, advanced "at a gallop through the line of fortifications", and captured a valuable pontoon bridge.[34] And when Winslow fell ill in February, Benteen was given temporary command of the brigade. As the Federal XVII Corps started to return to Vicksburg, Benteen's brigade in the rear came under attack by a numerically superior Rebel force. Benteen

---

33. Mills, *Harvest,* 64.
34. War Department Records, Ibid, 70-73.

quickly deployed his units and drove the enemy brigades into retreat. "Splendid Benteen!" General McPherson enthusiastically gushed, "You never get sick and I always know where to find you!"[35] On his return to Vicksburg, Benteen was promoted to Lieutenant Colonel on 27 February, effective 14 February 1864. With Bowen's dismissal from the Army, Benteen filled his slot and became commander of the 10th.

The 10th Missouri, with Benteen now commanding, continued to engage in skirmishes with the rebels. On 1 May, the brigade was transferred to Memphis and immediately saw action at Bolivar, Tennessee. In July, the 10th was decimated when the three-year volunteer enlistments expired and most of the men, who had not seen home since December 1862, opted out. Benteen's 10th would finish the war with never many more than 300 men out of an authorized 1200.

In the fall of 1864, Confederate Major General Sterling Price led about 12,000 troops, known as the Army of Missouri, on a campaign with orders to take St. Louis, Jefferson City, Kansas City and Ft. Leavenworth, and then invade Illinois. Price advanced into Missouri from Arkansas on 19 September 1864, after first taking a licking from a small number of well entrenched Federals at Pilot Knob on the way north. With that exception, his march north was amazingly successful. But the reinforcement of St. Louis by 6000 Union troops forced him to proceed with a backup plan to capture Missouri for the Confederacy. He skirted the defenders at St. Louis and headed for Jefferson City. Major General Alfred Pleasonton was sent to Jefferson City to command Union forces. He immediately recognized a need for seasoned troops to combat Price. He called for Winslow's brigade, which

---

35. Mills, *Harvest*, 74

was now in St. Louis. Union troops were now in pursuit and the state militia was mobilized.

Price drove westward along the Missouri River, taking out the railroad as he went. He took or occupied several towns, bypassing Jefferson City. Price captured Independence, Missouri, east of Kansas City, on 21 October, driving out the Union troops under Major General Samuel R. Curtis. Curtis set up defenses south of Kansas City at Westport, waiting for Price to make his move and for Pleasonton to join up.

Pleasonton's cavalry arrived at Independence on the night of 22 October and waited to attack. Sending Winslow's brigade on a scout, they located a ford on the Big Blue River on the southeast flank of Price's army. Price now faced Union troops on two fronts. Despite an escape avenue to the south, he attacked Curtis and the fighting was fierce, neither knowing precisely where Pleasonton was and if, when, or where he would engage.

Winslow's brigade halted at the ford and reconnoitered. The Rebels were positioned on a hill about a half-mile beyond the west bank of the river and, unknown to Winslow, skirmishers were under cover along the river bank as well. Winslow ordered his artillery to shell the hill while he sent a forward unit of militia across the river. The Rebel skirmishers opened fire, wreaking havoc on the fording troops in the stream. The day had dawned cold and the water was frigid. Nonetheless, they were spurred on by their commander and reached the west bank, firing as they waded ashore, sputtering and shivering, forcing the skirmishers to fall back and re-deploy. The Confederates withdrew a few hundred yards and now Winslow's entire brigade lunged across the ford. On the west side, they dismounted and launched their assault, driving the skirmishers back until the brigade was finally pinned down under heavy fire at the base of the Rebel-held hill.

Winslow then took a round in the left leg; he relinquished command of the brigade to Benteen, and retired from the battle to find medical aid back on the east side of the river. It was now Benteen's brigade and up to him to make the best of it. But now the troops were showing some reluctance to advance and "...by dint of great urging and exertion of authority" Benteen got his men to attempt to take the hill, but after about an hour they had made little headway against the heavy Confederate fire pouring down from above.[36]

Meanwhile, an additional militia brigade forded the river and fell in behind Benteen's brigade and General Pleasonton arrived to pitch in with his troops. The impasse did not last long. The 4th Iowa detachment, on the left flank of Benteen's brigade, broke loose, and surged up a ravine toward the crest. The Southerners re-formed their line to meet the threat, thus giving Benteen's 10th Missouri the freedom of action to reinvigorate their own assault. They swarmed to the top of the hill with the rest of the brigade and the Rebels were put into full retreat.

Benteen stopped long enough to have the brigade's horses brought forward. He began a mounted pursuit of the Rebels, pausing to feed his mounts in a cornfield. But the sound of battle ahead cut his halt short and he rushed the brigade forward. He quickly encountered Pleasonton's militia brigades falling back under a Confederate counterattack. After a short, fruitless attempt to rally the militia, he charged with the 10th Missouri and routed the Rebels, effectively driving them from Missouri into Kansas. The battle of Westport would be called the Gettysburg of the West.[37]

---

36. War Department Records. Ibid, 85.
37. Ibid, 86.

Pleasonton and Curtis palavered and decided to join forces to pursue the Confederates and finish them off.[38] But they argued over who should take credit for the victory and the decision came late. The Rebels had at least a half-day's running start. Nonetheless, Price was unable to make good time because his wagon train, burdened with plunder from his Missouri raid, could only plod along. The Union troops hit the trail in pursuit. The weather was abysmal, and the pace was fast so that the horses, with scarce water and without forage, soon became jaded. After about forty miles of chase, they made camp just before it rained.

The next day, 25 October 1864, broke "...dull and dreary..." but cleared by mid- morning.[39] Benteen's brigade was given the lead in the chase under orders to engage the enemy upon contact. That contact came first at Mine Creek, some 80 miles south of Westport. The Rebels formed a line on the bank of the stream but were located by the brigade's forward skirmishers. Benteen ordered a charge. But the 10th Missouri, unaccountably, faltered and would not advance despite Benteen's vehement protestations and persistent orders to charge.

> Colonel Benteen's order to charge was instantly obeyed. The Tenth Missouri started forward with their 'yell' and their bugles sounding, but when they had covered half the distance, the enemy showing no sign of breaking, they hesitated and stopped. Their Colonel urged them with great spirit and they made spasmodic efforts to brace up, but failed.... Again and again Benteen ordered the charges, and many of his regiment made brave efforts to overcome the singular balk. Some got

---

38. Ibid, 87. Kansas governor Carney was also at the meeting. A true politician, he urged that the Kansas militia under Curtis be released in order that they could go home to vote. Curtis obliged when Pleasonton agreed to join him in the chase.
39. War Department Records, Ibid, 87-88

forward a little farther, but the line could not be moved. He persisted most heroically in trying to break the unfortunate situation. He rode directly in front of his men, within pistol shot of his enemy, hatless, white with passion, waving his sword and shouting the order to charge. His trumpeters repeated it, and all the trumpets in the column answered with the same piercing notes. Then for a few moments, the two opposing lines of men simply stood, glaring at each other.[40]

The 4th Iowa Cavalry Regiment, held up behind the reluctant 10th Missouri, had no choice but to advance around them. They charged with abandon on the Rebel's right side. The 3rd Iowa followed, attacking the center of the line. The 10th Missouri was sucked along in their wake giving courage to the militia brigade on Benteen's right flank (and whom Benteen had earlier had implored "for God's sake" to join him in his charge) which now took heart as the enemy began to break. Under the weight of the combined forces, the break turned into a rout. The Confederate Generals Cabell and Marmaduke were captured along with all the artillery.[41] In the rout, numerous Rebels were unhorsed crossing the swiftly flowing Mine Creek and attempting the slippery far bank; many drowned.[42] A vicious, running fight among individuals ensued. At the Little Osage River, eight miles south, Confederate General Jo Shelby formed a rear guard. Benteen had halted near Mine Creek to rest the regimental horses. Then he continued the pursuit. By mid-afternoon he faced Shelby, but he was low on ammunition and his horses were too spent for a charge. He waited for reinforcements, but they did not come. The infuriated Benteen watched the Rebels slowly withdraw toward the Marmaton River

---

40. Graham, *Myth*, 159. Graham quotes here the 4th Iowa Cavalry Regiment historian.
41. Ibid.
42. Mills, *Harvest*, 90.

and Missouri where Price ordered his stalled wagon train burned during the wee hours of 26 October.[43]

Price was beaten but the Yankees wanted him out of Missouri. Benteen kept up the chase, reluctantly, under orders. He wanted to get back into the thick of the fighting in the east. He wrote several requests to have his orders changed but with little luck. Finally, on 8 November, General Curtis met up with him near what is now Muskogee in the Indian Territory where Benteen had trailed Price and the remnants of his army. While meeting with Benteen, Curtis wrote Governor Willard P. Hall of Missouri:

> I have had the cooperation of a Brigade of Cavalry commanded by Lieutenant Colonel F. W. Benteen of the 10th Missouri Cavalry, who has exhibited the most fearless and distinguished success in the field of battle... I hope you will aid me in securing for him a Brigadier's commission, which he well deserves – and is most competent to fill.[44]

Returning from Indian Territory, Benteen's cavalry units were assigned to the Cavalry Corps, Military Division of the Mississippi, which was commanded by twenty-seven year-old Major General James Harrison Wilson, one of the many Civil War "Boy Generals". Wilson was preparing for a Confederate assault on Nashville, which was readily repulsed. He then set his sights on a raid through Alabama. Meanwhile, in mid-December, Winslow received a promotion to Brevet Brigadier General. The next most senior officers, Colonel John W. Noble of the 3rd Iowa Cavalry and Lieutenant Colonel Benteen were not elevated, primarily because there were so few men remaining in the brigade that such promotion would have resulted in an unwarranted top-heaviness

---
43. Ibid, 91-92.
44. Ibid, 95.

and no Generals were needed to command elsewhere. The 10th Missouri had fewer than 600 men and Benteen would finish the war a Lieutenant Colonel.

Two divisions under Wilson and including Benteen's (Winslow's) brigade halted north of Selma, Alabama, on 2 April 1865 and made ready to assault the well-defended Confederate manufacturing and munitions fortress. About 5,000 troops, well armed and fortified, defended the city and knew of Wilson's progress toward them. His would not be a surprise attack. The fortifications precluded a cavalry attack, but fortunately for Wilson, his men were more than capable of fighting on foot. The Rebels were overcome by a multi-pronged assault, and by mid-evening Selma fell to the Union troops. Benteen and his men acquitted themselves well; they charged the defenses under heavy fire then "scaled the works and waved their hats in triumph."[45] It was a victory in no small part owed to the aggressive use of superior firepower in the hands of temerarious cavalry.[46] In all, about 2,700 Confederates were captured along with their equipment and cannon. Their commander, Lieutenant General Nathan B. Forrest, escaped but Benteen's 10th Missouri did not lose a man. It was a significant victory at Selma, but one which would be remanded into obscurity.[47]

After the destruction of Selma, Wilson's units headed eastward toward Columbus, Georgia, where they arrived on 16 April 1865. Columbus was almost as important a manufacturing site for the Confederacy as was Selma. Sherman, on his infamous march

---

45. Hinricks in, Mills, *Harvest*, 104.
46. Mills, *Harvest*, 106. The Union troopers were armed with repeating Spencer carbines, pistols, and sabers. The Rebels had few, if any, comparable repeating firearms.
47. Ibid, 105-06. The victory got small shrift in the papers largely because no northern reporters witnessed the battle and because on that same day Grant took Richmond.

through Georgia, had bypassed Columbus but the defenders had prepared for its defense by fortifying its east side. Wilson's approach from the west caused consternation and hurried construction of defenses on the western reaches of Girard (now Phoenix City, Alabama), Columbus's twin city across the Chattahoochee River, connected by five bridges.

General Wilson ordered General Upton to attack after dark. Colonel John Noble's 3rd Iowa was to lead the assault on foot. Benteen's 10th Missouri and the 4th Iowa were held in mounted reserve. Noble's troops charged ahead without meeting strong resistance. Believing the Confederate defenses were now breached, Upton ordered Benteen and the 10th Missouri to charge and take the 14th Street footbridge. Noble's charge, however, had swept by the main defenses, which caught Benteen and his men essentially broadside. His formation broken, Benteen's command became scattered in the dark. Two companies made it through to the bridge, and captured a sizeable number of its defenders. But now Captain McGlasson, commanding the two-company detachment, found himself in an impossible advanced position, forcing him to release his prisoners and return to his own lines.[48]

In the excitement, confusion, and frustration accompanying the reorganization of the 10th, Benteen and Captain Hinricks, one of his company commanders, had words. While they upbraided each other, Captain Lot Abraham with Company D of the 4th Iowa, took the bridge. Benteen, now in command again of his reorganized cavalry, crossed the bridge into Georgia. The remaining defenders, militiamen mostly, were killed or routed. The battle of Columbus was over.

---

48. Ibid, 109-10.

Generals Upton and Winslow singled out several of the 10th Missouri's officers for citation. On 7 June General Wilson would append to the official reports: "I would also request that Lieut. Col. F. W. Benteen, Tenth Missouri Cavalry, be brevetted Brigadier-General for gallant and meritorious services, not only during the recent campaign in Georgia and Alabama, but for distinguished and conspicuous bravery in the pursuit of Price out of Missouri."[49] It was a sterling recommendation but nothing would come of it.[50]

His commanders had increasingly counted on Benteen, proven to be reliable and unflinching under fire, during the course of the war. He had participated in significant ways in eighteen major battles, including Wilson's Creek, Pea Ridge, the siege of Vicksburg, the fight at Tupelo, and the victory at Selma; he would be awarded brevets up to Lieutenant Colonel in the Regular Army after the war for his actions at the Battle of the Osage and the charge on Columbus.[51] Nonetheless, personality and character traits began to emerge during the war that would later bring him grief. And the lack of recognition for the major Union victory at Selma and for his role there and elsewhere, effectively instilled in him a resentment that his battlefield accomplishments in the Civil War were not given the same recognition as the much publicized exploits of others with whom he would serve in the Regular Army on the western frontier.[52]

Although his actions under fire were admirable, he did have his difficulties with some of the trivialities attendant military service. Hardly a shrinking violet, his first run-in with a military superior came on 18 April 1862. Bowen was by mid-April exhausted.

---

49. War Department Records. Ibid, 114.
50. Ibid, 115.
51. Utley, *Life,* 250.
52. Mills, *Harvest,* 105-06.

He requested, and was granted, a thirty-day leave to rest and recuperate from the wrist wound he received at Pea Ridge. Captain Stanford Ing of B Company was appointed his temporary replacement. Ing delivered a written special order from the acting assistant adjutant of the Army of the Southwest for a Corporal in Benteen's company to report to headquarters as an orderly.[53] Furious, Captain Benteen grabbed the order from Ing's hand and scribbled on it, needing both sides:

> Corporal Weaver declines the polite invitation to leave his mess, and feels highly insulted at his rank being not attended to. Adjutant, Corporal Weaver cannot and shall not come, nor do I recognize the right of any one to detail the men of my Co. by name – they have taken of some of the best of them and if they want them all, my resignation is at their service. The company is small enough, without furnishing servants for Staff Captains, as one of them is at present.

Ing wrote Benteen up, the charges for the same offense included "...disrespectful behavior towards his commanding officer...", and "...conduct prejudicial to good order and military discipline...."

Nothing was to come of it,[54] but this kind of spontaneous sarcastic anger was to pepper his career and exact a toll on his reputation as an officer and gentleman.

A family drama also played out during the war. Old Charley Benteen had taken to running guns on the Mississippi for the Confederacy. In August of 1862, the gun running steamboat *Fair Play* with Charley aboard was captured by a Union flotilla near Vicksburg. The civilians aboard were eventually released, but inex-

---

53. Ibid, 35. The "acting assistant adjutant of the Army of the Southwest" was Henry Zarah Curtis, son of General Curtis.
54. Ibid, 35-36. Ing would resign his commission in mid May of 1862.

plicably, Charley Benteen remained incarcerated for the duration of the war. Some years later, in 1875, Frederick Benteen's seven-year-old son Freddie let the cat out of the bag: his dad had interceded to have granddad locked up for his own good. Charley fumed but understood and the matter was dropped after he wrote to his son who was posted on the prairie, "Some little boys talk too damn much."[55] It is not perfectly clear as to how large a role Benteen played in the capture of Charley if any,[56] but it is likely that Benteen engineered his father's lock-up for his own well being.[57]

After the Confederate surrender, Benteen mustered out to take up residence in the Atlanta area, buying a farm there. But the war had changed him and the trumpet beckoned. In September of 1866, following the implementation of the Army Act of 1866 expanding the Regular Army, Benteen applied for a commission in the Regular Army. His credentials and references were impeccable.[58] Benteen accepted a commission as Captain in the newly formed 7th Cavalry, by letter dated 24 November 1866, after first

---

55. Ibid, 39-45. Benteen was well connected with a number of officials who could have seen to Charley's lockup. Among his close associates and good friends were Captain John Noble, 3rd Iowa Cavalry, Judge Advocate General for the Army of the Southwest and Captain Edward F. Winslow of the 4th Iowa Cavalry, Provost Marshal of the District of Eastern Arkansas.
56. Asay, *Gray Head,* 3-4. Asay argues convincingly that the story that son Fred Benteen related to Graham was likely a faulty reconstruction of an imperfect childhood memory as it conflicts significantly with documented facts. It gave live ammunition to Benteen's critics, however.
57. Mills, *Harvest,* 39-45.
58. Ibid, 124-25. Benteen's character references were Generals Curtis, Pleasonton, and Upton and the mayor of St. Louis and the governor of Missouri. According to Mills, the story of his declining a majority in a colored regiment was told by Benteen to a correspondent in 1891 and is unsubstantiated by any written Army record. It may have been a verbal offer or it may not be true, which Mills doubts. Mills points out that Benteen's admission in 1891 was made "ruefully" and "he did accept a majority in a colored regiment seventeen years later with minimal reluctance."

declining a Major's billet in the 10th Cavalry because he did not want to command colored troops, in part because of prejudice and in part because such assignments were not considered prestigious.[59] It was a decision he later came to rue. Benteen's father, old Charley, with whom he had now completely reconciled, would manage the farm. Kate, pregnant with their second child, would remain in Atlanta until the baby was born and would be old enough to travel to join Captain Benteen in his new assignment at Fort Riley, Kansas.[60]

---

59. Asay, *Gray Head*, 5.
60. Mills, *Harvest*, 125.

CHAPTER 3

THE FIGHTING SEVENTH

Following the tragedy of the American Civil War, Congress authorized the formation of thirty new Army regiments on 28 July 1866. Four of these regiments were horse units and among those, the newly created 7th Cavalry Regiment was assigned to Fort Riley, Kansas, for the protection of the railroad, frontier settlers and westward-migrating pioneers. Major John W. Davidson of the 2nd Cavalry, already posted to Fort Riley, oversaw the early formation of the regiment, shuffling several hundred roughshod recruits into companies, and late in 1866 the officers of the 7th began to report for duty.

Many of the newly reporting officers had served only with Volunteer units in the Civil War and were unfamiliar with Regular Army custom and dress code, to the amusement of the Regulars.[1] In January 1867, Benteen headed west by train

---

1. Reedstrom, *Bugles*, 2.

to join his new outfit in the frontier Army as the senior Captain.[2]

Back in the summer of 1861, about the time Benteen began drilling Union volunteers into shape in Missouri, a spanking new Second Lieutenant with whom fate would forever link him in history was making a remarkable name for himself in Virginia, as a Union cavalry officer. Both of these men shared in common a rare virtue: incredible valor and coolness under fire. In most other respects they were as different as night and day.

George Armstrong Custer was born in New Rumley, Ohio, on 5 December 1839. His father called him Armstrong, but his own baby pronunciation shortened it to Autie, a moniker that stuck with family and close friends until his death. At age 10 he was sent to live with his married half-sister Lydia Reed, in Monroe, Michigan, about 25 miles north of Toledo.[3] He was a popular lad, well known as a practical joker and as time went by, one who apparently cut a swath through the teenage girls in both Michigan and Ohio as he alternated homesteads between his sister's and mother's. He was smart enough at school, but excelled only at subjects that were of keen interest to him. However, he was set on getting a good education and badly wanted an appointment to West Point, which would provide him with just that education, and at a cost he could bear. Unfortunately, his father and family were well known Democrats and the local congressman was neither a Democrat nor fond of them. Nonetheless, characteristically,

---

2. Mills, *Harvest*, 125. Of the four new cavalry regiments, two – the 9th and 10th – were filled with Negro troops (USCT, United States Colored Troops) and two – the 7th and 8th – were manned by whites.
3. Custer's early life, Civil War and frontier Indian fighting exploits are chronicled in Merington, *Custer Story,* Kinsley, *Soldier's Story,* Monahan, *Life,* Urwin, *Custer Victorious,* Van de Water, *Glory-hunter,* Whittaker, *Life,* and Connell, *Morning Star.* The books of Van de Water and Whittaker are remarkable in their contrasting treatment of the Boy General. Whittaker, Custer's first biographer, also was a major player in the controversy that surrounds his demise. Connell weaves a particularly fascinating tale.

Custer took the bull by the horns and got an interview and an appointment. Congressman John H. Bingham later was able to (and did) take credit for identifying at such an early age such an able soldier.[4]

Custer graduated from the U.S. Military Academy at West Point on 24 June 1861. The Civil War had started and he was eager to get to the battlefields, but as his newly commissioned classmates marched off to do battle, he remained behind under arrest for failing to exercise his duty in breaking up a fight between two incoming cadets. Fortunately for Armstrong, this was wartime and Regular Army officers were in demand. He was court-martialed but not much came of it; his West Point commanding officer vouched for him and he was let off with a reprimand and sent packing to Washington for assignment. There he met briefly with his former roommate, Jim Parker, who had not graduated. He was shocked to learn that Parker had accepted a commission in the Confederate Army. He was unable to dissuade Parker and convince him to return to the Academy. Custer, for whom the abstractions of a principled stand meant little, later stating that the most meaningless subjects he studied at the academy were philosophy and ethics, remained puzzled over Parker's decision throughout his lifetime.[5]

Custer quickly skyrocketed to fame with his reckless daring-do on the battlefield and by his twenty-fifth year was he commanding as a Major General a volunteer cavalry division. He was the true golden boy of the U. S. Army and the public: tall, slim, fit, golden-haired, and in possession of an enormous walrus mustache. Although none less than General Sheridan pushed for a postwar permanent rank of Major General for Custer, Republi-

---

4. Monaghan, *Life*, 9-10.
5. Ibid, 42-44.

cans in the catbird seat in Congress would have none of it; his Democratic Party lineage and his friendship with southerners after the hostilities ceased were well known. His appointment as General of volunteers expired on 31 January 1866 and he reverted to his regular army rank of Captain.[6] Nonetheless, in Washington a short time later Custer, while trying to get himself a fat assignment, prevailed on Secretary of War Stanton to give regular Army commissions to his brother Tom and friend and civil war comrade George Yates.[7]

Assigned to the newly formed 7th Cavalry in November 1866, with a rank-skipping promotion to Lieutenant Colonel, Custer arrived in early 1867, bringing along his comely and devoted wife Libby (Elizabeth), George Yates, his brother Tom, his black maid Eliza, four horses and a black jockey who rode them in races, and assorted dogs, both pets and hunting hounds.[8] As a Lieutenant Colonel (through the strong sponsorship of General Phil Sheridan, under whom he had served in the Civil War) he effectively became the commanding officer as the Regimental Colonel, Andrew Jackson Smith, had been seconded to other duties.[9] So it was he and Libby who received in their quarters the Regiment's new senior Captain, the sardonic, opinionated Frederick Benteen, on 30 January 1867. The courtesy visit did not go well. Custer dominated the conversation, broke out his scrapbook, and carried on at length about his wartime exploits. He made a deprecatory remark about his rival Wilson, Benteen's Civil War commander and hero, and Benteen was offended by it and by the short shrift that Custer paid to Wilson's highly regarded cavalry campaign.

---

6. Ambrose, *Crazy Horse,* 252.
7. Ibid, 253.
8. Ibid, 257-58.
9. It was generally assumed that the Regimental Commander was kept on detached service by Sheridan for Custer's benefit, Utley, *Life,* 274.

The perspicacious Mrs. Custer politely interceded before things got out of hand, but damage was done.[10] "...[T]he impression made on me at that interview was not a favorable one. I had been on intimate personal relations with many great Generals and had heard no such bragging as was stuffed into me that night."[11] Custer and Benteen were still on outwardly friendly terms when, a short time after that first disastrous meeting, Benteen cleaned out the pot at a card game in the Custer residence. He referred to Custer as "a rotten poker player"[12], and also collected a $150 IOU from his Lieutenant, Weir, writing later that it was never paid.[13]

In addition to his fighting experience as a cavalry commander, Benteen brought to the 7th a genuine concern for the troops under his command, a characteristic not generally attributed to the acting Regimental Commander, Custer. He later wrote that

> ...Gen. Custer had in use a hole deeply dug in the ground about 30 x 30 feet, by about 15 feet deep, entrance by ladder, hole boarded over: *this was the guard house,* and a man even absent from a call was let down. [There were so many of them] I don't know how the prisoners laid down.[14]

Nor did Benteen condone any bullying of troops by the non-commissioned officers. He presided over the court-martial of Sgt. John Ryan in 1876 at Fort Rice, Dakota Territory, who was con-

---

10. Mills, *Harvest,* 129. Mills wrote that this initial visit "...wasn't the low point in the Custer-Benteen relationship by any means, but it was a bad beginning."
11. Benteen, letter to Golden, in Carroll, *Letters,* 247.
12. Mills, *Harverst,* 130.
13. Benteen, letter to Goldin, in Carroll, *Letters,* 248.
14. Ibid, 257-58.

victed of tying up a soldier by the wrists for cutting a halter strap. Ryan was reduced to the ranks.[15]

Both Benteen and Custer had proved to be courageous under fire, both were at times unbearably egotistical, and both were hubristic and prone to brag about their military accomplishments,[16] yet two more differently flawed personalities could not have been juxtaposed. Custer's "manner and tone [were] usually brusque and aggressive; or somewhat rasping" and "it was not his habit to unbosom himself to his officers";[17] Benteen's style and speech were described as that of a courtly Virginia gentleman.[18] They would clash throughout their association and surrogates would carry on the feud well after their deaths.

The white settlers' southern route west cut straight through the Southern Plains Cheyenne Indians' homeland, to their great aggravation, and as the westward flow along the Santa Fe Trail continued unabated and even accelerated, the Cheyenne and their cohorts, the Arapaho, became increasingly bellicose. In February 1867, various companies of the 7th were posted to forts on the Kansas and Colorado frontier with the regimental headquarters and Companies A, D, M, and Benteen's company H, remaining at Fort Riley. The troopers were a hodge-podge of German and Irish immigrants, with a mix of lads from the cities, towns and farms east of the Mississippi River, and a fair share of rogues. In general, it was a "motley assortment."[19] They were overseen by a cadre of tough veteran Regular Army non-commissioned officers, tempered in the fire of the Civil War; some had service time back to the Mexican War. The First Sergeants were expected by their

---

15. Ryan, letter to Libby, in Rickey, *Beans and Hay,* 139-140
16. Asay, *Gray Head,* 29.
17. Godfrey, Last Battle," *Century Magazine,* 17.
18. Bentley in Asay, *Gray Head,* 6.
19. Rickey, *Beans and Hay,* 50

officers to administer company affairs, which they did through the duty Sergeants and Corporals. They meted out discipline, sometimes with their fists when necessary, except in grievous cases serious enough to warrant officer's attention and possibly court-martial.[20]

Officer billets had not yet been completely filled and new officers continued to report for duty as the first half of 1867 progressed. One, Joel Elliott, arrived on 23 May 1867 as a twenty six year old Major, a rank probably granted to ward off the wrath of his politically powerful sponsor, Governor Oliver P. Morton of Indiana, after his initial application for a commission was misplaced. There was some initial consternation and resentment among the officers of the 7th, but Elliott's pleasant and captivating personality soon won them over. He and Benteen became particularly good friends.[21]

As the regimental officers began to trickle in, it was only natural that cliques would form. In general, there developed an "in-crowd," those in Custer's favor, and an "out-crowd", those less highly regarded by their acting commander or those who did not highly regard the acting commander. These distinctions were further sharpened as the factions could also in general be classified as teetotalers and imbibers. Custer did not drink, smoke, nor, at Libby's request, swear. The same cannot be said of many of his officers. The officer corps of the 7th seems to have had its fair share of miscreants and drunkards. A short list of some of the notables includes Major Wycliff Cooper, who, after "exhausting his supply of whiskey…in a fit of delirium tremens, shot himself in the head with his pistol."[22] Captain Charles Cooper was "cash-

---

20. Ibid, 60-62.
21. Mills, *Harvest,* 130-31.
22. Utley, *Life,* 254.

iered following conviction on charges of drunkenness on duty and misappropriation of public property."[23] Captain Myles Keogh, who "sometimes became so boozy" that his striker "concluded that the safest place for the valuables and the family funds was in his own quarters."[24] Captain Samuel Robbins, was court-martialed "for offenses involving repeated public drunkenness: he had openly cohabited with a woman in Louisville's Galt House, he had beaten Lieutenant A. E. Smith's horse and then Smith himself, and he had knocked down a quartermaster Sergeant who declined to drink with him."[25] Lieutenant H. Walworth Smith, "…was charged with embezzling $1,200 and promptly deserting from camp near Fort Hays."[26] Lieutenant David Wallingford, was court-martialed; the court "found his behavior with 'a notorious prostitute or lewd woman' in the Perry House and American House hotels in Sheridan, Kan., an offense 'to the scandal and disgrace of the military service'" and dismissed him from the Army.[27] Captain Albert Barnitz summed it up:

> …there appears to be a premium offered for drunkenness in the army! Almost *all* the old officers drink a great deal. …a man is not regarded as sociable who does not keep a sort of open house and have something for his friends to drink, and he has a very small chance of becoming popular with the drinking class, unless he indulges a little himself – in fact, they are rather inclined to regard him with some distrust.…[28]

---

23. Ibid.
24. Libby Custer, Ibid, 264.
25. Ibid, 272.
26. Ibid, 276.
27. Ibid, 280.
28. Barnitz, in Utley, *Life,* 203. Barnitz, who did not like Custer but who also did not drink, kept a gift bottle of whiskey in his kit, "to cure snake-bites."

Custer tried to get his officers to cut down on the devil's spirits but was not very successful. It is likely that Benteen, a drinker, did not care for Custer's prodding on the subject, which may have contributed to the early coolness between them.[29] It was probably Custer's moral obligation as commanding officer to attempt to curtail those activities but likely that was not his motivation. He did not imbibe and preferred that others did not. Of the drinking class, Captain Robert M. West may not have been typical, but certainly he was not anomalous. West, an extremely capable officer commanding Company K, was a "distinguished man, but given at times to hellish periodical sprees."[30] He too became a bitter foe of Custer. To West's great distaste, Custer had ordered him while at Fort Hays to shave the heads of six soldiers who had gone to the sutler's store, absent without leave. Subsequently, Custer ordered that two deserters from West's troop were to be shot.

The Army was posted at a number of forts, distributed across Kansas in the rough form of a horizontal **Y**. At the base to the east was Fort Leavenworth on the Missouri River. Westward, at the confluence of the Republican and Kansas Rivers was Fort Riley followed by Fort Harker on the Smokey Hill River along the railroad route west from Fort Leavenworth. The northern branch of the **Y** was comprised of Fort Hays and Fort Wallace in a line along the Smoky Hill River. The southern branch comprised Fort Zarah, Fort Larned and Fort Dodge, all along or near the Arkansas River.

The westward advancement of the settlers and the Army's presence along the frontier were insult enough for the Indians, but the reprehensible Treaty of Medicine Lodge seemed to be the last straw. It was a masterpiece of chicanery. The Cheyenne were

---

29. Asay, *GrayHead*, 7-8.
30. Benteen, letter to Goldin, in Carroll, *Letters*, 252-53.

promised farm implements, livestock, construction of a gristmill, firearms and ammunition, and a community house to be built on the reservation where additional annuity goods could be delivered. All this was in exchange for their confining hunting to a reservation south of the Arkansas River and for stopping the raids on whites in western Kansas. However, in order to encourage the Chiefs to sign, the government's interpreters were instructed to tell the Cheyenne that they could continue to hunt anywhere in western Kansas as long as there were buffalo and provided they didn't harass the settlers.[31] The Treaty itself was never read to the Indians, and they signed it "as a matter of form."[32] Major Joel Elliott, who provided escort to the treaty commissioners that executed the document, considered it a sham and reported that the Indian chiefs had no understanding of what they signed.[33] Since the Indians had been completely misled that they could roam western Kansas, the seeds of war were now sown. The Indians continued to hunt in western Kansas in violation of the written Medicine Lodge Treaty, believing what they were told on Medicine Lodge Creek. Soon the delivery of the goods promised began to falter or were delivered short. The Indians, who were constantly warring among themselves, began instead increasingly to attack the railroad and white settlements wherever they found them.

In April of 1867, General Winfield Scott Hancock, a highly decorated Civil War veteran, led an expedition in south central Kansas against the Indians, which turned out to be a "dismal failure."[34] Hancock ended up burning a village but the campaign produced nothing but the ire of the Indians. It was on this campaign

---

31. Hoig, *Washita,* 36.
32. Stanley, Ibid, 37. This was the Stanley of Dr. Livingston fame.
33. Ibid.
34. Utley, *Life,* 29.

that Custer realized how little he knew about Indian fighting.[35] Custer was patrolling western Kansas and into Nebraska and Colorado, and he was thoroughly frustrated at his inability to catch up with any Indians, despite the abundant signs that they were around in numbers. In early July he launched a scout from his camp on the Republican River, arriving a week later at Riverside Station, Colorado, about forty miles west of Fort Sedgewick. He telegraphed General Sherman, who was commanding troops there, for further orders. Sherman notified Custer that Lieutenant Lyman S. Kidder and a detail of ten men and a Sioux scout had been sent from Fort Sedgewick with dispatches for him. With no sign of Kidder, Custer retraced his route in search of the detail. On 12 July, his point men discovered a dead horse and evidence of a running fight along Beaver Creek. Following the trail, the mutilated and partially burned remains of the detail were discovered in a dry ravine. They had been dead about ten days. Only the dead Sioux scout was not scalped. They were buried in a common grave.[36] Grisly sights and distasteful duties were all too common on the frontier, which further compounded the bleak existence of the soldiers.

Custer's harsh command and discipline extended to pushing men and horses to their limits and beyond, without adequate rest. In August 1867 he would be court-martialed for being absent without leave, and for ordering an unnecessary forced march without adequate care and rest for the horses and men.[37] These incidents occurred during his foray through northern Kansas into Nebraska and Colorado. Custer's heart was not into chasing Indians and he had no luck in catching them. He became despondent

---

35. Ibid, 256.
36. Cooper, *Kidder Massacre*.
37. Frost, *Court-Martial*.

over the harsh conditions in the field, the difficulty in re-supplying his column, and the long absence from Libby. His men also had had enough and were deserting in droves. While encamped near Fort McPherson on the South Platte River in Nebraska, a number of troopers openly deserted. Furious, Custer ordered Major Elliott and a detail of troopers to give chase and "bring none in alive."[38] Six deserters were rounded up and brought back. Three were wounded and one died subsequently of his wounds. One of the wounded men and the dead trooper were from Captain West's company, further inflaming West's hatred of his commander.

Following a hard march to camp near Fort Wallace, the column was exhausted. Nonetheless, Custer without authorization mustered four officers and seventy-two men for a forced march to Fort Riley. While Custer was making his unauthorized return to Fort Riley, on a pretense of requesting new orders but, it was widely assumed, to see his wife and personally escort her to Fort Wallace, two men of a detail sent to find his missing spare mare and her keeper, were reported killed by Indians. Custer did not return to their aid or to recover the bodies, causing great controversy and consternation among his officers and men.[39] Captain Arthur B. Carpenter of the 37th Infantry subsequently sent a detail to recover the bodies. One body and one wounded soldier were discovered; the dead soldier was buried and the wounded trooper was carried back to post for recovery.[40] Charges were immediately brought against Custer for leaving his post without authorization to return to Fort Riley, and for other associated misjudgments. No sooner had General Hancock endorsed Custer's court-martial, when the infuriated Captain West added the addi-

---

38. Utley, *Cavalier,* 52.
39. Mills, *Harvest,* 145.
40. Millbrook, *Custer,* 141.

tional charge to the already long list of charges against Custer: that of summarily shooting deserters, causing the death of one and subsequently denying the other wounded troopers medical care while transporting them back to confinement.[41]

Custer was starting to develop a reputation for a complete disregard of his soldiers and for abandoning men in battle, a reputation that would follow, although not particularly bother, him throughout his short life. A major strategy in his defense was based on "self-justification and indignation" and "the outraged rhetoric of injured innocence, a posture that would at least have had the virtue of consistency."[42] He wrote a friend during a recess in the trial, apparently with some satisfaction, stating that "West is drinking himself to death, has delirium tremens, to such an extent the Prosecution will not put him on the witness stand."[43] His court-martial ended on 11 October 1867. Custer and West traded tit-for-tat for a while; West was responsible for a murder indictment lodged against Custer for shooting the trooper; this allegation dragged him into civil court after his court-martial, but the charges were dismissed. Custer in turn had West court-martialed for drunkenness, for which West received a suspension of two months from the Army.[44] But his own court-martial sentence sent Custer packing, "suspended from rank and command for one year, and forfeit...pay for the same time."[45] Benteen was relieved: "At all events, we were free of Custer till autumn of 1868."[46]

In March of 1868, General Philip H. Sheridan replaced General Hancock as department commander, a command change that

---

41. Utley, Ibid, *52.* Utley states that "Custer loudly denied these men medical attention and then quietly ordered the surgeon to care for them."
42. Barnett, *Touched*,142.
43. Merington, *Custer Story,* 211-12.
44. Utley, *Life,* 281.
45. Court-martial record, in Frost, *Court-Martial,* 246.
46. Benteen, letter to Goldin, in Carroll, *Letters,* 252.

did Benteen no harm inasmuch as they had known and thought well of each other since the Civil War when they were both Captains. From May to October 1868, Benteen was Commanding Officer at Fort Harker. It was there that Kate and infant Freddie, 11 months old, joined him for the first time to live together on an Army post, in quarters overlooking the parade ground. As they settled into Army life, Benteen developed a close association with a group of young officers who dined and likely drank together – a "mess of seven." The messmates are not all positively identified but included Benteen, Major Elliott, Lieutenants Owen Hale, Donald McIntosh and William W. Cooke and either Captain West or Captain Edward Myers.[47]

While commanding at Fort Harker, Benteen appropriated some horses for H Company and for his mess-mate Lieutenant Owen Hale's M Company that were intended for the 10th Cavalry. He substituted their worn mounts in exchange. The commander of the 10th was surprised that his new horses bore regimental brands of the 7th; there was uproar and a complaint went up the chain of command, all the way to General Sheridan. "I simply exchanged some horses for others I thought would suit us better," was Benteen's uncharacteristic understatement.[48]

In August, Benteen and his troopers, while visiting Fort Larned "were amusing themselves visiting the Indian camps and making friends with their foes of the previous summer" when a large, rabid wolf loped into the fort and "commenced biting a number of the military people there."[49] The wolf bit a sentinel, ran into the hospital and bit a bedridden man, pulled another from his bed and severely mauled him, took a finger nearly off of

---

47. Mills, *Harvest*, 147-48.
48. Carroll, *Cavalry Scraps*, 7.
49. Mills, *Harvest*, 150.

another, bit at some woman, then attacked one or two others in bed, and proceeded to Captain Nolan's house where he thoroughly abused a large dog. In passing Colonel Wyncoop's house, he leapt on the porch and bit Lieutenant Thompson several times before being dispatched by a guard whom he also tried to bite.[50] "...[I]t scared Thompson pissless...and well it might"; the wolf bit through Thompson's "pants, drawers and socks, thus getting rid of all the virus on clothes.... All the others bitten by the wolf, died of hydrophobia."[51]

About a week after the mad wolf episode, the news of Indians beating and killing settlers and ravaging their womenfolk along the Saline River made its way to Fort Larned.[52] Two troops, Benteen's H and Hale's M, were sent back to Fort Harker to better position themselves to engage the Indians. Benteen moved out rapidly with a small compliment of his men. Hale was instructed to follow with the rest of the force as fast as the horses could bear. Benteen covered the eighty miles to Fort Harker in two days. There he put together a force of about 40 men, made up of his own troops and spare soldiers from the fort. While he was preparing, he sent a non-commissioned officer and a scout to the Saline River. They reported back that night that the river was running too high to ford. Benteen took this to be a "cock-and-bull story" and struck out for the Saline early the next morning, 13 August.[53] Crossing the river without difficulty, they stopped for their morning meal.

Breaking camp about an hour later, Benteen and his scouts proceeded up a small knoll where they immediately accosted about 50 Indians who, unbeknown to Benteen at the moment,

---

50. Barnitz, in Utley, *Life,* 178.
51. Benteen, letter to Goldin, in Carroll, *Letters,* 277.
52. Hoig, *Washita* 46-47.
53. Benteen, in Carroll, *Cavalry Scraps, 1.*

were separated from a larger war party of over 200. He ordered his pack mules to be herded up and put under guard of a sergeant and 10 men.

The surprised Indians had just raided a homestead and were carrying off two young girls. But with jaded ponies and the cavalry galloping into their midst, the Indians had no choice but to turn their captives loose. Benteen had his 30-odd men in a column-of-twos, and although they were greatly outnumbered, apparently it gave the appearance that his force was much larger as they galloped into view in file over the rise. Finding the girls, he told them to keep moving downriver and galloped off after the Cheyenne. (A rescue party found the girls safe after they had spent a frightening night alone.) Benteen would halt and dismount his troopers periodically, who opened up with their Spencer repeating carbines "…as the Indians in their retreat kept well bunched…we would…pump five shots from the carbines into the mob, reload, and thus having given our chargers a breathing spell, would mount and get as close to the gang again as we dared, and repeated the same tactics…" Benteen kept after them for almost twenty miles, until dark.

The Indians were reluctant to stop and fight, likely because of their uncertainty about how many troops were pursuing them and, as Benteen later discovered, because they were carrying their dead and wounded. The dead included their war party chief, and thus Benteen surmised that their war "…medicine was a trifle mouldy." Benteen sent for his pack mules and quickly sent a report to Fort Larned: three Indians killed and 10 wounded without a single Army casualty. The running fight would make Benteen a hero with the settlers and more importantly provide the 7th Cavalry with its first unequivocal victory over the Cheyenne. He would receive his first post-Civil War brevet, to full Colonel, for his actions at the Saline River.[54]

Returning to Fort Harker, he met his old Civil War acquaintance, Phil Sheridan, whom he had not seen since the Civil War. Complimenting Sheridan on his rise to General Officer, Sheridan responded, "Benteen, I saw chances, in fact sought them, got the opportunities, and, well, I did the very best I could with them, and here I am. God bless you! Let's take a drink." It was an offer Benteen could not refuse.[55]

The rampaging Dog Soldiers, a Cheyenne warrior society – "the bravest, ugliest, most vindictive and determined Indians of our day"[56] – proved especially difficult to corral in the summer of 1868. They roamed freely across the plains, raiding at will. Lieutenant Colonel (Brevet Brigadier General) Alfred Sully, Commanding Officer of the Arkansas District, led an expedition in September 1868 against the Cheyenne. They departed Fort Dodge Kansas and headed south across the Arkansas River toward the Cimarron where they reckoned the Cheyenne to be in large numbers. There were some skirmishes but the expedition was not a success.

The attacks on the settlers and the taking of women and children by the Indians prompted the State of Kansas to appeal for military assistance. This aid came when Congress authorized the formation of the 18th and 19th Kansas Volunteer Cavalry. Significantly and in an unusual move for a politician, Samuel J. Crawford, governor of Kansas resigned to assume the colonelcy of the 19th at Topeka.[57]

The event that set the relationship between Custer and Benteen in an irreversible downward spiral took place on the bitter-

---

54. Mills, *Harvest*, 152.
55. Benteen, in Carroll, *Cavalry, Scraps*, 2-5.
56. Anonymous news reporter, in Hoig, Ibid, 32.
57. Godfrey, *Reminiscences*, 161.

cold morning of 27 November 1868 on the plains of northern Oklahoma where the Battle of the Washita was fought.[58] The Army brass was increasingly anxious for results on the plains. General Sherman, commander of the Military Division of the Missouri and General Sheridan, commander of the Military Department of the Missouri under Sherman, were set on bringing total war to the Plains Indians.

In the Fall of 1868, Generals Sherman and Sheridan organized a winter campaign to attack the Indians in their camps, reckoning that they would be made immobile by winter conditions. Sheridan spent the summer and fall in the field to oversee firsthand the efforts of the cavalry to keep the Indians on the run, and Benteen was assigned some of that time to escort him. In addition to his own Company H, he had Owen Hale's Company M under his command for this task. Sheridan complimented Benteen on the quality of his horses, stating it "was the finest mount he ever saw a troop of cavalry have."[59] At a rendezvous point where an infantry unit was to take over the escort, the foot soldiers were nowhere to be found. Sheridan then wanted to know if Benteen's horses were up to the task of continuing on to Fort Hays. Benteen, aware that Sheridan had seen the complaint about the horse incident at Fort Harker, replied that he wouldn't have swapped horses with the 10th if they were in poorer shape than the ones he had unloaded. Sheridan did not comment, but nothing more was ever heard of the unauthorized horse-trading.[60]

---

58. The discussion of the Washita fight is largely encapsulated from Hoig, *Washita* and Utley, *Cavalier.* Benteen's role in it is summarized from Mills, *Harvest.* For a short summary of the battle see also Keenan, *Indian Wars*, 243-44.
59. Benteen, letter to Goldin, in Carroll, *Letters,* 264.
60. Carroll, *Cavalry Scraps,* 6.

To achieve the goal of ending the Indian war in Kansas, Sheridan needed an aggressive field commander. But the 7th was thin on experienced leaders. The senior officers, Major Elliott and Captain William Thompson, were on leave of absence, so Benteen, a brevet Lieutenant Colonel (he was later to be awarded his brevet to the rank of full colonel for his actions at Saline River), was offered the command of the 7th in the field. Surprisingly, he rejected the offer and recommended instead that Custer be recalled early from his restricted duty in Washington, hoping that he would return instilled with more sense than when he left:

> I politely but firmly declined the compliment of being so selected, recommending...that Sheridan secure the remission of [the] unexpired portion of Custer's [court-martial] sentence, and let him join command, saying that perhaps he would have, and exhibit, more sense and judgment that he had during his former short tour in command. So Custer came.[61]

But that generosity of Benteen toward his commander would be short lived. On 24 September 1868, Sheridan telegraphed Custer who was serving out his suspension at home in Monroe:

> "Generals Sherman, Sully, and myself, and nearly all the officers of your regiment, have asked for you, and I hope the application will be successful. Can you come at once? Eleven companies of your regiment will move about the 1st of October against the hostile Indians."[62]

---

61. Benteen, letter to Goldin, in Carroll, *Letters*, 252. Benteen had been on good terms with Sheridan since the Civil War and would remain in good stead throughout his military career. The same cannot be said of Custer. Sheridan's admiration and fondness for his protégé had cooled by the conclusion of the winter of 1868-1869. Mills, *Harvest*, 184.

62. Merington, *Custer Story*, 216.

Could he come at once? Need Sheridan have asked? And "...he did not come back chastened, by any manner of means."[63]

On 10 October Custer and Benteen arrived at Camp Sandy Forsyth south of Fort Dodge on the Arkansas River in preparation for the impending winter campaign. Neither officer was so discomfited in their relationship that it precluded Custer's asking Benteen for a loan or Benteen's making one, albeit grudgingly. About two weeks after settling in at Camp Forsyth, Benteen was instructed by Custer to proceed only with an orderly through the 90 miles of Indian country to Fort Harker to bring back fresh horses and some recruits who were waiting there. And, by the way, could he send $100 to Mrs. Custer at Fort Leavenworth? Benteen was known in the regiment for having plenty of money on hand. "I then began to see why I was selected! ...I got to Fort Harker O.K. First duty performed was to send to Mrs. Custer my check on First Nat'l Bank of Leavenworth for $100."[64]

Benteen began his return to Camp Sandy Forsyth a few days later, accompanied by his orderly, two 2nd Lieutenants from Fort Harker, one of their wives, nearly 80 recruits and the horses. En route he discovered that a Mexican wagon train loaded with arms and ammunition was to have awaited his arrival at Fort Larned but instead had already departed and was ahead of him on the trail. He hurried to catch up. In a scenario that could have been confused with a Hollywood B-western, his column came upon the circled wagon train in the midst of an Indian attack. Hurriedly mustering about 25 recruits, Benteen charged the Indians (it is unknown if there was a trumpeter among the recruits to blow charge!); he "had the red scamps run off" before the rest of his detail could

---

63. Mills, *Harvest,* 154. Custer's sentence was not commuted, rather the balance was remitted. Graham, *Myth,* 204, note.
64. Benteen, letter to Goldin, in Carroll, *Letters,* 263.

join forces. It was a close call for the wagon train but no one was killed. The pursuit continued to the Arkansas River where it was called off with the Indians in full flight.[65]

Benteen was disgusted when he arrived back at Camp Sandy Forsyth to discover that Custer, ever the showman, had commandeered all the regimental horses and redistributed them to the companies so that each company was mounted on steeds of the same color. Benteen complained that his "$100 and horses went about the same time."[66] Also, about this time, Captain West tried to make peace with Custer. He had a heart-to- heart conversation with the regimental commander and then offered his hand as a gesture of sincerity. Custer stated that their past differences would not influence his official conduct toward him, but he refused to shake West's hand.[67]

That November, while the Army commanders strategized and their minions made preparations for the winter campaign, the Southern Cheyenne and Arapaho chieftains Black Kettle and Big Mouth rode to Fort Cobb in the Indian Territory to seek peace and protection from General William B. Hazen. They wanted to bring their followers to the sanctuary of the fort. Black Kettle was now an old man and although he had been an honored and respected chief, he was unable to control the young braves of his band. Just four years earlier his village had been massacred at Sand Creek, Colorado, by Colonel John Chivington and a force of militia volunteers. He presciently believed that his young bucks' warring on the whites would bring terrible retribution from the Army.

---

65. Ibid, 263.
66. Ibid, 264. Some 14 months later Benteen heard that Custer won big at the Faro tables and dunned him by letter for repayment, less a small amount owed for poker losses. Custer paid. Up to that point they were still playing cards together.
67. Frost, *Libbie,* 177.

And how right he was. Hazen told the chiefs that he was unable to accommodate their request to bring his people to the fort for safety; only Sheridan could authorize such a plan; they should make their peace overtures directly to him. The dejected chiefs returned to their camp on the Washita River.[68]

Sheridan's plan leading to the Washita battle called for a three-pronged pincer movement on the Indians. From Fort Lyon, Colorado, to the northwest, Lieutenant Colonel E. A. Carr would march with a column of seven troops of 5th Cavalry southeast, join with Captain Penrose's five troops of cavalry on the North Fork of the Canadian River, and march toward the Antelope Hills. From Fort Bascom, New Mexico, to the west, Colonel A.W. Evans, commanding six troops of 3rd Cavalry and two companies of infantry, would scout the territory south of the Red River. Lieutenant Colonel Sully of the 3rd Infantry would march from Fort Dodge, join Custer at Camp Forsyth and proceed southward to establish a new camp and base of operations in the Indian Territory.[69]

On 12 November Custer moved out to the south with eleven troops of cavalry and five companies of infantry (to escort the 400-odd wagon supply train). Camp Supply was ultimately located on the North Canadian River and the soldiers immediately began construction of the fort, which would comprise a log stockade harboring supplies, a pair of blockhouses, and a cavalry tent camp pitched outside.[70]

Lieutenant Colonel Sully was initially in overall command of the entire expedition, but at Camp Supply, a brief tussle over command broke out. Sully attempted to take command from Colonel

---

68. Anon., *Washita*. Utley, *Cavalier,* 64.
69. Godfrey, *Reminiscences,* 161.
70. Mills, *Harvest,* 159.

Crawford of the Kansas volunteers, who had been ordered to unite with the force at Camp Supply, by pulling rank as a Brevet Brigadier General. Not to be outdone, Custer issued an order taking command himself, inasmuch as he was a Brevet Major General and thus outranked both Crawford and Sully. It was a standoff until General Sheridan arrived on 21 November and supported Custer, putting him in charge and sending Sully back to Fort Harker to resume command of his district.[71]

Sheridan was convinced that the Cheyenne and Sioux would not stop raiding in Kansas until the Army had whipped them. Neither he, nor his boss General Sherman, were by any stretch rabid Indian-haters;[72] but in giving the order to proceed with the campaign, Sheridan told Custer to "kill or hang all warriors and bring back all women and children."[73] As for Benteen, he thought more of horses and Indians than he did most white folks and certainly did not share the common view of them as savages to be exterminated: "I cannot say that I have had much heart in warring on Indians, for I have always been impressed with the belief that they were more sinned against than sinning."[74] Custer likewise identified with the Indians, portraying them as noble fighters in defense of their way of life, but he gloried in the role of Indian

---

71. Ibid, 159-60. According to Utley, *Cavalier,* 63, when regulars and volunteers served together, Army regulations required brevet rank to take preference.
72. In a letter to Grant, Sherman wrote that the settlers wanted the Army to "kill all the Indians" but "I will not permit them to be warred against *as long as they are not banded together in parties large enough to carry on war."* (Italics added.): Lewis, *Sherman,* 596. In contrast, Sheridan was branded by a remark he denied ever making: "The only good Indian is a dead Indian." It tagged him an Indian hater and bigot. His opinion, however, was that the Indians could only be converted from their nomadic lifestyle to the domestic ways of the white man by force of arms. His maxim was simple: "protection for the good, punishment for the bad". Hutton, *Phil Sheridan,* 180-81.
73. Mills, *Harvest,* 160.
74. Benteen, in Mills, *Harvest,* 137.

fighter. Both men attempted to intervene to protect noncombatants, but neither had any compunction against engaging warriors on the battlefield when required.

Custer departed Camp Supply in search of a winter Indian encampment on the morning of 23 November 1868, following a blizzard that left a foot or more of snow cover on the ground. The band played *The Girl I Left Behind Me* while the troopers struck a southwesterly course. Some 40 sharpshooters were drawn from the regiment and placed under Benteen's next-in-command, Lieutenant Cooke. The weather turned bright and cold and by the second day, some of the officers and men suffered from snow blindness. Benteen and Company H provided the rear guard for the supply wagon train. Stomping through the deep snow that obscured the Indian trail, which Custer had hoped to follow, was seen to be a lost cause by the time they reached the Canadian River and camped. After an early reveille on the cold misty morning of 26 November, Custer sent Major Elliott with G, H, and M companies up the Canadian to scout for any signs of a trail, then crossed the Canadian where he ordered seven wagons with ammunition to be broken out from the main wagon train. Lieutenant Bell was placed in command of the ammunition wagons and Captain Hamilton, of Company A, was given escort duty for the balance of the wagon train. Ahead with Elliott, Captain Barnitz was on point and he soon discovered a war party trail, which headed south in the snow.[75] A short distance farther on, they found an abandoned campsite. The soldiers were confident that the trail would lead to a village. A courier was sent to inform Custer.[76]

---

75. Utley, ed., *Life*, 216. Barnitz wrote that they knew it was a war party because there were no signs of dogs. Dogs did not accompany war parties, only hunting parties.
76. Utley, *Cavalier*, 65. Mills, *Harvest*, 159-163.

Elated by the news that Elliott had found a trail, Custer sent the courier back on a fresh horse with instructions for the advance party to follow the trail until Custer and the regiment intercepted him. If Custer did not catch up by 2000 hours, Elliott was instructed to halt and wait. The regiment was off on a forced march within a half-hour and the ammunition wagon train struggled to keep up in the melting snow. The remainder of the wagon train and a small guard followed as best they could. They hit the Indian trail as dark was falling and by 2100 hours they caught up with Elliott's battalion, waiting on the trail. The temperature dropped drastically and the snow crusted over; men and horses suffered from the cold, hunger, and lack of rest. They halted for a brief rest break. They continued slowly and carefully along the trail until after midnight, when the regiment's Osage tracker, Little Beaver, let Custer know that he smelled smoke and that the village he sought was in the Washita River valley, just beyond the hills that lay before the regiment.[77]

Custer climbed a ridge on foot and, lying in the snow, surveyed the village of about 50 or so tepees. He returned to his officers, and one by one led them to the ridge-top and quietly went over the lay of the land with them. Then he assembled them all and laid out his plan of attack. He did not know if any other Indian camps were nearby, nor apparently was he concerned enough to order a reconnaissance to find any other villages.

Back at the rest stop, his Osage scouts urged him to wait until morning before attacking. But they were unclear about their reasons and Custer assumed that they wanted to know exactly how many encamped Indians they were dealing with before commencing battle. Even in the Civil War, his methods were to attack first

---

77. Utley, Ibid. Mills, Ibid, 164.

and worry about numbers later, and if out-numbered, fight his way back if he had to.[78]

His plan was simple, based on a surprise attack at dawn from all sides by four battalions. Benteen was assigned to Major Elliott's battalion along with Captain Barnitz's Company. They were ordered to swing north and bear down on the camp from the northeast. They were unaware of other Indian camps along the river in that direction, harboring perhaps as many as 2,000 warriors by some estimates.[79] Captain Myers with two companies would attack the village from the southwest, in a direction opposite that of Elliott. Captain Thompson, also with two companies, was to follow Myers but continue to swing easterly and attack from the southeast. Custer and the remainder of the regiment would charge over the ridge to complete the encirclement. Lieutenant Godfrey's orders were to charge straight through the village and take the Indian pony herd pastured on the other side. At first light, the band would give the signal to attack by playing the regimental tune *Garryowen*.

After much stumbling and backtracking in the dark, the battalions finally gained their positions just before dawn, except for Captain Thompson who was forced to remain farther back in the only cover available. Then an Indian stepped out of this tepee to investigate barking dogs; he spied soldiers to the northeast and fired a shot. The village began to muster and other shots followed. Custer ordered the band to strike up *Garryowen* and the fight was on.[80] Custer charged the village with his four companies and the surrounding soldiers attacked simultaneously. In the frigid pre-dawn, the band players' spit froze in their instruments after a

---

78. Monaghan, *Life,* 314.
79. Mills, *Harvest,* 165.
80. Ibid, 167.

stanza or so and the fighting 7th's stirring rendition of *Garryowen* ended unceremoniously in a disharmonious squawk. The Indian men leapt from their lodges armed and firing, but the soldiers were among them so quickly that they had no time to lay down effective fire. Sharpshooters, pre-positioned by Custer, began to cut them down. Women and children tended to remain in the tepees, where they believed they were relatively safe. Thompson was late in reaching the village because of the greater distance he had to travel so a modest escape path briefly presented itself and warriors and those women and children who did not remain in the tepees were quick to take advantage of it, but many were picked off by troopers in the village who had dismounted in order to fire more accurately.[81]

Benteen encountered a fleeing teenager and signed "peace" and for him to give up. He was answered with three shots in rapid succession; a bullet nicked Benteen's coat sleeve and his horse's neck, felling the horse. Benteen was pitched clear, rolled to a firing position and killed the boy. Custer used the incident later to chide Benteen about being a boy-killer. In writing about it in his official report, Custer also referred multiple times to Benteen as Major, knowing full well that he was a Brevet Colonel.[82]

As ordered, Godfrey and his platoon charged through the camp. He rounded up a number of horses, ponies and mules, turned them over to the platoon to his rear and continued on in search of more. A few miles farther, from a raised vantage point, he observed the tepees of a large camp. His sergeants urged a tactical retreat and he wisely agreed. This was the first indication that any of the 7th's officers had that Black Kettle's village was but one of a number of encampments along the river. On the return he

---
81. Ibid,168.
82. Ibid.

noticed Indians flanking him, out of range. Meanwhile, Captain Barnitz, chasing Indians through the gap presented by Captain Thompson's tardy arrival, was shot in the gut, receiving a severe wound. Major Elliott took up the chase with sixteen troopers, shouting to Lieutenant Hale, "Here goes for a brevet or a coffin." It was a prescient boast. Elliott pursued for several miles and then noticed that the Indians whom Godfrey had seen on his flank were now closing on his detail. He turned and headed back, but his horses were worn out and the Indians cut him off. He and his men dismounted, assumed the prone firing position in a circle and valiantly attempted to fight off the Indians, estimated to outnumber him ten to one.[83]

Godfrey reported his observations of the big Indian village to Custer, who put him "…through a lot of rapid fire questions." Godfrey looked after Barnitz, and then was summoned by Custer who inquired again about the big village. Godfrey informed him of his suspicion that firing he had heard on his return from his pony hunt may have come from Elliott's detail. Custer doubted it.[84]

As Custer began to take stock while the mop-up of Black Kettle's village proceeded, he realized that "From being the surrounding party we now found ourselves surrounded, Indians on all sides closing in on us."[85] Several officers and their men charged the perimeter and were successful in driving the Indians far enough back that they posed little threat. Benteen, with two companies, led at least one such charge and a trooper noted that it was "the prettiest sight I had ever witnessed."[86] While this was going on, a detail of soldiers emptied and stripped the tepees and piled all

---
83. Ibid, 170.
84. Godfrey, *Reminiscences,* 172.
85. Custer, in Merington, *Custer Story,* 222.
86. Cited in Wert, *G. A. Custer,* 277.

the bounty onto bonfires.[87] By now, somewhere around 875 Indian horses, ponies and mules had been rounded up. After picking out a few choice ones, Custer ordered the rest to be shot. As the troopers began the grim task, the captive Indian women set up a wail and the surrounding warriors, aghast a the prospect of losing their herd, started to close again on the soldiers, who were now running low on ammunition. Then Lieutenant Bell, regimental quartermaster, broke through the ring of surprised Indians with seven wagons and an ambulance bearing blankets and ammunition.[88] Destruction of the Indian's belongings, supplies, and herd continued well into the afternoon. But where was Elliott? Custer sent out Captain Myers and a detail to look for him. They rode about two miles south without discovering anything and returned with that news.

Custer believed that his position was now untenable and he feared for the safety of his main wagon train back on the trail. The wounded were gathered up, the prisoners herded together, and the troopers began a march downstream toward the other encampments. This feint caused the Indian warriors to race to their own lodges, fearful that a repeat of Black Kettle's disaster was in store. At dark, the 7th left the Washita River valley and struck for Camp Supply.[89] Benteen, upset about the waste of horseflesh but more so about enormous number of bullets whizzing around and endangering the soldiers on the perimeter, was convinced that Custer, preoccupied with the destruction of the

---

87. Ibid, 276. Officers allowed the women and elderly to collect some personal items.
88. Mills, *Harvest,* 171. Mills writes, "Bell's dashing ride was greatly appreciated, arriving as he did in the nick of time, and it set a precedent that would later have a very important effect on Benteen's career seven and a half years later." The implication is, of course, that Benteen should have done likewise at Little Big Horn.
89. Wert, *G. A. Custer,* 277.

Indian camp, was in effect abandoning Elliott and his men. He spoke to Custer but was sarcastically rebuffed.[90] The fallout caused by Elliott's loss would have serious ramifications for the 7th Cavalry.

Custer sent glowing reports of the victory to Sheridan by courier and the regiment marched triumphantly into Camp Supply on 2 December. Sheridan was pleased with the results of the campaign and highly congratulatory of Custer, but when he inquired about Elliott, Custer told him that without a guide, Elliott probably became lost and would soon straggle in. Sheridan didn't believe it, but let it go as there was little he could do about it. It did, however, substantially temper his enthusiasm for Custer's deeds.[91]

On 7 December Sheridan led an expedition, with Custer in immediate command, of the 19th Kansas and 7th Regiment south to subdue the rest of the wayward Indians. On 11 December, they came across the mutilated remains of Elliott and his men. Following an Indian trail south, the columns arrived at Fort Cobb, Indian Territory, on 17 December. Benteen checked in sick.[92] While ill at Fort Cobb, he received word that his wife had given birth to a daughter who died shortly thereafter.

Benteen's disgust at what he considered to be Custer's malfeasance on the Washita would have to vent. He wrote a letter on 22 December, highly critical of Custer's behavior at the Washita, to his civil war friend, William J. DeGress of St. Louis, who subsequently submitted it to the *Missouri Democrat,* for anonymous publication. It hit the streets on 8 February 1869 and on 14 February, the *New York Times* reprinted it. Custer was furious when he was made aware of it. Sometime in late February, Benteen admit-

---

90. Mills, *Harvest,* 172.
91. Utley, *Cavalier,* 70.
92. Mills, *Harvest,* 177-83. Benteen's medical record shows his malady was diagnosed as "chronic rheumatism."

ted to Tom Custer that he wrote the missive, but it is unclear whether Tom informed his brother. That night Custer gathered his officers in his tent. Pacing and waving a rawhide riding-crop, he told them that someone had belittled his actions at the Washita, and if he knew who it was, he would whip him. Benteen stepped outside the tent and checked his pistol, rotating the cylinder and re-holstered it loosely. Re-entering, he approached Custer and said, "General Custer, while I cannot father all of the blame you have asserted, still, I guess I am the man you are after, and I am ready for the whipping promised." Flustered at the sight of the burley officer before him, hand on pistol, Custer stammered, "Colonel Benteen, I'll see you again, sir!"[93] That, as it turned out, was the end of it, although the breach in the relationship between the men was now irreparable. But for the remainder of their association, the two officers did nothing more than snipe at each other, albeit venomously at times. Despite the bad blood, Benteen never attempted to transfer from the regiment nor did Custer seek his transfer.[94] Benteen's dislike of Custer was not totally or evenly reciprocated. Custer could be petty and Benteen did get some unwelcome assignments from his commander but he admitted after Custer's death that Custer would have liked to have been a friend,

> Everybody – I mean most of the captains and all of the subalterns in the 7th, seemed to be positively afraid of Custer. However, without parade, when he did anything that was irregular to me, or infringed on 'regulations,' where I was concerned, I always went to him in 'propria persona' and had the matter adjusted at once. Custer liked me for it, and I always surmised what I afterwards learned, de facto, that he wanted

---

93. Ibid, 184. Benteen, letter to Goldin, in Carroll, *Letters*, 266-267; 280-281
94. Mills, Ibid.

me badly as a friend; but I could not be, tho' I never fought him covertly."⁹⁵

The 7th spent most of the remainder of the 1868-1869 winter/spring campaign operating from a camp on Medicine Bluff Creek in the Indian Territory, which was eventually named Fort Sill by General Sheridan. The women captured at Black Kettle's village were still with them, ostensibly as interpreters to communicate with hostile Indian villagers. Custer apparently took a fancy to a particularly comely lass. There was

> ...an informal invitation from Custer for officers desiring to avail themselves of the services of a captured squaw, to come to the squaw round-up corral and select one! Custer took first choice, and lived with her during the winter and spring of 1868 and '69.⁹⁶

Her name was Mo-nah-se-tah, daughter of Little Rock, the chief second in command to Black Kettle. Custer clearly was enamored and fairly gushed with admiration. She

> ...was an exceedingly comely squaw, possessing a bright, cheery face, a countenance beaming with intelligence, and a disposition more inclined to be merry than one usually finds among the Indians. She was probably rather under than over twenty years of age. Added to bright, laughing eyes, a set of pearly teeth, and a rich complexion, her well-shaped head was crowned with a luxuriant growth of the most beautiful silken trusses, rivaling in color the blackness of the raven and extending, when allowed to fall loosely over her shoulder, to below her waist.⁹⁷

---

95. Benteen, letter to Goldin, in Carroll, *Letters,* 199.
96. Ibid, 271.
97. Custer, in Quaife, ed., *Life,* 415.

Benteen had great sport with Custer's indiscretion. He referred to Custer's young mistress as 'Mona', claimed that "Custer slept with her all the time," was observed "copulating with her,"[98] and was much amused when

> "...the squaw 'calved' at site of the present Fort Sill. The issue was, however, a simon-pure Cheyenne baby, the seed having been sown before we came down on their fold at Washita."[99]

Mona was quite pleased with her high status as Custer's bunkmate. In contrast to Custer's assessment that "she was inclined to be merry," Benteen noted that she had a "hellish temper"[100] and when her Cheyenne husband showed up at the fort, she "gave him the marble heart", laying into him with: "Go away, you poor one-blanketed Indian man! You must swappy for some older squaw to keep your lodge-fire going and your back warm! Custer heap good!"[101]

The Washita expedition ended with the loss of two capable officers, Captain Louis M. Hamilton and of course, Major Joel Elliott, and the serious wounding of Captain Albert Barnitz. Two other officers and thirteen enlisted men were also wounded; two died of their wounds. Barnitz was brevetted to Colonel for "distinguished gallantry" at the Washita. Hamilton posthumously also received a brevet. Barnitz applied for and received a disability retirement in 1870.[102] Captain West, now concerned "that Custer would catch and salt him away surely," got a promise from Sheridan of the sutlership at Fort Sill and resigned his commission

---

98. Benteen, cited in Mills, *Harvest*, 178.
99. Benteen, letter to Goldin, in Carroll, *Letters*, 271.
100. Benteen, cited in Mills, *Harvest*, 178.
101. Benteen, letter to Goldin, in Carroll, *Letters*, 271.
102. Utley, *Life*, 243-44.

effective March 1, 1869. He died of sunstroke before he could take up his duties at his new post store.[103]

The 7th remained involved with bringing wayward Indians onto the reservations and the regiment roamed the southern plains relentlessly pursuing them. When the campaign concluded in April of 1869, Custer ordered Benteen to remain at Fort Dodge, Arkansas, as commanding officer, despite his knowledge that Benteen's wife was seriously ill and had lost an infant daughter that winter. Custer also knew that he still owed Benteen $100; Benteen bitterly complained that "Custer paid me off for the [Missouri *Democrat*] letter in almost spot cash" by keeping him at Fort Dodge and not paying the debt.

At Fort Dodge Benteen was visited by the department's inspector general, Colonel William G. Mitchell. In the course of their conversations, he allowed as how Custer had banished him for the published letter, which he showed to Mitchell. Mitchell read it, and promised to come to Benteen's aid when he returned to Fort Leavenworth.

He did just that, and on 2 June, Benteen and H Company, orders in hand, left Fort Dodge for good. En route to the cavalry camp outside Fort Hays to await formal assignment to the fort, Benteen learned that Colonel Samuel D. Sturgis was appointed commanding officer of the 7th cavalry and Fort Hays. "I gave 3 hearty cheers!" he recalled,[104] mistakenly believing that he was finally free of Custer and his capriciousness. Sturgis would be seconded to other duties.

In July 1869, 2nd Lieutenant Charles C. DeRudio, an Italian immigrant and Civil War veteran, reported for duty with the 7th.

---

103. Benteen, letter to Goldin, in Carroll, *Letters,* 253. Mills, *Harvest,* 201. Utley, *Life,* 281.
104. Carroll, Ibid, 270.

DeRudio had attended the Royal Austrian Military Academy in Milan and was considered both a competent officer and a competent purveyor of tall tales. Before coming to the United States, he supposedly led an adventurous life as a French army officer in Algeria, a dock worker in England, an exile in Switzerland, and a radical fighter in Paris against Napoleon III's *coup d'etat*. In the 7th, DeRudio passed himself off as a Count; Benteen liked him and his young English wife and enjoyed his stories while admitting that "The 'Count' was always a fearful liar!" Nonetheless, "I treated him as a gentleman, which he was not!"[105]

Major Marcus Reno, an 1858 graduate of West Point and distinguished Civil War veteran, reported for duty at Fort Hays in March of 1870. He and Benteen were not on warm terms. Shortly after his arrival, they got into a scuffle at the post trader's when Reno "attempted to bully" Benteen. Benteen slapped Reno's face and called him a "dirty S.O.B.", offering him "satisfaction," which Reno declined to accept. Although Benteen gained Reno's respect for the incident, Benteen said, "My opinion of Reno was not an exalted one."[106] Both DeRudio and Reno would play significant roles in the future of the 7th Cavalry.

Custer and Benteen did gain respite from their mutual aggravations. In February 1871, the 7th was shipped off to various posts in the South to maintain order in the wake of the rise of racist groups such as the Ku Klux Klan. About that time, Captain Thomas H. French joined the regiment. A pudgy man with "a squeaky voice" and a penchant for booze, French had risen from the ranks in the Civil War and was considered one of the bravest officers in the 7th Cavalry. He would become a close compatriot of Benteen, who was always an admirer of good soldiers and sol-

---

105. Mills, *Harvest,* 194.
106. Benteen, letters to Berry, in Carroll, *Letters,* 196-99.

diering.[107] Occupation duty was not a happy time for the cavalry regiment, but they made the most of it. While in Nashville, and away from Custer, Benteen, an avid baseball fan, sponsored the Benteen Baseball Club. The sly old fox had under his command an enlisted man, Joseph McCurry, a pitcher of "professional caliber."[108] How the play of this ringer influenced side bets on the games is unknown, but it seems likely that Benteen, the superb poker player, capitalized on his trooper's talent.

While in the South, Benteen's garrison in Nashville was under the command of Brigadier General Alfred H. Terry, a man whom Benteen would admire throughout his life. Terry likewise was impressed with the Captain and his troopers, and when he was assigned to command the Department of the Dakota in 1873, it was on the basis of his first-hand knowledge of Benteen's soldiering abilities that he requested the 7th be assigned to him in the Northern Plains. To the relief of all in the regiment, it was transferred to Dakota Territory in April 1873. But the journey from the South was difficult with much illness and disease among the soldiers as well as the horses. Throughout the posting in Dakota Territory, Custer and Benteen would continue to clash over the disciplining of men and officers.[109] Benteen's dislike extended to Custer's wife and those feelings were mutual. To his credit, Custer made a great effort not to let his personal animosities interfere with the normal social intercourse of an Army post, although he was unabashedly nepotistic and well known for playing favorites in his official duties. But the necessity of separating official and unofficial life on the post escaped Custer's wife, Libby. By the time the 7th had begun to settle in at Fort Lincoln in the Dakota Terri-

---

107. Ibid, 202.
108. Ibid.
109. Ibid. Darling, *Dakota*.

tory, Libby's hatred of Benteen had likewise settled in. Regardless, the players were now in place to participate in one of the greatest events in the history of the U. S. Army.

Five years earlier, on the night of 26 November 1868, as Custer laid out his plan to his officers for the attack on Black Kettle's village, Captain Thompson inquired as to the consequences of finding more Indians than the regiment could handle. Custer gruffly replied that there weren't enough Indians in the country to whip the 7th Cavalry.[110] But he hadn't taken the time to reconnoiter and discover how many more might be camped along the Washita before attacking Black Kettle, and when large numbers of warriors appeared from the camps downstream he was forced to withdraw to protect his supply train. He was exposing his habit of being "too impetuous" and "without deliberation" that so irked General Sheridan.[111] Major Elliott and his troopers paid the price. He would make the same mistake and the same statement five-and-a-half years later at the Little Big Horn, but the consequences would be much more costly.

---

110. Utley, *Cavalier,* 65.
111. Hutton, *Phil Sheridan,* 32.

Hunkpapa Sioux Medicine Man and Chief Sitting Bull (Courtesy of Western History/Genealogy Department, Denver Public Library)

Lt. Colonel George Armstrong Custer (Courtesy of Western History/Genealogy Department, Denver Public Library)

Hunkpapa Sioux Chief Gall (Courtesy of Western History/Genealogy Department, Denver Public Library)

Major Marcus A. Reno (Courtesy of Western History/Genealogy Department, Denver Public Library)

Top left: First Lieutenant Edward S. Godfrey
Left: Trumpeter John Martin
Above: Captain Tom McDougall
(Photos courtesy of Western History/ Genealogy Department, Denver Public Library)

TERRENCE J. DONOVAN

CHAPTER 4

PLENTY OF INDIANS FOR US ALL

The Laramie Treaty of 1868 between the government of the United States and the major Northern Plains tribes of Sioux and Cheyenne concluded the bloody Red Cloud's War. The provisions of the treaty were favorable to the Sioux, and the Great Sioux Reservation, encompassing all of what is now South Dakota west of the Missouri River, was created. The treaty called for abandonment of Forts Phil Kearny, Reno, and C. F. Smith, which had been established to protect the whites' westward migratory route known as the Bozeman Trail, and for closure of the trail itself.[1] There was also an enormous parcel of land loosely defined as "that country north of the North Platte River and east of the summits of the Big Horn Mountains" established as unceded Indian Territory, that was set aside for the benefit of the Indians.[2] A number of the Indians settled near the Bureau of Indian Affairs agencies to partake of the white man's "generosity." Others, under

---

1. Keenan, *Indian Wars*, 25.
2. Utley, *Controversy*, 18.

the Hunkpapa Sioux medicine man Sitting Bull, elected to roam the unceded territory despite entreaties by the government to settle down. It was an agreeable impasse soon made untenable by the continued westward flood of white men.[3] The Army was ordered to rein in the wayward wanderers and return them to the reservation.

Sitting Bull, by dint of intelligence, spirituality, and personality, was a key representative and highly respected leader. Among all the other chiefs, he could best see the handwriting on the tepee buffalo-hide wall and, better than most of his kindred fellows, foresee the disaster this westward migration meant to the nomadic way of life of his people; the white man's encroachment was relentless. And he detested the "Laramie Loafers" – agency Indians – who lived off the Indian Agency's largess.[4]

Custer, meanwhile, was suffering from President Grant's wrath. He had entangled himself in politics, testifying before the Clymer committee investigating corruption among the Army's post traders. Based on hearsay, Custer implicated General Grant's brother, Orville. Incensed, Grant had Custer arrested in Chicago, essentially for being AWOL from Washington. Back in Washington, Custer was ordered to stay there, which he did not do, but traveled to Chicago to implore Sheridan to intercede with Grant and let him participate in the upcoming campaign against the Sioux. He was Sheridan's protégé and Sheridan admired his audacity in the field but considered him impetuous and without deliberation, leading a charmed life.[5] After having his plea for reassignment to his command turned down by Sheridan, Custer again disobeyed orders to remain in Washington and traveled to

---

3. Ibid.,19.
4. Utley, *Indian Frontier,* 236-39.
5. Hutton, *Phil Sheridan,* 32.

St. Paul to plead his case with General Terry. Terry was swayed and wrote a positive endorsement to Custer's appeal to President Grant. It went up the chain of command through Sheridan. Sheridan gave in, and coolly endorsed Custer's request:

> The following dispatch from General Terry is respectfully forwarded. I am sorry Lieutenant-Colonel Custer did not manifest as much interest in staying at his post to organize and get ready his regiment and the expedition as he now does to accompany it. On a previous occasion, in 1868, I asked executive clemency to enable him to accompany his regiment against the Indians and I sincerely hope that if granted this time, it may have sufficient effect to prevent him from again attempting to throw discredit upon his profession and his brother officers.[6]

General Sherman added his endorsement; Grant gave in and Custer was directed to join his regiment at Fort Abraham Lincoln, at Bismarck, Dakota Territory. He was under orders not to take any newspaper correspondents with him, which he characteristically ignored. As the Regiment prepared to depart on the campaign, Marc Kellogg, a Bismarck *Tribune* reporter and editor, was invited to tag along.

The Dakota column of the Army's three-pronged foray into Indian country left Fort Lincoln on 17 May 1876, Crook from the south, Gibbon from the northwest and Terry from the east. Twelve companies of the frontier Army's finest moved out with all the hoopla of victors off to gather their spoils. Elements of the 6th, 17th, and 20th Infantry Regiments marched along escorting the supply wagons and three Gatling guns. Custer permitted Libby and Margaret (his sister and Lieutenant Calhoun's wife) to ride

---

6. O'Connor, *Sheridan*, 338-39. Mills, *Harvest*, 226-27.

along for the first day. They would return to the fort under escort the next morning. As nepotism and favoritism were Custer hallmarks, also in the clique were brother Captain Thomas Custer, who was a company commander and right-hand man; brother Boston Custer who had been signed on as a civilian guide; and nephew Harry Armstrong "Autie" Reed, only 18 years old, who was signed on as a herder.[7] The regimental band played *Garryowen* and *The Girl I Left Behind Me*. It was all quite splendid. Although General Terry commanded the expedition, Custer took the lead, as he took great pride in marking the route and choosing campsites.[8] At the first afternoon's camp at the Heart River, the troops were paid their overdue wages. This delayed payday was Terry's and Custer's way of keeping them out of the whorehouses and bars of Bismarck at the start of the campaign.[9] Outwardly everyone appeared to be in high spirits, but some undercurrents were beginning to flow; surgeon De Wolfe wrote his wife from the first bivouac that night that he didn't care much for Major Reno but gave no reasons.[10]

The column journeyed westward battling rough ground, monstrous northern-plains thunderstorms, treacherous stream crossings, prairie fires, and ever-present campsite rattlesnakes.[11] The campaign's Northwest prong, the Montana column under the command of Colonel Gibbon, was already in the field along the Yellowstone River at the mouth of Little Porcupine Creek. Gib-

---

7. Willert, *Diary*, 8. Autie was Custer's half-sister Lydia's son.
8. Ibid, 3-5.
9. Liddic and Harbaugh, *Camp*, n. p. 107.
10. De Wolfe, in Willert, *Diary*, 7.
11. Kennedy, interview with Wheeler, in Liddic and Harbaugh, *Camp*, 155. Kennedy says he was bitten by a rattlesnake before the column got to the Little Missouri River. Willert, *Diary*, details numerous encounters with rattlesnakes and rattlesnake clearing-drives by the troops beating the bushes and ground ahead as they advanced in a skirmish line at the campsites along the march.

bon had been probing daily the surrounding countryside for hostiles. His orders were to prevent hostile Indians from crossing the Yellowstone River from the south and escaping into the wild country to the north.

On the early morning of 17 May, the same day that Terry and Custer departed Fort Lincoln, Gibbon's Chief of Scouts, Lieutenant James Bradley, and his detachment, reported discovery of a camp of Indians on the Tongue River about 30 miles up the valley from its confluence with the Yellowstone. Bradley reckoned that the camp was small enough that Gibbon's column, consisting of the 7th Infantry and elements of the 2nd Cavalry, could successfully attack the camp the next dawn if it was done with surprise. That would require a forced march of some 35 miles. No sooner had Gibbon accepted Bradley's recommendation to attack than preparations were made. But the Yellowstone was swollen with spring runoff and the troops encountered great difficulty to get the command across to the southern shore. Several horses were drowned in the attempt and after much frustration, the forced march to the Tongue was called off and camp was re-pitched at the mouth of the Porcupine. But hostile Sioux and Cheyenne were in the area and soon began to taunt the soldiers from the south bank, hoping to lure them into a trap. Bradley concluded that he couldn't be sure if the Indians knew the soldiers had attempted to cross the river, "but it is fair to presume that they did. If so, it would of course have been impossible for us to surprise their camp."[12]

The steamer *Far West*, skippered by Captain Grant Marsh, came upriver from its temporary tie-down at the camp at Glendive Creek and anchored at the confluence of the Powder and Yellowstone Rivers on 5 June. A new camp, dubbed Camp Supply, would

---

12. Bradley, in Willert, *Diary*, 14.

be established here. Custer with an advance party arrived there about mid afternoon on 7 June. General Terry rode up early that evening and the rest of the Dakota column straggled in after him with the rear guard reaching camp at about 2100 hours. Terry moved his headquarters to the *Far West;* Custer and his command continued up the Powder about 25 miles and set up their camp.

On 3 June Gibbon had passed on intelligence from his scouts to General Terry and his Dakota column that a large camp of Indians was seen on 27 May up the Rosebud valley, that his hunting parties had been attacked several times, and three members of his command had been killed on 23 May. War parties were seen regularly from his camp and the Indians showed no fear.[13] Terry now knew that a large number of Indians were on the Rosebud. But he could not know of the pending battle they would wage with Crook or its disastrous outcome. Camp Supply was established.

Around this time, early June, the Indians held their celebratory Sun Dance in their camp on the Rosebud. Following this ritual of pain and suffering, Sitting Bull had a vision, perhaps a dream, of soldiers falling upside down into his camp. He interpreted this vision as a premonition of soldiers attacking his village and being defeated.[14]

On 9 June Terry sent for Gibbon, who rode to meet with him. The *Far West* proceeded upstream to meet him. They met along the north bank around noon and Gibbon was taken aboard. Gibbon gave the General a detailed intelligence briefing of his encounters with the Indians over the past weeks and together they formulated a strategy. Gibbon would move back west along the Yellowstone to the Rosebud confluence to prevent hostiles, who

---

13. Gray, *Campaign,* 84-85.
14. Vestal, *Sitting Bull,* 150-151.

could be under pursuit from Crook, advancing from the south by now, from crossing the Yellowstone and escaping into the nether land north of it. The 7th Cavalry would insure that the Indians didn't bolt back eastward into the Powder River Valley, as remote as that possibility seemed. Terry and Gibbon then steamed back to Gibbon's camp on the Tongue confluence. After leaving Gibbon, Terry returned to Camp Supply on the *Far West*, ordered that the camp at Glendive Creek be relocated to Camp Supply, and proceeded to ride in a driving rain up the Powder Valley to join Custer.[15]

The next day, with his intelligence on the Indians' whereabouts now two weeks old, Terry concluded that with Gibbon to the west, he would look east for the Indians, along the Powder River.[16] Reno was selected to lead a wing of the 7th Cavalry on the reconnaissance. He was ordered to search up the Powder to its confluence with the Little Powder, then scout the Mizpah Valley back to its juncture with the Powder, and if no Indians were discovered, cross over to Pumpkin Creek, then to the Tongue River, and back downstream to rejoin his regiment in about ten days. Custer seethed. The hostiles were up the Rosebud, not the Powder, and the entire regiment should be looking for them.[17] Terry's plan at the time was to swing the Seventh to the south and then pinch the Indians between Custer's cavalry riding down and Gibbon marching up the Rosebud – if the Indians were still there. But he had to be certain that they had not turned back to the east.

Both Reno and Custer wanted to lead the scout; there would be glory and distinction to the one who first made contact with the wayward Indians. But Terry did not hold that there was a high

---
15. De Wolf, *Diary and Letters,* 9
16. Willert, *Diary,* 110-111; 117.
17. Ibid, 117.

probability that any Indians would be found in or around the Powder River and for that reason, sent Reno on the scout. Terry likely believed the Indians were where Gibbon said they were, on the Rosebud.[18] Reno was elated, however; his unspectacular career needed a boost. His picking up the Indian trail or making contact could just be what he needed. He soon decided, "to overstep the limits of his orders, to accept the risks of the detachment's advance into the hostiles' recent proximity, to discover...whether the hostiles had moved...when, how far and where...."[19] In the evening of the seventh day of his scout, with no Indians anywhere in sight on his explorations of the area prescribed in his orders, Reno and his column crossed the divide between the Tongue River and Rosebud Creek and rode westward into the Rosebud valley. There the soldiers discovered the remains of a large Indian camp, probably the one that Lieutenant Bradley and his scouts had seen on 27 May. They arrived at the abandoned campsite near dark, but Reno persisted in pursuing upstream in

---

18. Ibid, 124.
19. Ibid, 149. Reno's written orders, signed by Captain Smith, Acting Assistant Adjutant General, and dated 10 June 1876, read:
Major M. A. Reno, 7th Cavalry, with six companies (right wing) of this regiment and one gun from the Gatling battery, will, proceed at the earliest practicable moment to make a reconnaissance of the Powder River from the present camp to the mouth of the Little Powder. From the last named point he will cross to the headwaters of Mizpah Creek, and descend that creek to its junction with the Powder River. Thence, he will cross to Pumpkin Creek and Tongue River, and descend the Tongue to its junction with the Yellowstone, where he may expect to meet the remaining companies of the Seventh Cavalry and supplies of subsistence and forage.
Major Reno's command will be supplied with subsistence for twelve days, and with forage for the same period at the rate of 2 lbs. of grain per day for each animal.
The guide Mitch Bouyer and eight Indian scouts, to be detailed by Lieutenant Col. Custer, will report to Major Reno for duty with this column.
Acting Assistant Surgeon H. R. Porter, is detailed for duty with Major Reno. By command of Brigadier General Terry.

the fading light, along the cold but easily visible trail of deep ruts left by dragged lodgepoles. They camped just before midnight.[20]

On the next morning, 17 June, the hostiles whose trail Reno so eagerly pursued engaged General Crooks's command on the upper Rosebud. It was a hard-fought battle and the Indians held numerical superiority and were well-armed. The situation looked bleak for Crook until the Indians' field position was flanked and they were surprised from the rear by Captain Anson Mills of Crook's 3rd Cavalry. They withdrew, but Crook had all he wanted, taking a good whipping.

Meanwhile, some 50 miles or so to the north, Reno, unaware of Crook's dilemma, followed the Indian trail for a couple of hours, ominously impressed with the enormous number of hostiles responsible for it. He called a rest halt about mid-morning. He sent his scouts ahead but they could find no signs that the trail freshened. Short of rations and running out of time to join up with Custer and the rest of the 7th, Reno did an about-face and headed back down the Rosebud in the late afternoon. This was a prudent move. He had disobeyed orders by exploring Rosebud Creek, and if the large camp of Indians he was trailing discovered him, his command wouldn't have a chance of surviving the encounter. But he now knew that the Indians were either making their way to the Little Big Horn Valley or continuing to the south up Rosebud Creek. Reno set up camp for the night at about 2000 hours.[21]

After a rough ride, Reno's reconnaissance column reached the confluence of Rosebud Creek and the Yellowstone River late in the day on 18 June. They were on the south bank about four miles upstream from Gibbon's camp on the north bank and Gib-

---

20. Ibid, 150.
21. Ibid, 172-173.

bon's scouts had seen them coming. They eventually made contact through makeshift signal flags and written messages carried back and forth across the raging Yellowstone current by two of Gibbon's Crow scouts. After sunrise on 19 June, Reno continued down the south bank of the Yellowstone toward the Tongue to join Custer who was bivouacked on its east bank at the confluence. It was tough going; the pace was slow and the horses became jaded, the men were worn out. Reluctantly, Reno decided to camp for the night even though the ground was unsuitable. He sent a note, along with one he was carrying from Gibbon, forward to General Terry.

News of Reno's proximity soon reached Custer's command, and rumors were rampant in his camp that Reno had found the Indians' trail.[22] Terry sent word back to Reno to halt and hold where he was. With the poor maps of the day, and lack of solid intelligence from Reno as to the whether the Indians were tracking southwestward along the Rosebud to the Little Big Horn or continuing southerly, Terry had to formulate a plan as best he could. But given what he did know, he would send Custer and the mighty 7th Cavalry on the Indians' trail in the Rosebud Valley. Reno's scout had shown that the Indians hadn't doubled back to the east. Now he could unleash Custer to head westward into the Rosebud drainage.

With his incomplete map laid out before him and his officers, Terry pondered where the Indians were. The trail that Reno had followed went southwest along the course of Rosebud Creek. If the Indians had continued in that direction, they would have crossed over the divide into upper Tullock's Creek or possibly into the Little Big Horn Valley. Even if the Army didn't know precisely

---

22. Godfrey, *Reminiscences*, 129-130.

where the hostiles were, Terry was confident that Custer and his cavalry could catch up with them.[23]

Meanwhile Custer was seething. It was obvious to him that Reno had willfully disobeyed orders with his foray into the Rosebud Valley, and then to add to his disobedience, he failed to determine the numbers of hostiles and the precise direction of their travel. Custer was ordered by Terry on 20 June to proceed to Reno's camp at the mouth of the Tongue River. Custer rode as rapidly as the badlands terrain would allow, eager to deliver a dressing-down and perhaps file charges against his second in command. When he arrived at Reno's camp near midday, the steamer with General Terry also pulled up, and Reno was preparing to meet with the General on board. What transpired between the two is unknown, but when Custer climbed aboard, the fireworks erupted and a bitter exchange between Reno and Custer ensued. General Terry in his quiet manner finally told Custer to shut up.[24] But Custer wasn't completely silenced. He retired to his tent where he wrote a letter to Libby after playing poker for much of the night. Custer was also sending reports back to the New York *Herald* as an "anonymous correspondent", referring to himself in the third person. He then composed a scathing piece as an installment to *Herald*. It was a piece that would damn Reno forever.[25]

> ...Major Reno, whose departure with six companies of the Seventh Cavalry to scout up the Powder Rive was mentioned

---

23. Willert, *Diary,* 189-190.
24. Thompson, in Willert, *Diary,* 193-194. Reno had no use for Custer. He told a Chicago *Times* reporter during the 1879 Court of Inquiry "...I had no confidence in his ability as a soldier. I had known him all through the [Civil] war...." Willert suggests because of his strong feelings and personal history, that Reno was likely not intimidated by Custer and probably did not take Custer's verbal abuse quietly.
25. Willert, *Diary,* 206-207.

in my last letter, moved under written orders, which in substance directed him to scout up the Powder River as far as the mouth of the Little Powder, then across to the headwaters of Mizpah Creek, down that creek to near its mouth, then across to Pumpkin Creek, down that stream to its junction with Tongue River, then down Tongue River to its mouth on the Yellowstone, where he was informed the main part of the expedition would be by the time of his arrival at that point.

In the opinion of the most experienced officers it was not believed that any considerable, if any, force of Indians would be found on the Powder River; still there were a few, including Major Reno, who were convinced that the main body of Sitting Bull's warriors would be encountered on Powder River. The general impression, however, is and had been, that on the headwaters of the Rosebud and Little Bighorn rivers the "hostiles' would be found.

It was under this impression that General Terry, in framing the orders which were to govern Major Reno's movements, explicitly and positively directed that officer to confine himself to his orders and instructions, and particularly not to move in the direction of Rosebud River, as it was feared that such a movement, if prematurely made, might 'flush the covey', it being the intention to employ the entire cavalry force of the expedition, when the time arrived, to operate in the valleys of the Rosebud and Big Horn Rivers. Custer and most of his officers looked with little favor on the movement up the Powder River, as, among other objections, it required the entire remaining portion of the expedition to lie in idleness within two marches of the locality where it was generally believed the hostile villages would be discovered on the Rosebud, the danger being that the Indians, ever on the alert, would discover the presence of the troops as yet undiscovered – and take advantage of the opportunity to make their escape. Reno, after an absence of ten days, returned, when it was found, to the disgust and disappointment of every member of the expedition, from the commanding general down to the lowest private, that Reno, instead of simply failing to accomplish any good results, has so misconducted his force as to embarrass, if not seriously and permanently mar, all hopes of future success of the expedition. He had not only deliberately, and without a shadow of an excuse failed to obey his written instructions issued by General Terry's personal directions, but he had acted in positive disobedience to strict injunctions of the department commander. Instead of conforming his line of march to the valleys and water courses laid down in his written orders he moved his command to the mouth of the Little Powder River, then across to Tongue River, and instead of following the latter stream down to its mouth, there to unite with the main command, he, for some unaccountable and thus far unexplained reason, switched off from his prescribed course and marched across the country to the Rosebud, the stream he had been particularly cautioned not to approach.

He struck the Rosebud about twenty-five miles above its mouth, and there – as Custer had predicted from the first – signs indicating the recent presence of a large force of Indians were discovered, an abandoned camp ground of the Indians was found, on which 380 lodges had been pitched. The trail led up the valley of the Rosebud. Reno took up the trail and followed it about twenty miles, but faint heart never won fair lady, neither did it ever pursue and overtake an Indian village. Had Reno, after first violating his order, pursued and overtaken the Indians, his original disobedience of orders would have been overlooked, but his determination forsook him at this point, and instead of continuing the pursuit and at least bringing the Indians to bay, he gave the order to countermarch and faced his command to the rear, from which point he made his way back to the mouth of the Tongue River and reported the details of his gross and inexcusable blunder to General Terry, his commanding officer, who informed Reno in unmistakable language that the latter's conduct amounted to positive disobedience of orders, the sad consequences of which could not yet be fully determined. The details of this affair will not bear investigation.

A court-martial is strongly hinted at, and if one is not ordered it will not be because it is not richly deserved. The guides who were with Reno report that the trail where the latter was abandoned indicates that the Indian village...was moving in such deliberate manner and left so recently that Reno's command could have overtaken it in a march of one day and a half. Few officers have ever had such a fine opportunity to make a successful and telling strike and few ever failed so completely to improve their opportunities.

Of course there was but one thing to do and that was to remedy as soon as possible the effects of Reno's blunder. ...Yesterday, Terry, Gibbon and Custer...with unanimity of opinion, decided that Custer should start with his command up the Rosebud valley to the point where Reno abandoned the trail, and take up the latter and follow the Indians as long as a far as horse flesh and human endurance could carry his command. Custer takes no wagons or tents with his command, but proposes to live and travel like Indians; in this manner the command will be able to go wherever the Indians can...Custer advised his subordinate officers...that it would be well to carry an extra supply of salt, because, if at the end of fifteen days the command should be pursuing a trail, he did not propose to turn back for lack of rations, but would subsist his men of fresh meat – game, if the country provided it; pack mules if nothing better offered. The Herald correspondent will accompany Custer's column and in the event of a 'fight or a foot race', will be on the ground to make due record thereof for the benefit of the Herald readers...[26]

If Reno had any kindly inclinations toward his commanding officer, they were now put to rest. But despite the animus and conflict, for better or worse, Reno had discovered the trail and

---

26. Graham, *Myth*, 236-237.

Terry now revised his strategy. A two-pronged pincer deployment – Gibbon from the north, Custer from the south – would squeeze the hostiles' area of mobility and restrict their options; they would be forced to surrender or fight on the Army's terms. Gibbon would reposition to the mouth of the Big Horn, into which the Little Big Horn flowed, and then proceed up the valley until encountering the Indians or Custer. The north-flowing Big Horn River, flush with spring runoff, would prevent an Indian escape to the west.

On 22 June, Custer received his written orders from General Terry. They were all he could hope for, a *carte blanche*. An elated Custer sat in his tent and read Terry's directive.

> HEADQUARTERS DEPARTMENT OF DAKOTA
> (In the Field)
> Camp at the mouth
> of the Rosebud River
> June 22, 1876
>
> Lieutenant Col. Custer, 7th Cavalry
> Colonel:
> The Brigadier General commanding directs that as soon as your regiment can be made ready for the march, you will proceed up the Rosebud in pursuit of the Indians whose trail was discovered by Major Reno a few days ago. It is, of course, impossible to give you any definite instructions in regard to this movement, and were it not impossible to do so, the Department commander places too much confidence in your zeal, energy and ability to wish to impose upon you precise orders which might hamper your action when nearly in contact with the enemy. He will, however, indicate to you his own views of what your action should be, and he desires that you should conform to them unless you shall see sufficient reason for departing from them. He thinks that you should proceed up the Rosebud until you ascertain definitely the direction in

which the trail spoken of leads. Should it be found to turn toward the Little Big Horn he thinks you should still proceed south-ward, perhaps as far as the headwaters of the Tongue, and then turn toward the Little Big Horn, feeling constantly however, to your left so as to preclude the possibility of the escape of the Indians to the south or southeast by passing around your left flank. The column of Col. Gibbon is now in motion for the mouth of the Horn. As soon as it reaches that point it will cross the Yellowstone and move up at least as far as the forks of the Big and Little Big Horn. Of course, its future movements must be controlled by circumstances as they may arise, but it is hoped that the Indians, if upon the Little Big Horn, may be so nearly enclosed by the two columns that their escape will be impossible. The Department commander desires that on your way up the Rosebud you should thoroughly examine the upper parts of Tullock's Creek, and that you should endeavor to send a scout through to Col. Gibbon's column with information of the result of your examination. The lower part of this Creek will be examined by a detachment of Col. Gibbon's command. The supply steamer will be pushed up the Big Horn as far as the forks if the river is found to be navigable for that space, and the Department commander desires you to report to him there not later than the expiration of the time for which your troops are rationed, unless in the meantime you receive further orders.

Respectfully,
s/E. W. Smith
Captain, 18th Infantry
Acting Assistant Adjutant General[27]

---

27. Overfield, *Little Big Horn*, 23-24.

Custer would depart on 22 June up the Rosebud and then to the headwaters of the Little Big Horn – whose precise whereabouts were uncharted on Terry's map. From there, Custer would ride down the Little Big Horn closing any southerly or easterly routes by which the Indians might flee. Somewhere between Custer and Gibbon, Terry hoped they would find the Indians.

During the march on 23 June, Custer in his hot pursuit of the Indian trail in the Rosebud valley had spread out the command with the pack train falling, in Benteen's mind, dangerously behind. He had worked hard escorting the packs and devised a plan for deployment of the guard in such a way as to keep a tighter rein on the mule train. He would have to approach Custer with it, confident that the General would ignore his advice or reject it outright. On the morning of 24 June, Benteen spoke with Custer, telling him that during the previous day's march, the pack train had become strung out far behind his command and without orders, he had taken the initiative by organizing a marching plan to mitigate the situation.

To Benteen's surprise, Custer was grateful for his recommendation, replying, "…I am much obliged to you, Colonel, and I will turn over the same order of march for the rear guard to the officer who relieves you…"[28]

It was about dusk on 24 June when the regiment halted on Rosebud Creek near the present town of Busby. Benteen, with the pack train's escort, was the last to ride into the temporary campsite. His good friend, Miles Keogh, called to him "…come here old man, I've kept the nicest spot in the whole camp next to me,

---

28. Benteen, in Graham, *Myth,* 178. Willert, *Diary,* 236, suggests that Custer's willingness to accept Benteen's recommendations for the mule train had more to do with his preoccupation with pursuing a hot trail than any concern for the packs and their escort.

for your troop, and I've had to bluff the balance to hold it..." Benteen happily obliged.[29]

At about 2100 hours, the three Crow scouts returned to camp with the information that the Sioux trail up the Rosebud had abruptly turned west and crossed the divide into the valley of the Little Big Horn River. The scouts had followed the trail to the top of the divide but could not discern anything beyond, as they were looking into a setting sun.[30]

Custer knew of the Crow's Nest from the Crow scouts; it was a high promontory just south of a saddle in the divide between Davis Creek, which drained into the Rosebud, and Reno (Sundance) Creek, an ephemeral stream that drained into the Little Big Horn.[31] The Crows had used this high point to scout Sioux camps in the Little Big Horn valley when they were on horse-stealing raids. The Crow's Nest was a high, rounded feature on the Little Chetish Mountains (Crow for Wolf or Wolf Hair Mountains[32]) that comprise the divide between the Rosebud and Little Big Horn valleys. From its perch much of the Little Big Horn valley and the intervening terrain could be scouted without obstruction. "Its value was not the result of any great elevation, for it was little if any higher than some of the other points nearby, but resulted largely from its location in regard to the bluffs and other topographical features of the Valley."[33]

With the trail heating up and Custer desiring to close on the hostile Sioux, he decided on a night march to the base of the divide, beginning at 2300 hours. Lieutenant Varnum, Chief of

---

29. Benteen, in Graham, *Myth*, 178
30. Utley, *Cavalier*, 47.
31. Red Star, in Graham, Myth, 32. Varnum, letter to Camp, in Hammer, *Camp*, 60.
32. White-Man-Runs-Him, interview with Scott, in Graham, *Myth,* 14.
33. Stewart, *Luck,* 272-273.

Scouts, Bouyer as interpreter, and Charlie Reynolds[34], with five Crow and eight or ten Arikara ("Rees") scouts, were sent ahead to the Crow's Nest to attempt to locate the Sioux camp from that vantage as soon as morning light permitted. Custer told Varnum that he would have the command bivouacked near the base of the Crow's Nest by morning and he would be expecting Varnum's report there. Fires were ordered put out after supper. Benteen tried to get some sleep after eating, having a premonition that he would enjoy precious little sleep in the near future, but was kept awake by DeRudio telling stories of his military escapades in "some other country." No sooner had Benteen "rudely" quieted the bull session than the orderly trumpeter notified him of officer's call, which was held about 2130 hours. The night was pitch black. Lieutenants Godfrey and Hare, unhappy about giving up much-needed sleep, "…groped our way through horse herds, over sleeping men, and through thickets of bushes, trying to find headquarters. No one could tell us, and as all fires and lights were out, we could not keep our bearings. We finally espied a solitary candlelight, toward which we traveled and found most of the officers assembled…."[35] Benteen located his boots in the dark and got them on, then stumbled around trying to find headquarters. He commented to Keogh when the order to report came that he was sure Custer had a night march in mind; so certain was he that he ordered First Sergeant Joseph McCurry to see to the horses and equipment and be ready to move the company out quickly. But before he could locate the meeting place in the dark, he met an officer who told him that the call was over and they were to march at 2300 hours.[36]

---

34. Varnum, in Willert, *Diary*, 243.
35. Godfrey, in Graham, *Myth*, 136.
36. Benteen, in Graham, *Myth,* 178-179. Benteen referred to such a premonition, which he professed to have often, in his correspondence as a "Pre."

Custer informed those present that because they were closing in on the Sioux, he would march at night and conceal the regiment the next day near the divide separating the Rosebud and Little Big Horn drainages while he awaited further intelligence from the scouts. Then that night, they would approach the newly discovered village and attack at dawn on 26 June. Sometime between 2330 and 0030 they began to move out.[37] Custer ordered Girard, along with Half Yellow Face and Bloody Knife, to take the lead with him. While they waited for the scouts to pick up the trail, Custer told Girard to ensure that no camp Sioux got away to the South and to have his scouts follow any left-hand trail no matter how small. Custer's concern about Indians escaping to his left would fuel a controversy that would keep historians and history buffs busy for over a century with no resolution in sight. During the course of the conversation with the commander, Girard was asked what numbers of Indians he expected they would have to fight. He ventured that Custer could expect to encounter no less than 2,500 hostile Sioux.[38]

They marched about two-and-one-half to three hours in the dark and halted. The pace was rapid[39], even though the night was "...dark as pitch...."[40] Benteen wrote that "...the gait was a trot...I kept the ding-donging of the tin cup, frying pan – or

---

37. See Gray, *Campaign,* 220-243 for a time-motion synopsis. Participants place the precise time variously from 2300 on 24 June to 0100 on 25 June. The time and distances used here for the climb to the divide on the night of 24-25 June are taken generally from Gray who converted all times to local sun time.
38. Girard, in Nichols, *Reno Court,* 85. Girard later revised his estimate downward to 1,000-1,500 warriors.
39. Ryan, in Graham, *Myth,* 241.
40. Windolph, in Graham, *Myth,* 179. A number of the officers and men commented that the night was too dark to see what was ahead of them; they marched in the direction of the rattle of tin cups, carbines, and skillets carried by the troopers ahead of them.

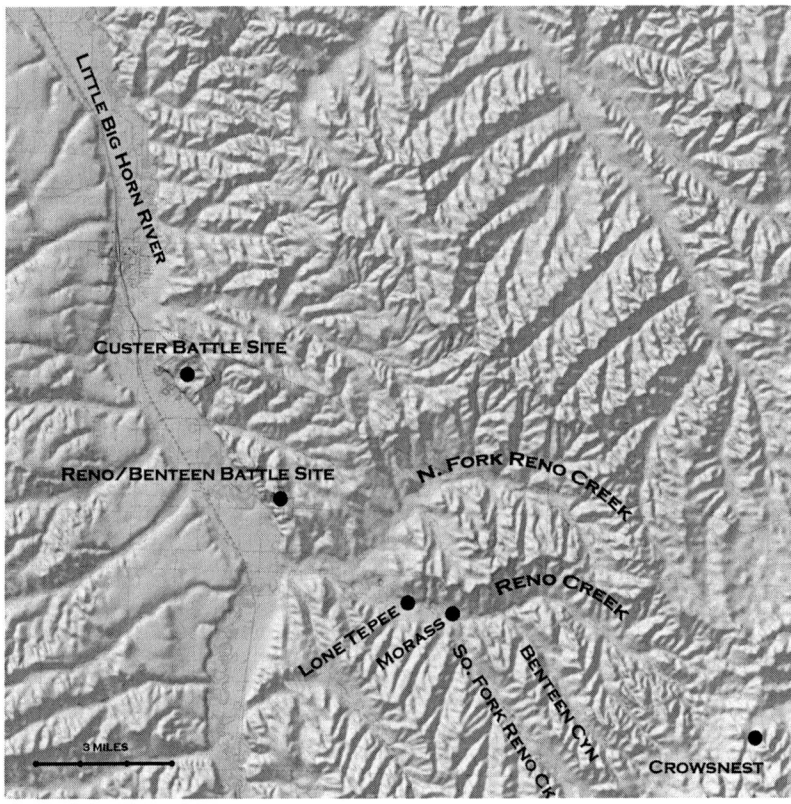

Figure 4-1: The relative flatness of the Little Big Horn River valley is sharply contrasted with the surrounding mountains through which the 7th had to travel.
(North is toward the top of the page.)

something; that was my guide as to direction; the pounding of that on the saddle of the horse on the left of the troop preceding mine, being all I had to go on...."[41]. The Indian scouts had estimated that they could get over the divide in about two hours but it was too dark to make that kind of progress. Realizing that he wasn't going to cross the divide before daylight, Custer called a halt just as first light appeared in the east, around 0245. Unable to recon-

---

41. Benteen, in Graham, *Myth,* 179.

noiter in the dark, the General was concerned that there would be no cover for the command when daylight broke, but the scouts informed him that there was plenty of brush for concealment. Many of the bone-weary men napped on the ground without unsaddling their horses or making coffee, as they were instructed to do.[42]

After sunrise (ca 0415 hours) they ate breakfast and cat-napped again. During the halt, Custer's scouts, white and Indian alike, warned him of the large size of the band ahead as indicated by the trail they were following, but he discounted these warnings.[43] Early that morning, before moving on, Bloody Knife, several Ree scouts, and a half-breed interpreter squatted in a circle with Custer, talking in an agitated and disturbed fashion. He appeared to be preoccupied. Then Bloody Knife said something that got Custer's attention. "What's that he says?" Custer queried.

The interpreter responded with, "He says we'll find enough Sioux to keep us fighting two or three days."

Custer smiled and said, "I guess we'll get through with them in one day." His opinion apparently would change after an encounter with the Crow scout White Man Runs Him at the Crow's Nest later that morning.

Varnum and his scouting party had arrived at the Crow's Nest sometime around 0230 or 0300 hours on the morning of 25 June. Varnum got in a short nap before the sky began to lighten enough to see well, but some of the other scouts were restive and did not sleep. In June, near solstice, the sun rises early in the big sky of Montana. Around daybreak two of the Crows had scaled the Crow's Nest and returned to the scouting party below the summit

---

42. Willert, *Diary*, 252.
43. Stewart, *Luck*, 280. Stewart cites numerous sources for the ominous warnings of the scouts.

to report that they had sighted the hostile encampment. Varnum was awakened and they all climbed to the lookout. Crooked Horn told Red Star, "Look sharp, my boy, you have better eyes than I." Red Star searched the valley. He could see a "dark object" and above it light smoke rising up from the tepees. "It was at the upper end of the village, the tepees were hidden by the high ridge [the ridge that ultimately would become the Reno-Benteen battlefield] but the smoke was drawing out and up. Beyond the smoke he saw some black specks he thought were horses."[44] Varnum, his eyes burning and enflamed from lack of sleep and trail dust, could not make out what the scouts were seeing. The Crows handed him a "cheap spyglass" and coached him to look for the large pony herd on the west escarpment resembling "worms crawling on the grass." Varnum still saw nothing in the Little Big Horn valley. He did make out two lodges far down Reno Creek. Could there be more, hidden from view?

By now it was almost 0500 hours; Varnum dispatched the Rees Red Star and Bull back to Custer with a note stating that smoke from the hostile village was visible 20 miles away along the Little Big Horn. The two scouts headed for the smoke of the regiment's cooking fires, about ten miles off, a sight that aggravated the Crows considerably, and they questioned the common sense of the commander who was supposedly making a stealthy approach to the hostile encampment.[45]

Red Star and Bull arrived back at the halt close to 0730 hours. Meanwhile Sergeant Curtis was sent back on the trail with a small detail to retrieve supplies that had fallen from the pack mules. Custer sat down with Red Star, who was enjoying a morning cup

---

44. Red Star, in Willert, *Diary,* 252. Girard, in Nichols, *Reno Court,* 137, testified that "We had a good view of the Indians and ponies. We could not distinguish one from the other. We saw a large, black mass."
45. Varnum, in Graham, *Myth,* 60-61.

of coffee, and asked Red Star by signing if he had seen the hostile Indians. Red Star answered in the affirmative and handed him the note.

The General was eager to see the purported village site for himself and in particular get the lay of the land from high ground.[46] Custer, speaking through Girard, told Red Star to saddle up and take him to Varnum and the lookout party. The scout dutifully left his coffee and went for his horse. Custer rode through camp bareback and gave orders to march at 0800 hours. The General, Girard, Bloody Knife, Red Star, Bob-tailed Bull, and Little Brave then rode off to join Varnum. The rest of the column hit the trail at about 0845 hours, under the command of Reno, and proceeded at a walk. Following Custer's orders, they moved forward nearly four miles to a place of concealment in the timber and brush along Davis Creek close to the divide. On the back trail, Sergeant Curtis found the lost boxes they were looking for, but surprised a Cheyenne Indian trying to open one of them. The Indian galloped off out of range but then tagged along as an outrider along the adjacent ridge. Curtis returned to the main column and promptly reported this news to Captain Yates who passed it up the chain of command. Tom Custer rode off to find his brother and inform him of the news.[47]

Right after the Rees left to report to Custer, the scouting party spied a mounted pair of Sioux a little over a mile away near

---

46. Gray, *Campaign,* 234. Gray makes a point that apparently was missed by others. "Custer would be anxious to see the village and its location for himself, especially if the note from Varnum had disclosed that he could not verify it. It was even more important that Custer seize this perfect opportunity to study the lay of the land, over which he planned to approach the village that night."
47. Godfrey, *Last Battle,* 21. Moylan, in Nichols, *Reno Court,*214. Willert, *Diary,* 262, says that Custer was informed of the incident after he returned to the regiment from the Crow's Nest.

the base of their lookout. Varnum, Bouyer, Reynolds, and two Crows attempted to intercept them on foot but they were called back by a signal, an imitation of a raven's caw, from the lookout. The two Sioux then rode off down Davis Creek toward Custer's camp and there was concern that they would spot the smoke of the soldiers' column, which Varnum could see, or perhaps overtake the two Ree messengers and do them in. Bull's mount was small and jaded and he could not keep up with Red Star who, carrying the message, did not wait for his compatriot.[48]

Varnum's scouts then saw six Sioux near Tullock's Creek to the northeast. They galloped after them and the hostiles headed off in the direction of the Sioux village. The Sioux party then split up and successfully evaded their pursuers. After the chase ended and the scouts returned to the Crow's Nest, the Sioux were seen, circling away from the Crow's Nest. General Custer and his party arrived at the Crow's Nest where Varnum met him near the base and told him that the Sioux had spotted the troops and that the scouts had seen the Indians turn, separate and race for their village.[49] At the Crow's Nest, Custer climbed up far enough to scan the Little Big Horn valley and attempt to view the Indian encampment:

> Charley Reynolds and Custer went ahead, leaving the others behind. Reynolds pointed where Custer was to look; they looked for some time and then Gerard [sic] joined them. Gerard called back to the scouts, "Custer thinks it is no camp." Custer thought Reynolds had merely seen the white buttes that concealed the lone tepee [down where Varnum had seen the two lodges]. So Reynolds pointed again, explaining Custer's mistake, and after another look, Custer nodded that

---

48. Red Star, in Graham , *Myth,* 32. Stewart, *Luck,* 273.
49. Varnum, in Graham, *Myth,* 61

he saw signs of the camp. Next, Reynolds pulled out his field glasses and Custer used them and nodded his head again.[50]

The scouts, sighting the thin wafted smoke, indicated that the Sioux village was downstream of the mouth of Reno Creek but Custer could not see it. Nonetheless, the General undoubtedly spent useful time at the Crow's Nest observing the countryside with the benefit of having the knowledgeable Bouyer and the Crows at hand.[51] From the Crow's Nest the intervening terrain – the course of Reno Creek and its tributaries, the high ground vantage points to the south of the drainage – are laid out panoramically, giving a synoptic overview of the approaches to the battlefield and its environs. And surely Varnum discussed with Custer the two lodges, which he had seen downstream on Reno Creek, and any surmised significance that they may have held. If Custer did not believe that a large concentration of hostiles was in the Little Big Horn valley, he could not discount that they may have been strewn out in a series of smaller camps along the river and its tributaries.

Custer now faced a conundrum. If there were Indians on the Little Big Horn upstream of the mouth of Reno Creek or along the Reno Creek itself near its juncture with the Little Big Horn, as Varnum had seen and reported, then any attack from the valley of Reno Creek could drive them south, away from Gibbon's approaching column. Further, if the upper Little Big Horn valley or its tributaries contained satellite camps, of whatever size, their warriors could circle to Custer's rear as he attacked down the valley toward the main village. These satellite villages, if they existed, potentially could be anywhere – in Reno Creek near the two

---

50. Red Star, in Graham, *Myth,* 33.
51. Gray, Campaign, 239.

lodges, in the South Fork of Reno Creek, or God knows where. Since he didn't completely buy into the "big encampment scenario", he would have to address, in formulating his plan of action, the dispersed camp thesis. Back with the group, Custer listened to the scouts' report of the column's discovery. White Man Runs Him (also known as Big Belly) asked the General through an interpreter what he thought of the Sioux encampment. Custer replied, "This camp has not seen our army, none of their scouts have seen us." White Man Runs Him countered with, "You say we have not been seen. These Sioux we have seen at the foot of the hill, two going one way, and four the other, are good scouts, they have seen the smoke of our camp." Custer angrily retorted, "I say again we have not been seen. That camp has not seen us. I am going ahead to carry out what I think. I want to wait until it is dark and then we will march, we will place our army around the Sioux camp." White Man Runs Him was not happy. "That plan is bad, it should not be carried out."

The General, in some sort of denial, at first resisted, disagreeing with the obvious fact that his troops had been discovered, but then reluctantly accepted it even though it meant he would have to attack as soon as possible under less than ideal conditions and without the element of surprise. Custer stubbornly tried to cut off the conversation with, "I have said what I propose to do, I want to wait until it is dark and then go ahead with my plan."

But the Crow scouts insisted that the Sioux scouting party had seen the command and would get the news back to the main camp. They wanted a daylight attack now and to capture the Sioux horses, leaving the Sioux afoot and unable to make a rapid escape.

Custer capitulated. "Yes, it shall be done as you say." He then rode off with his party back to the regiment. They met Tom Custer on the way back. The General was angry that Tom had left the column and that the command had moved forward without his direct orders.[52] But he had left word for the march to resume at 0800 hours and that it did. Tom bore his brother's rebuke and then relayed the information from Sergeant Curtis about Indians on the back trail. After rejoining the command, Custer held officer's call. The skeptical commander told the assembled group that he had just come down from the mountains and that although the scouts reported seeing an enormous camp in the Little Big Horn valley with ponies, tepees, and smoke, he couldn't make it out even with his field glasses. He ventured that he didn't believe there was a village in the valley.[53] Custer didn't doubt that the Indians were in the Little Big Horn Valley but,

> ... it was impossible for him to discover more of the enemy than had already been reported by the scouts. In consequence of the high bluffs which screened the village, it was not possible in following the trail to discover more. Nor was there a point of observation near the trail from which further discoveries could be made....

However, it was clear that the Seventh had been discovered and the news was traveling down to the Little Big Horn. But how fast? Custer believed he had to move quickly to preclude the Indians' scattering and escaping and he acted on that notion

---

52. Red Star, in Graham, *Myth* 33. According to Gray, *Campaign,* 225, White Man Runs Him was also known to the Rees as Big Belly, as was Half Yellow Face. Big Belly is used by some authors but leads to confusion. For example, Sandoz, *Battle,* 57, says it was Half Yellow Face that confronted Custer on the morning of 25 June. Red Star says it was Big Belly without explanation as to which Big Belly. It is well documented that Half Yellow Face was not in Varnum's scouting party.
53. Godfrey, in Graham, *Myth,* 135.

> ...as there was no use in trying to surprise them...we would press on as quickly as we could and attack them in the village if possible...The Indians would not stand against a whole regiment of cavalry...as soon as they learned of our advance they would try to get away....[54]

He then ordered the command to move out and indicated that the first company commander to report he was ready would take the lead. Benteen and the other company commanders were still under the marching orders issued by Custer earlier in their trek, which specified that,

> ...a non-commissioned officer and six men from each company should be with the pack [train] and not more, and that each man should have 100 rounds of ammunition in his cartridge belt and saddle pockets. I suppose that every officer there could have told him that those requisitions were being carried out, but as the others went for formality's sake, I went to my company and said to the first sergeant, 'There are so many men with the packs?' 'Yes, sir.' 'And you have so much ammunition?' all of which I knew without his answering.[55]

---

54. Edgerly, in Graham, *Myth,* 219. Note that Edgerly wrote *attack them in the village.*
55. Benteen, in Nichols, *Reno Court,* 402, testified that at the officers' call, "General Custer told us that he had just come down from the mountains, that he had been told by the scouts that they could see a village, ponies, tepees and smoke. He gave it to us as his belief that they were mistaken, that there were no Indians there, that he had looked through his glass and could not see any, and did not think there were any there. Other instructions were given, those were that the officer who first reported to him that his company was carrying out the condition of an order that was given two days before should have the advance." Reno (p. 560) told a similar story. "[Custer] called the officers together and I attended of course. He said the Indian scouts had reported there was a large Indian village in view from the top of the mountain. He did not believe such himself as he had looked with his glass. He then announced that the column would be formed by companies in accordance with the manner in which they reported themselves ready and it was so done."

And,

> ...I notified him [Custer] at once that in my troop the requirements were being strictly adhered to. I feel quite sure it wasn't expected of me, but he stammered out, 'Well Col. Benteen, your troop has the advance.' [56]

Custer apparently applied compartmentalized reasoning to all the intelligence now gathered and at his disposal. His scouts told him that the Sioux were already arrayed in the valley of the Little Big Horn. Although he reluctantly agreed that it might be so, perhaps to cut off debate, it would mean then that he would have accepted the estimate of the large numbers of Sioux to be reasonable. But in his heart of hearts he probably was not convinced because he discounted the danger implied by such numbers in formulating his plan of attack. And he only reluctantly accepted the fact that his command, in the face of overwhelming eyewitness accounts, had been discovered, thus losing the element of surprise. What his conscious or subconscious motive was for such self-delusion is lost to history. But he had no doubts that he was in for a fight. He sent his orderly, John Burkman, who had been up during the night on guard duty, back with the pack train, telling him that he was tired and, "...we're going in to a real fight... You'll get in at the tail and share in the glory. There'll be plenty of Indians for us all."[57]

The column, with Benteen's Company H in the lead, headed for the divide. As they crossed over the divide sometime close to 1200 and began to descend down Reno Creek, Custer rode up to Benteen, who was mounted on his horse Dick, a fast walker, and admonished him for setting too fast a pace as the regiment was

---

56. Benteen, in Graham, *Myth*, 179.
57. Wagner, *Neutriment*, 37.

becoming strung out. He took charge, and after a short distance, called a halt where he and Lieutenant Cooke dismounted. They were now about a hundred yards beyond the crest, fifteen miles or so from the Little Big Horn. Custer finalized his plan. He had been slow to accept his scouts' argument for a large Indian encampment in the Little Big Horn valley, but he had seen for himself, as had Varnum, evidence of a campsite near the mouth of Reno Creek and perhaps near its confluence with the South Fork as well. That much he knew was fact, and when the hostile Indians became aware of the regiment's advance from the divide, the odds were that they would race south and southwestward to escape, negating General Terry's grand pincer strategy. They would scatter, with the noncombatants in particular making a run for it. His years as an Indian fighter taught him that if he could round up the non-combatants, the braves' will to fight would disappear.

Custer and Cooke now cast the regiment's tactical battle plan. They dismounted, and as Custer detailed his plan, Cooke wrote and sketched furiously on a page torn from his field notebook. Mitch Bouyer and Charley Reynolds joined them. The details of the grand plan went to the grave with all of them, but the early execution was straightforward. The regiment was divided into battalions and a rear guard to be left with the packs; Benteen was given command of a battalion of 125 men, consisting of Companies H, (his own); D (Captain Weir commanding); and K (Lieutenant Godfrey commanding) and ordered to proceed on a left oblique scout. The Captain was ordered to prevent any hostiles from dispersing in the south tributaries of Reno Creek. Benteen was not happy with division of the command in the face of a numerically superior enemy and said as much. Custer cut him short, reminding him that he had his orders.[58] Any shortcomings

---

58. Windolf, *in* Hunt, *Custer,* 188.

in Custer's plan would have to be compensated for by his famous luck.

Reno, aware that since his scout up the Rosebud he was thoroughly ensconced in Custer's outhouse, had not bothered to advance when the officers gathered around Custer to receive their orders. Cooke had to ride back to tell him that he was given command of a battalion comprised of Companies A (Captain Moylan commanding); G (Lieutenant McIntosh commanding); and M (Captain French commanding). Reno was incredulous that Custer would give him a battalion command after their bitter exchange on the *Far West*.[59]

Custer retained command of the last battalion of five companies. As a testament to Custer's penchant for military show, each of the companies in his battalion rode horses of uniform color: C, sorrel horses (Captain Tom Custer commanding); E, gray horses (Lieutenant Smith commanding); F (Captain Yates commanding); I (Captain Keogh commanding); and L (Lieutenant Calhoun commanding) all rode bay horses.

Captain McDougall with Company B would provide the rear guard and one corporal and six men from each of the twelve troops would escort the pack train under command of Lieutenant Mathey, along with the civilian packers.

It would take an estimated two hours for Custer to ride down Reno Creek to the Little Big Horn. If Benteen on his oblique route encountered the Sioux and notified him, Custer could support him. Likewise, if Custer first made contact, Benteen possibly could be summoned to engage.[60] How much detail was laid out to Benteen is unknown, but with the icy relationship between the commanding officer and his senior captain, and according to Ben-

---

59. Willert, Diary, 265.
60. Ibid, 267.

teen's writings and testimony, not enough to put him at ease. He was much less comfortable with the prospect of a divided regiment than he was about traipsing about on a scout through inhospitable country. An unhappy Benteen was dispatched on his mission and shortly thereafter Custer was advancing the Seventh Cavalry Regiment on a hot trail to destiny.

TERRENCE J. DONOVAN

CHAPTER 5

ACROSS THE RIVER...AND INTO THE TREES

Benteen and his battalion had started out at a brisk walk with Lieutenant Gibson and six troopers galloping in the lead in order to scout from the high ground along their route. Custer struck out with his command and Reno's battalion down Reno Creek. The pack train and its escort plodded along after Custer, bringing up the rear. Benteen's battalion had not proceeded very far, just about halfway to the base of the first ridgeline, when Sergeant Henry Voss, regimental chief trumpeter, rode up with a message from Custer. Benteen was to continue beyond the first low ridgeline regardless of any sightings of Indians by Gibson. But by the time they reached the base of the ridgeline, the regimental Sergeant Major, William Sharrow, galloped up with further revised orders from Custer. The scouting battalion was to continue to a second ridgeline, and in the absence of signs of Indians, proceed into the second valley. Implied in these rapid amendments to Custer's original orders to Benteen is the probable fact that, as Custer proceeded down Reno Creek, his understanding of the topographic detail (originally gleaned from his perch at the Crow's Nest) deepened.

He realized that the low ridgelines just a short distance from the divide were too distant from the Little Big Horn and the mouth of Reno Creek and also not high enough to afford a satisfactory scout. And their narrow intervening valleys were insufficient to harbor large numbers of Indians. Benteen later offered several versions of his orders, but it is likely that the sum of his orders (original and revised) was to push on to a line of bluffs about four miles distant from the divide along the east side of the South Fork of Reno Creek. From there he (actually, Gibson) could see the Little Big Horn and could engage any hostiles trying to break out via the South Fork from any camp that might exist on lower Reno Creek.[1]

As Benteen's men struggled over the rough ground to the south, they were afforded occasional glimpses of the main column. It must have been a hell of a sight: nearly two-thirds of the Frontier Army's finest Indian fighting regiment whooping, hollering, and occasionally shooting while at a gallop down Reno Creek.[2] Any wayward Sioux on the highlands bounding the drainage must have surely wondered what the Great Spirit hath wrought. So much for surprise if there were any surprise left to be had.

---

1. Benteen, in Graham, *Myth*, 179. Mills, *Harvest*, 254, also suggests that Custer's improved knowledge of the lay of the land as he marched down Reno Creek prompted his revising his orders to Benteen. However, he makes no mention that Custer's initial impression of the topography was probably gained at the Crow's Nest. Perhaps he regarded it as self-evident.
2. Godfrey *Last Battle*, 22. Godfrey wrote that while on the oblique scout "we could see occasionally the battalion under Custer, distinguished by the troop mounted on gray horses, marching at a rapid gait. Two or three times we heard loud cheering and also some few shots, but the occasion of these demonstrations is not known."

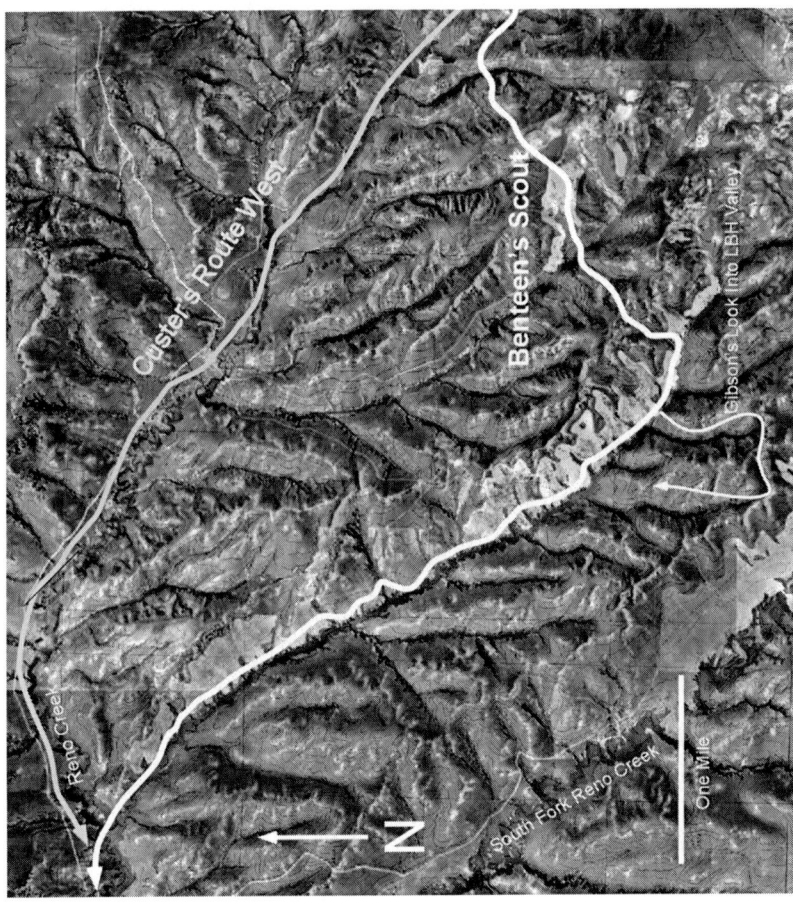

Figure 5-1: Comparison of the terrain that Benteen's scouting expedition encountered versus the relatively easy ride Custer and his men had as they galloped down Reno Creek. Before he could proceed down Benteen Canyon, several ridges had to be slowly crossed.

Benteen was both discouraged by, and wary of, his scouting assignment. He believed the mission itself was "senseless"[3] and was concerned that removed from the main command as he himself was, the possibility loomed large that Major Joel Elliott's disastrous foray at the Battle of the Washita eight years prior was about to be repeated. Benteen's memory of Elliott's small detail of troopers riding out too far from the main command and becoming surrounded and annihilated, while Custer had been distracted, had reinforced his distrust and low opinion of Custer's abilities as a commander.

> From being a participant in the battle of the Washita, Nov. 1868, and from seeing the manner of the 7th Cavalry were handled there, by Custer, I formed an opinion that at some day, a big portion of his command would be 'scooped' if such faulty measures were persisted in.[4]

Difficulty in negotiating the rough terrain prevented Gibson's scouting detail from easily staying ahead of the battalion and they had to halt frequently to let Gibson take high ground and scan the countryside ahead with field glasses. When they finally reached their objective, the bluffs overlooking the South Fork, Benteen held his command in the valley on the eastern side while Gibson traversed the bluffs and scouted. When he rejoined the battalion, the Lieutenant reported that he could see no Indians anywhere. That was enough for Benteen and he turned his column down the valley, to intercept Custer's trail on Reno Creek. He was satisfied that he accomplished what he had been ordered to do. He wrote both in his official report and to his wife immediately after the ensuing battle that he was ordered to the left to explore the bluffs

---

3. Byrne, in Mills, *Harvest,,* 254
4. Benteen, letter to Barry, in Mills, *Harvest,* 254.

four or five miles distant, pitch into anything he might find, and notify Custer.[5] He also told a New York *Herald* reporter after the fight that if he found no Indians on this jaunt, and satisfied himself that there were none to be found, then his supplementary orders gave him discretion to return to the command's main trail. Lieutenant Gibson corroborated this interpretation of Benteen's orders in a contemporary letter.[6]

The might of the mid-day sun was at its peak when they reached the main trail a little over two hours after striking out from the divide and just ahead of the pack train.[7] That timing would have placed them on the main trail somewhere between 1400 and 1420. As they joined the trail, Boston Custer passed them by heading towards the Little Big Horn, waving happily and voicing a greeting to Lieutenant Edgerly, but he did not speak to anyone else in Benteen's command. Boston had ridden back from Custer's battalion to exchange his horse, had spoken briefly with Captain McDougall at the pack train,[8] and now he was hurrying down Reno Creek to join the fun with his older brothers and other kin with the main body of the Seventh.

Benteen's task now was to find his commanding officer and the regiment. He could see from the shod hoof tracks that Custer was following the days-old hostiles' trail, broad and deeply rutted by dragged lodgepoles, down to the river. But precisely where Custer and Reno were was anyone's guess. Nothing indicated that Benteen's battalion should proceed at a rapid gait.

---

5. Benteen, *Official Report; Stewart, Luck,* 318.
6. *New York Hearld,* August 8, 1876.
7. Estimates of the time Benteen spent on the oblique scout vary widely. The most likely estimate is that of Darling, *Scout.* See Ch. 7.
8. McDougall, interview with Camp, in Liddic and Harbaugh, *Camp,* n., 81.

The worn and weary battalion, exhausted from their trek over inhospitable terrain, followed the regiment's track along the Indian trail down the Creek perhaps a mile or more at an easy pace, assumed to be a walk.[9]

Shortly beyond they reached a ponding of water, a "morass", where they halted to water their horses and fill their canteens.[10] The water was alkaline and as a trooper indicated, would "…take the hide off your tongue…" but it was cool and wet.[11] They spent about twenty minutes at the morass watering horses and filling their canteens. Benteen's horse, Dick, was known to strike off on his own after drinking whenever the bit was removed from his mouth. Since he could ill afford to chase his mount across the countryside, Benteen " …lariated old Dick to a stump of ironwood before removing the bit; and after drinking [Dick] pulled taut on the stump, and looked as if to say, 'Well, I didn't much care to go off this time anyway.'"[12]

At some point during the halt, they heard gunfire off to the west and Weir became "uneasy," suggesting to Godfrey that he prevail upon Benteen to mount up the battalion and move out. But Godfrey would have none of it, reckoning that Benteen was allowing the men to fill their canteens and would likely put him in his place and tell him to mind his own business.[13] Weir said, "I am going anyhow," and set out with his company. Benteen was probably ready to move out anyway but it's likely that Weir's move prompted him, and Benteen followed immediately with the remaining two companies and quickly took the lead following

---

9. Godfrey, in Willert, James, *Diary,* 295. Godfrey referred to the pace at this point as "very leisurely".
10. Stewart, *Luck,* 382. Nichols, *Court.* Benteen in his Reno Court testimony used the term morass for the watering hole.
11. Stewart, *Luck,* 382.
12. Benteen, in Graham, *Myth,* 180.
13. Godfrey, in Hammer, *Camp,* 75.

Custer's trail.[14] Benteen didn't say anything to Weir about the unauthorized advance,[15] suggesting that he may indeed have been ready to depart anyway.

As the battalion pulled out, the lead mules of the pack train, sensing water, were now in a dead run to the morass despite their handlers' best efforts (and vehement curses) to restrain them. All of the regiment's men and stock suffered from thirst in the oppressive heat. Benteen continued, apparently unhurriedly, through a deserted Indian camp site, one of a number of abandoned sites that the hostiles had left in Reno Creek as they migrated toward the west side of the Little Big Horn River over the past week.

While Benteen had reluctantly detoured on his scout south of the main column, Custer, in character, was letting no moss grow under his feet, riding down the north flank of Reno Creek at a smart trot. Downstream, where the flood plain widened and flattened, Custer signaled with his hat for Reno and his battalion to cross to the south side. Although separated by the streambed, the two columns were not a great distance apart and they could converse.

Custer must have had in his mind early on, perhaps from the time he climbed Crow's Nest, that since he could not see the evidence of the large encampment that the scouts tried to point out to him, it was then likely that the Indians were not somewhere on the floodplain of the Little Big Horn but rather along the lower reaches of Reno Creek, as indicated by Varnum in his report of his reconnaissance. This presented the further possibility that the Indians might attempt to flee south up the Little Big Horn or even up the broad South Fork near whose confluence with Reno Creek

---

14. Godfrey, letter to Shoemaker, in Mills, *Harvets*, 255
15. Ibid.

Varnum had seen lodges.[16] The line of bluffs five miles away from the divide bounds South Fork on the east, and when Custer reached a lone tepee, holding a ceremonially prepared dead Brave, likely killed in the fight with Crook the previous week, it "seems obvious"[17] that he thought it was all that remained of the Indian encampment from which the Indians were now fleeing toward the Little Big Horn. All signs supported the interpretation that they were in the vicinity of a large camp that had been abandoned recently and hastily.[18] In fact, the lone tepee marked the site of the camp of the group Varnum and the Indian scouts saw riding off from their lookout at the Crow's Nest.[19]

The column continued down the trail to about a mile or so above the Little Big Horn when dust from the valley of the Little Big Horn was interpreted by Girard, who had ridden to a nearby small knoll for a better view, as further evidence that the Indians were scrambling to escape. Girard testified that he signaled with his hat, and "then hallooed to General Custer, 'Here are your Indians, running like devils!'"[20] Custer ordered his Indian scouts after them, but they balked. Believing that the hostile Indians were in flight, and with his Indian scouts refusing to pursue, Custer issued his orders to Reno (through Cooke) to attack the hostiles from the south and bring the "fleeing" Indians to battle. "General Custer directs you to take as rapid a gait as you think prudent and charge the village afterwards, and you will be supported by the whole out-

---

16. The possibility exists that the historical record focuses on the Little Big Horn River valley because that is where the Indians were found and that was what was fixed in the participants' minds.
17. Stewart, *Luck*, 329.
18. Terry, report of 2 July 1876, in Graham, *Story*, 113.
19. Stewart, *Luck*, 323.
20. Girard, in Gray, *Campaign*, 273-75, points out that this activity happened further down Reno Creek and not at the lone tepee. Nichols, *Reno Court*, 84.

fit."[21] That was Reno's recollection, but Custer at that moment did not know the location of the village. Lieutenant Wallace was probably more accurate in his account, stating that Cooke had said, "The Indians are about two miles and a half ahead, on the jump, follow them as fast as you can and charge them wherever you find them and we will support you."[22] Reno moved his troops out at a "slow lope," directing them to "[k]eep your horses well in hand."[23] But as Reno's battalion started off, Lieutenant Varnum rode up and gave his scouting report to Custer that a large Indian village was in the Little Big Horn River valley. Varnum with his Indian scouts, and Girard with his, then joined Reno's column, which now proceeded at a brisk trot. Mitch Bouyer and his Indian scouts remained with Custer. It is reasonable then, that Custer probably thought that the lone tepee represented the remains of the large village and when he received Varnum's report, it was his first intimation of an existing large hostile encampment, issued from a source (Varnum) he could trust and believe.[24]

This new intelligence probably prompted Custer to change his plans, and at some point, rather than follow Reno as he had been doing and cross the Little Big Horn, he turned towards the bluffs, after pausing to water his horses at the North Fork of Reno Creek. He had plenty of evidence of a big gathering of Indians corroborating Varnum's report: he was following a large, easily visible lodgepole trail, larger than the one trailed by Reno.[25] Cooke, who had relayed to Reno Custer's orders, accompanied the Reno column to the River, arriving there about 1500. He then

---

21. Reno, Nichols, *Reno Court,* 561.
22. Wallace, Nichols, *Reno Court*, 21.
23. Herendeen, Nichols, *Reno Court.* Others state the pace ranged from a trot to a gallop.
24. Stewart, *Luck,* 329.
25. Martin, in Stewart, *Luck.*, 330.

turned to rejoin Custer. Unfortunately, Reno remained in the dark about Custer's change in plans. Custer may have sent a written message to Reno but if he did, its contents are unknown. Reno denied receiving any further communication from Custer after being ordered to charge the village in the river valley. However, Reno did not hold it against Custer for not notifying him of any change in plans. He would write in his report after the battle, "General Custer was fully confident that the [Indians] were running or he would not have turned from me."[26]

At the ford slightly upstream from where Reno Creek empties into the Little Big Horn, Reno's column stopped briefly. The men took this opportunity to water their horses and fill their canteens.[27] Girard, warned by his scouts that hostile Indians were headed their way, told the battalion commander, "Major Reno, the Indians are coming up the valley to meet us."[28] But Reno was unsure of Girard and had little confidence in him, so there was some further hesitation while he mulled it over, all the while looking at Girard; finally Reno gave the command to advance.[29] They crossed in a column of twos and at the far side of the river, the battalion was regrouped in a column of fours; they then continued at a trot past the timber onto a well-trodden floodplain. At some point, now aware that there was a large force of Indians ahead of him about two miles downstream, Reno sent Trooper McIlhargy with a message to Custer advising him of the situation. A little farther down the valley, perhaps a half-mile or so, Reno changed the disposition of his command, placing Troops A and M abreast, and keeping G trailing in reserve to the rear of the advancing troops.

---

26. Ibid, 334-35.
27. Hare, in Nichols, *Reno Court,* 276; Taylor, *With Custer,* 35.
28. Girard, in Nichols, *Reno Court,* 114 .
29. Ibid. As it turned out, this was probably a false alarm because the Indians were taken by surprise when Reno charged. Stewart, *Luck,* 346.

He sent another trooper, a cook named Mitchell, with a second message to Custer regarding the strength of the hostiles. Now advancing at a gallop, with Varnum and his scouts on his left flank, Reno led the charge toward the village.[30] Trooper William Taylor of Company M recalled that as they charged down the valley floor, Reno and Benny Hodgson were riding side by side a short distance behind. Taylor glanced back to see Reno "taking a bottle from his lips. He then passed it to Lieutenant Hodgson. It appeared to be a quart flask, and about one half or two thirds full of an amber colored liquid."[31]

As they closed on the village, Reno, seeing dust clouds kicked up at the southern perimeter of the village, believed that he was about to be met by a large defensive force, and while still at the gallop, ordered Company G onto to the line on the left flank.[32] The valley down which they raced was bounded on the right by the heavily timbered banks of the meandering river, and on the left by the high, grassy terrace where the Indian pony herd now grazed. The condition of the ground was poor; the pony herd had previously eaten the grass and the soil was cut and ground by hooves; the surface was soft, ashen-like and dusty, and it was difficult for the officers to maintain their troops in a line. Fine dust was driven in the air, giving the Indians ahead clear notice of the charge that was in progress.

As the cavalry approached the village and the Indians began to take fire from the troopers, they rapidly readied for a counterattack. Many headed for the pony herd, others went out to meet Reno either on foot or on horses that had been picketed by their

---

30. Reno, in Nichols, *Reno Court,* 561.
31. Taylor, in Nichols, *Reno Court,* 36. At the Court of Inquiry Reno admitted to having several drinks during the fight but was exonerated of the charge of drunkenness.
32. Wallace, in Nichols, *Reno Court,* 46.

tepees.[33] The troopers could now see heavy dust in the direction of the village and knew that the Indians were advancing to meet them.[34] The Indians were riding back and forth to set up a thick, covering dust cloud.[35] It was clear that the Indians were not in retreat, but in fact were coming out in strength to fight.

Visibility was reduced by dust and smoke, slowing Reno's advance, and he feared that the Indians were prepared to flank him if he continued. He became increasingly uneasy and hesitant. Other Indians were working their way to his left, attempting to get to his rear. Reno now surmised that if he advanced into the village, his command would easily be wiped out. He ordered his officers to halt and form a skirmish line across the valley floor. They halted at a place where a stretch of timber, following an old river meander, jutted out towards the plain, and which had obscured their view of much of the village behind it. According to First Sergeant John M. Ryan of M Company, "This was our first view of the Indian camp from the skirmish line."[36] At this point Reno estimated (probably too high) that he faced 500-600 hostile Sioux and Cheyenne.[37] The short skirmish line extended roughly perpendicularly onto the valley floor from the abandoned dry, brushy, riverbed channel (a cut-off oxbow) on the troopers' right flank. They were just yards from the timbered bank of the Little Big Horn.[38] No sooner had the skirmish line formed than Indians began to emerge from a ravine, or coulee, about 400 yards in front.[39]

---

33. Stewart, *Luck,* 347.
34. Wallace, in Nichols, ed. *Reno Court,* 47.
35. Hare, Nichols, *Reno Court,* 277.
36. Ryan, in Graham, *Myth,* 242.
37. Reno, in Nichols, *Reno Court* 562. Estimates of the number of hostile Indians have a wide range.
38. Nichols, *Reno,* 175.
39. Hare, in Nichols, *Reno Court,* 277.

With every fourth man deployed as a horse-holder, Reno knew that his effective firepower was substantially reduced and he was seriously outnumbered by a determined foe. Lieutenant Wallace estimated that the skirmish line "took up a few hundred yards."[40] Another estimate is that the line was about 250 yards long.[41] Estimates of the number of troops under Reno, including civilians and Indian scouts, range from 110 or 115,[42] to as many as 165.[43] With about 100 men on the line at the standard five yards separation, the skirmish line would have stretched about 500 yards onto the valley floor. If the line was only a few hundred yards, then the men were more bunched than the tactics of the day called for. The horse-holders and their charges withdrew to the cover of the timber along the river. The troopers slowly advanced on foot, firing rapidly as they went.[44]

As they neared the village, they met increased resistance and the advance stopped. It was now getting hot for Reno and his men, and Reno was desperately awaiting Custer's promised support. He was becoming heavily engaged. His troopers were firing rapidly and ammunition was being expended at an alarming rate.

> At this particular place there was a prariedog town and we used the mounds for temporary breastworks. We got the skirmish line formed and here the Indians made their first charge. There were probably 500 of them coming from the direction of their village. They were well mounted and well armed.

And,

---

40. Wallace, in Nichols, *Reno Court,* 23.
41. Willert, *Diary,* 287.
42. Wallace, in Nichols, *Reno Court,* 20.
43. Nichols, *Reno* 174.
44. Herendeen, in Nichols, *Reno Court,* 252.

"They tried to cut us through our skirmish line. We fired volleys into them repulsing their charge and emptying a number of their saddles. ...Lieutenant Hodgson walked up and down the line encouraging the men to keep cool and fire low."[45]

Private William E. Morris gave his account,

> We were perfectly cool, determined, and doing good execution and expected to hear Custer attack. We had been fighting lying down about fifteen minutes when one of our men came from the timber and reported that they were killing our horses in the rear.[46]

Despite this account, many of the new recruits, of which there were an abundance distributed throughout the companies, did not perform as well, firing wildly and rapidly, and some hunkered down in fear.[47] Nonetheless, there was sufficient firepower from the soldiers to keep the Indians from breaking through the line, but Reno's command was soon flanked and there were now hostile Indians to his rear. "...When they could not cut through us, they strung out in single file, lying on the opposite side of their ponies from us, and then they commenced to circle. They overlapped our skirmish line on the left and were closing in on the rear to complete the circle."[48] Worse, Reno was informed that they were infiltrating the timber and going after the horses.[49] His situation was becoming dire. Where was Custer and his support?

---

45. Ryan, in Graham, *Myth,* 242.
46. Morris, letter in, Brady, *Fighters,* 402.
47. A number of officers and noncommissioned officer so testified. Nichols, *Reno Court.* See also Brininstool, *Troopers,* 48.
48. Ryan, in Graham, *Myth,* 242.
49. The number of Indians infiltrating the woods is much debated. See, for example Carter, letter in Graham, *Myth,* 318.

Without Custer's support and with the hostiles flanking him, Reno desperately needed to regroup and find cover. He ordered G Company, which was nearest the dry river channel separating them from the cottonwoods lining the river, to cross into the woods to assess the extent of infiltration by the Indians.

Lieutenant Varnum thought that someone said this move was to better position the company to assault the village, so having released his Indian scouts, who were now trying to pillage the Sioux and Cheyenne pony herd, he rode to join them in the charge. The timber was underlain by thick underbrush through which cut winding animal paths, and it took some time to find Reno. Reno directed Varnum to return to the line, assess the situation and report back to him. As he rode back he met Lieutenant Hodgson and told him to find Reno and give him a report, while he would continue and subsequently update Reno. Captain Moylan and A Company were further out in the valley, and he repositioned his men to fill the gap left by Company G's movement into the timber.

When Reno crossed the Little Big Horn to start his advance, Custer had already turned north, away from Reno Creek; on the bluffs overlooking the river, he finally got a view of the Indian encampment and the large number of inhabitants. Now Custer had his own dilemma. He had told Reno he would support his attack, apparently without fully understanding the lay of the land. As Reno retreated to the timber along the Little Big Horn, Custer and his battalion arrived at the base of a high bluff now known as Weir Point. He halted the column, and along with his Trumpeter John Martin and adjutant Lieutenant Cooke, rode up on the bluffs bounding the river to get a look at the village.

Through his field glasses he may or may not have seen Reno's engagement, but likely did not; the dust and smoke hid the unhappy fact that some or all of Reno's men were by now probably taking cover in the timber and precluded him from making a full assessment of the fight. But now he could see just how large the Indian encampment was. "It was a big village, but we couldn't see it all from there, though we didn't know it then; but several hundred tepees were in plain sight."[50] Part of the village was hidden from view by the high bluffs ahead of them. Even without seeing the village in its entirety, Custer knew he would need all of his troops to carry out a successful attack. Because of the size of the village and the density of the lodges, Custer was unable to discern much movement within it, and even though Reno was fully engaged, the General was convinced that he had caught the village unaware and unprepared. Trumpeter Martin stated, "There were no bucks to be seen; all we could see was some squaws and children playing and a few dogs and ponies." The Hunkpapa Sioux Chief Gall corroborated Martin's testimony, saying, "The women and children were hastily moved downstream where the Cheyennes were camped."[51] Custer waved his hat, as did Cooke, possibly as a signal to Reno and, according to Martin, at his command waiting near the base of Weir point, and shouted, "Hurrah, boys, we've got them! We'll finish them up and then go home..."[52] It would turn out not to be his most prescient moment.

In the village, women, children, old men – noncombatants – began to scamper around, many herding the ponies, but moving generally away from Reno, downstream toward the end of the village where the Cheyenne were camped, in a northerly and northwesterly direction towards the western escarpment and tributary gullies of the Little Big Horn.

---

50. Martin, in Graham, *Myth,* 289-290.
51. Gall, in Graham, *Myth,* 88.
52. Martin, in Graham, *Myth,* 290.

Varnum testified later that about the time Reno deployed his skirmish line he saw Lieutenant Smith's Company E (the Gray Horse Company) moving along the bluffs on the other side of the river.[53] DeRudio stated that he saw Custer, Cooke, and someone else he did not recognize, on "the highest point of the bluff" waving their hats.[54] Custer's orderly, Trumpeter Martin, was probably the third man. Chief Gall, and presumably other hostile Indians in the village, also saw the soldiers on the bluffs along the east side of the river.[55]

Custer, relying on his experience at the Washita eight years earlier, now probably solidified his plan: Capture the women and children and the fight is over. The warriors' resistance would melt At this point it must have occurred to Custer that there was no suitable ford of the river for the battalion immediately below the bluffs; from his present position he would have had to return to where Reno crossed, which would be tactically unacceptable if he were to round up the noncombatants, or continue downstream along the bluffs to find another crossing[56] and thereby possibly encircle the camp between his command and Reno's. Unfortunately for Reno's battalion in the valley, Custer appears not to have made a full assessment of their circumstances before he left his vantage point to join his waiting command.[57] He opted to head downstream. With the enemy concentrated in the valley below, Benteen could now be summoned from his scout along with the pack train. From his vantage point on the bluffs, Custer likely reckoned that Reno was in fact achieving his objective because few warriors could be seen in the village. There was no need now

---

53. Varnum, in Nichols, *Reno Court,* 157.
54. DeRudio, in Nichols, *Reno Court,* 337.
55. Gall to Brady, in Willert, *Diary,* 286.
56. Hein, in Graham, *Myth,*336.
57. Willert, *Diary,* 286.

to go through with any pincer movement because given the disposition of the Indians, it would not entrap the enemy between the battalions. But from the size of the village, Custer knew that, as his scouts had told him earlier that morning, there were "heap Indians" out there. He would need reinforcement.

He returned with Cooke and Martin to his column and after conferring with Cooke, the five companies rode on at a rapid gait toward the head of a ravine called Medicine Coulee. Custer issued an order to his brother, Captain Tom Custer to send someone back after Captain McDougall and the packs. Tom ordered his sergeant, Daniel Kanipe to find the pack train and tell McDougall "…to bring it straight across the country. If the packs come loose, cut them and come on quick…" adding, "…If you see Captain Benteen, tell him to come quick…."[58] Two versions of what happened next were given by Trumpeter Martin, the last soldier of Custer's command to see him alive.[59] In his early version, he said that Custer gave him verbal orders to go back on the trail and find Benteen and the ammunition packs and hurry them up: "Orderly, I want you to take a message to Colonel Benteen. Ride as fast as you can and tell him to hurry. Tell him it's a big village and I want him to be quick, and to bring the ammunition packs."[60] Custer had no idea as to where Benteen might be; the mission Benteen was sent on must have looked pretty ludicrous by now. But with luck, perhaps he had already returned to the main trail. As Martin checked his horse, Cooke, not trusting the English of the immigrant Italian Martin (nee Martini), held him up, scribbled the message in his notebook and tearing the page out, handed it to the trumpeter, telling him to ride fast on the same trail they came

---

58. Windolf, in Hunt, *Custer,* 82.
59. See Stewart, *Luck,* 340-41.
60. Martin, in Graham, *Myth,* 290.

down. Martin last glimpsed the command galloping down the ravine.⁶¹ But in his 1879 testimony, Martin gave a different version:

> General Custer turned around and called his adjutant and gave him instructions to write a dispatch to Captain Benteen. I don't know what it was. Then the adjutant called me. I was right at the rear of the General. He said, 'Orderly, I want you to take this dispatch to Captain Benteen and go as fast as you can.⁶²

Martin struck out on the back trail. He then heard shots to his rear. He stated that shots were fired at the soldiers by Indians who were now hiding in ambush back on the trail. The Indians also were waving blankets and robes, attempting to spook the cavalry horses. His horse was jaded but he proceeded as fast as he could. A short while later, approaching the hill from which Custer scouted the valley, Weir Point, he encountered Boston Custer with his fresh horse in a headlong run to join up with his brother's command. He halted only long enough to ask the trumpeter where the General was. Martin gestured toward the route Custer had taken, telling Boston that he would find him just beyond the next ridge.⁶³ Boston charged on and disappeared into history. Continuing along the back trail, Martin could see the action in the valley; Reno's men were withdrawing from their skirmish line and the Indians were in full attack. Some Indians spied him and fired "four or five" shots. One hit his horse in the hip, but Martin did

---

61. Ibid.
62. Martin, in Nichols, *Reno Court,* 390. Martin is not considered a reliable source by most historians. Apparently "his intellectual and language difficulties were many," Stewart, *Luck,* 340-41.
63. Martin, in Graham, *Myth,* 290.

not know it at the time. As he crossed the North Fork of Reno Creek, he began anxiously looking for Benteen.[64]

Down in the timber along the Little Big Horn, chaos and confusion were beginning to reign. Reno ordered the Company G skirmishers to cross a clearing in the woods and proceed toward the village tepees that were in plain sight. As they reached the outskirts of the village they were rebuffed by "...about two hundred yelping, yelling redskins...."[65] They were forced to withdraw to the cover of the cottonwoods. As they did so, the Indians attempted to encircle; Reno realized that further withdrawal would allow the hostiles to turn his right flank toward the spot where the timber widened toward the meandering river channel bounding its east side. Reno rode toward the valley plain to check on the situation there, and as he emerged from the woods, he met Lieutenant Benny Hodgson. Hodgson informed him that Captain French's M Company at the far end of the line on the plain, which did not extend to the high bench bounding the valley, was having its left flank turned. Reno immediately thought that perhaps they could set up a defensive position along the banks of the brushy dry riverbed that would afford some cover. He and Hodgson set about passing the word along the line to withdraw to the dry channel. Captain Moylan's A Company, nearest to it, was able to accomplish a "flanking maneuver to the right" and quickly take advantage of its cover. When Varnum got to Moylan's position, the Company had fallen back to the woods and were now at, and parallel to, its fringe, using the brush as cover, rather than extending the line out into the valley. Moylan called out that his horses, with all the extra ammunition, were now beyond his left flank and in danger of being cut off by the Indians infiltrating through the

---

64. Ibid.
65. DeRudio, in Graham, *Myth,* 253.

woods. Varnum said he would bring them up. He found the A Company horse-holders and instructed them to move up toward the line. The other companies followed in the confusion without specific orders. Varnum returned to Moylan in time to hear him call out that he was out of ammunition. Every alternate man was ordered back to the horses to replenish from their saddlebags, then to return and allow the others to do likewise.[66] And still no sign of Custer.

Captain French's position was several hundred yards out in the open valley. When French got the word and ordered his men to withdraw to the channel, "About half of M Company had to face to the left again in order to change front...as this attack was being made from that direction by Indians closing at the time the line was being withdrawn."[67] Some of French's men were near panic, turning their backs to the Indians and racing toward the cover of the channel, inviting catastrophe. French coolly instructed them to face about and conduct an orderly withdrawal: "Steady men – fall back, slowly; face the enemy, and continue your fire." This they did briefly until some of the troopers could mount and get out of the timber and begin their headlong gallop to the river.[68] As the troopers reached the limited cover of the channel, Reno believed that his position was still untenable; he had no confidence that Custer would come to his aid, nor did he know where Benteen was. It was increasingly clear to him that Custer was not about to show himself anytime soon.[69] The timber to the rear of his men in the channel was being infiltrated, endangering the horses and the spare ammunition, which they carried. Each man had begun the fight with 100 rounds for his carbine and 24 car-

---

66. Varnum, in Nichols, *Reno Court,* 141-43.
67. Moylan, in Nichols, *Reno Court,* 217.
68. Morris, letter in Brady, *Fighters,* 403.
69. Reno, in Nichols, *Reno Court,* 585. Nichols, *Reno,* 178-79.

tridges for his pistol distributed between his person and in his saddlebags.

By this time, Reno was keenly aware that his command had expended a significant amount of ammunition. His casualties were still low, but if he were to stay where he was, his position would soon be indefensible; they were short of ammunition and if he were forced to send troops into the timber to protect the horses and the channel soldier's rear, he would have to spread his men too thin, affecting their command and control by his officers and sergeants; it would be a recipe for disaster. He would have to break out. Reno had a brief conference with Moylan wherein "…he designated a point across the river at some high hills where we would go to establish ourselves…and await further developments."[70] Moylan returned to this troop, and unable to mount and form them up with any semblance of order due to the restrictions of the timber, moved them out on to the plain to form in column-of-fours. Meanwhile, as Lieutenant Wallace testified, "After waiting some time word was passed down that we would have to charge them. We were surrounded, no assistance had come and we would have to get on higher ground…"[71] Reno called over the scout Bloody Knife to confer with him, and as the Indian started signing, a volley was fired by the Indians. A private was hit in the back of the neck, crying out, and Bloody Knife took a ball in the head, splattering blood and brains over Reno, only feet away. Apparently flustered, Reno ordered the men to dismount, "…and the soldiers had just struck the ground when he gave the order to mount."[72] It was confusing to say the least. The surgeon Dr. Por-

---

70. Moylan, in Nichols, *Reno Court*, 217.
71. Wallace, in Nichols, *Reno Court*, 204.
72. Herendeen, in Nichols, *Reno Court*, 255.

ter stated, "I heard him tell someone that we had to get out of there, that we had to charge the Indians."[73]

Despite the fact that not all his Company commanders received the order, among them Lieutenant McIntosh and Lieutenant DeRudio, Reno led a mounted withdrawal out of the timber and onto the plain, back toward the river. Those who never received word of the retreat were left, along with the wounded, to fend for themselves. In the mad dash for the river, there was no organized rear guard or covering fire.

The soldiers were now in panic mode. The Indians rode abreast and amongst them firing, using their clubs and hatchets, and physically pulling the men from their mounts. Lieutenant Benny Hodgson, somewhat incredulous about Reno's decision to leave the timber, questioned a colleague, "What is this, a retreat?" The reply was, "It looks most damnably like a rout."[74] Indeed it did.

A few officers attempted to bring order to chaos. Reno and A Company were in the lead; M Company then followed headlong for the river and the bluffs just beyond. French rode after his men, firing his pistol at the Indians as they drew alongside. Varnum cried out for the men not to run, that there were wounded on the field who should not be abandoned, but it was to no avail.[75] Lieutenant Hare was equally vocal in urging the men not to panic, shouting, "If we've got to die, let's die like men!" And, after emitting a Rebel yell, bellowed "I'm a fighting son-of-a-bitch from Texas!" followed by, "Don't run off like a pack of whipped

---

73. Porter, in Nichols, *Reno Court*, 190.
74. Roe, in Stewart, *Myth*, 373-374.
75. Graham, *Story,* 46. Stewart, *Luck,* 370. Stewart writes that Varnum urged the men to hold and not let them "whip us." In either event, Varnum was rebuked by Reno for admonishing the men to stay and fight with, "I am in command here, sir."

curs!"[76] The battle cry ". . .gave Reno the cue and recovering himself, he said, 'Captain Moylan, dismount those men.' Moylan didn't obey at once, and Reno repeated the order. So, A Company dismounted and deployed as skirmishers" on the far side of the bank.[77]

Lastly, after seeing mounted troopers abandoning the cottonwoods, poor McIntosh and G company finally left the cover of the timber and, with the swarming Indians, "…as thick as trees in an apple orchard…"[78] already in hot pursuit of A and M Companies, had little chance to gain the river unscathed. The Indians essentially rode into them. McIntosh's horse was killed, and a trooper who apparently elected to remain in the cover of the timber, offered his horse to the young officer[79] but McIntosh himself was felled before reaching the riverbank, where the soldiers had bunched up waiting to ford at a place where the steep bank had been worn by the horses of the preceding troopers. There, for the Indians, it was like shooting ducks in a barrel.

The valley side of the river was bounded by a steep, nearly vertical bank. The river itself was on the order of 40 or so feet wide and the far bank below the bluffs posed an additional obstacle, another high near-vertical cut bank. Some troopers forced their mounts to leap into the deep water and rode them across; other dismounted and as the horses and men fought to gain the far bank, they eventually wore both banks sufficiently to ease the escape for those that followed.

---

76. Benteen interview in Atlanta Journal, 24 May 1897, cited in Mills, *Harvest,* 261.
77. Morris, *Major Reno,* 27.
78. Wallace, in Nichols, *Reno Court,* 28.
79. Willert, *Diary,* 312.

The stream where I crossed was 40 or 50 feet wide. The water was almost up to a horse's back, it came to the saddle pockets. The bank of the side we ran from was 4 or 5 feet high, a straight cut bank, and on the other side about the same. After some of the horses had gone down the bank and caved it in, it made a pretty good crossing.

When I got there everybody was rushing in, trying to get across as fast as they could; the Indians were firing into them. Every man seemed to be looking out for himself, trying to get across as soon as possible.[80]

There was no line formed on the bluff side of the bank to provide cover for the crossing of the remainder of the battalion, but French did dismount and fire his rifle toward the Indians on the valley-side bank. Troopers scrambled up the steep bluffs with the Indians firing at them all the way. Dr. James DeWolf was killed during the scamper up the bluffs. Lieutenant Benny Hodgson was wounded on the plain when a bullet hit him and his horse, dropping him. A trooper rode by and offered him his stirrup as a handhold. Hodgson held on all the way to the other side of the river but on the far bank he was shot again and killed.[81] At the top of the bluff, the routed troopers regrouped.

Reno's conduct during the valley fight was immediately criticized by a number of his cohorts. Later, he was attacked for his decision to leave the timber as that freed up the Indians to attack Custer,[82] but such sniping is largely second-guessing. Much of the criticism is based on hearsay, but the testimony given by the 7th's officers at the Reno Court of Inquiry suggests that they were by

---

80. Porter, in Nichols, *Reno Court,* 197-98.
81. Wallace was of the opinion that a small contingent of Indians was on the bluffs and it was they who killed DeWolf and Hodgson. Nichols, *Reno Court,* 54.
82. See, for example, the discussion in Evans, *Last Fight,* 205-39, and references therein.

any means not lavish in offering praise of Reno's conduct; rather they were timid and reserved in offering criticism.[83] The harshest criticism at the Court by participants in the valley fight came from civilian scouts.[84]

Implicit criticism is also buried in the officers' testimony that they heard no bugle calls sounding retreat or verbal commands ordering withdrawal, and the retreat to the bluffs across the river was at best disorganized and at worst may have resembled a rout.[85] What the officers said and wrote privately amongst themselves and to others of course is a much different story. Lieutenant DeRudio reportedly said, "If we had not been commanded by a coward we would have been killed."[86] Lieutenant Godfrey was equally as harsh,

> I believe that Reno was dismayed when he saw the showing in front of him, and when he failed to see the "support" promised, I think he lost his nerve, and then when his Ree scouts stampeded and he found his force being surrounded in the bottom, I believed he abandoned himself to his fears, then stampeded to the hill and lost his reason, throwing away his ivory handled pistols.[87]

But Godfrey, as good an officer as he was, did not participate in the valley fight, so his opinion was formed from hearsay. Not everyone shared DeRudio's viewpoint. Private Morris forcefully defended his battalion commander, remembering him as "a brave and gallant officer" who was "cruelly libeled."[88] On balance it

---

83. See, for example, Wallace's testimony, in Nichols, *Reno Court*, 53. Carter, *Memorandum* Graham, *Myth,* 336-37.
84. Herendeen, in Nichols, *Reno Court,* 284-86.
85. Ibid.
86. Mathey, in Nichols, *Reno Court,* 551-52.
87. Godfrey, letter in Brady, *Fighters,* 375.
88. Morris, letter in Brady, *Fighters,* 401.

seems, however, that some criticism may be warranted, not necessarily of Reno's *decision* to leave the timber, but of the *manner* in which the withdrawal was conducted. Captain French was especially vehement, saying that he contemplated shooting Reno during the retreat from the valley fight.[89]

The conclusion that Reno's retreat from the valley was a less-than-orderly military withdrawal with organized rear guard covering fire brings to bear the equally ominous charge that he was drunk, or at least had been drinking, and thus was impaired to some degree.

Nonetheless, like so much of the Custer story, these are arguments that cannot be resolved by either side.

---

89. French, letter in Graham, *Myth,* 341-42.

TERRENCE J. DONOVAN

CHAPTER 6

HIGH GROUND

Benteen's battalion had not proceeded far from the watering hole (the morass) down the main trail before they encountered Sergeant Daniel Knipe of Company C who was backtracking on the trail with the message for McDougall to get the packs up to Custer in a hurry. Benteen indicated to Knipe where the packs were, back at the morass.[1] He galloped off without giving Benteen any of the essential details. Knipe didn't tell Benteen that Custer had ordered Reno with his three companies to cross the Little Big Horn and attack the Indians, presumably fleeing down the western floodplain. Nor was Benteen told that Custer had turned

---

1. Knipe, in Hammer, *Camp,* 96. states that he told Benteen that "They want you there as quick as you can get there – they have struck a big Indian camp." Benteen wrote that Knipe did not impart that information to him, rather Knipe's instructions to "bring packs" were directed to the commander of the pack train, R. H. Nichols, *Reno Court,* 404. Willert contends that Knipe did not report to McDougall with the packs because he lost his nerve at the prospect of encountering hostiles, and merely proceeded up the trail and then turned and followed Benteen's battalion at a safe distance, Willert, *Diary,* 334-335.

downstream and was trekking northward along the River's East bluffs.

While Martin followed the back trail up Reno Creek to find Benteen, Custer by now had reached the mouth of Medicine Tail Coulee, where elements of his command probed the ford in the Little Big Horn, but they were either driven back or turned back to look for better advantage; meanwhile, slowly, sporadically, the Indians had begun to disengage from Reno after routing him and moved downstream to meet this new threat posed by Custer's column.

By heading north, away from Reno's engagement with the Indians, Custer may have been attempting to round up the noncombatants, the women, children, and elderly, which, if successful, would certainly have taken the fight out of the warriors, as it did at the Washita.[2] But the record of much of the Little Big Horn battle is vague at best and twisted at worst.

On the back trail, Martin encountered Benteen below the watering hole and gave him the note from Custer, scribbled by Cooke:

---

2. Fox, *Archaeology*. The noncombatant thesis draws mainly from Fox and his colleagues' archeological reconstruction and forensic evidence of the battle melded with data from this study. Although there exists voluminous historical documentation, much of it is conflicting (or at least the interpretation of the documentation is conflicting). The evidence uncovered by archaeological studies at the battlefield and the integration of that evidence with eyewitness accounts given by cavalry and Indian participants and observers, however, provides new insight. And because these studies provide *physical* evidence of events, they must be given substantial weight. (Interpretation of that evidence is, of course, another thing.) Analysis of the archaeological discoveries and their interplay with personal accounts yields a compelling summary of events. In addition, see Scott, *Perspectives* and Scott and Fox, *Insights*. Benteen believed that Custer intended to enclose the Indian camp in a pincer between his battalion, attacking from the North, and Reno's on the South. Benteen, letter to Kate, in Graham, *Myth,* 187.

Benteen
Come on. Big village. Be quick. Bring packs.
W.W. Cooke
P.S. bring packs[3]

Benteen noticed that Martin's horse had been shot. Martin thought he was just tired but Benteen said, "Tired out? Look at his hip. You're lucky it was the horse and not you."[4] Weir rode up and Benteen showed him the note. The junior officers Edgerly, Gibson, and Godfrey joined them while they pondered the note. Edgerly heard Benteen say, "Well! If he wants me in a hurry, how does he expect that I can bring the packs? If I am going to be of service to him I think I had better not wait for the packs...."[5]

"Where is Custer?" Benteen wanted to know from Martin. And was he engaged?[6] Martin indicated he was about three miles down the trail. He was given another horse and instructed to stay with the battalion. Benteen had little complimentary to say about the trumpeter, describing him as

> ...a thick headed, dull witted Italian, just about as much cut out for a cavalryman as he was for a King; he informed me that the Indians were "skidaddling"; hence, less the necessity for retracing our steps to get the Packs, and the same would be gained by awaiting the arrival of them where we then were.

But with this intelligence on the situation he "...did neither; but took the trot!"[7] The packs were in sight about a mile behind.[8]

---

3. Benteen, in Graham, *Myth, 180*.
4. Martin, in Graham, *Myth, 291*.
5. Edgerly, interview with Camp, in Hammer, *Camp, 55*.
6. Martin, interview with Camp, in Hammer, 101.
7. Benteen, in Graham, *Story, 180*.
8. Martin, in Graham, *Myth*, 291. There is some question as to whether the pace was at the trot. See Ch.7.

When they reached the spot where Custer's and Reno's trails parted, Benteen said to Gibson, "Here we have the two horns of a dilemma."[9] Despite the "dilemma", he must have known, or could easily find out from Martin, which trail was Custer's.

Arriving at the ford where Reno crossed the Little Big Horn on to the flood plain, Benteen could see that rather than the Indians skidaddling, "...there were 12 or 14 dismounted men on the river bottom...being ridden down and shot by 800 or 900 Indian warriors." Concerned now that Martin's information was faulty, Benteen wheeled to the left and approached three or four Absarka or Crow scouts, quickly learning that "Otoe Sioux, Otoe Sioux...Heaps of them" were in the valley.[10,11]

From his position with the scouts, Benteen could see the first of the remnants of Reno's shattered battalion making their way to the top of the bluffs. He ordered his battalion to the bluffs, approaching with pistols drawn. There, he deployed his three companies along a skirmish line at the top of the bluffs to provide covering fire for the routed soldiers of Reno's command making their way across the river and up the hill. Hiding in the brush along the river bank with Girard, DeRudio noticed that the warriors were not pursuing across the river, although a number had been on the north bluffs taking pot shots at the soldiers as they climbed up. He heard heavy firing downstream, which was later determined to be Custer's location; the hostiles heard it too and most began to disengage from Reno and head downstream

---

9. Gibson, interview with Camp, in Hammer, *Camp, 80*.
10. Benteen, in Graham, *Story 180-81*.
11. Edgerly, interview with Camp, in Hammer, *Camp, 55*, note. Edgerly said that the battalion went nearly down to the ford, near enough to see Reno's troops climbing the bluffs.

toward the firing. A few stayed hidden in the ravines around the bluffs.[12]

Benteen and his officers were astonished at the sight before them. Reno approached Benteen, obviously in a state of distress, without his hat with "...a red handkerchief about his head, which gave him a rather peculiar and unmilitary appearance"[13]; he demanded that Benteen halt his men and wait for him to get reorganized.[14] Reno's companies were in shambles, disorganized and demoralized having just suffered a rout. Captain Moylan, Commander of Company A was "blubbering like a whipped urchin, tears coursing down his cheeks."[15] An excited Lieutenant Hare, who had been with Varnum and the scouts in the valley, approached Lieutenant Godfrey, commanding Company K with Benteen's battalion, "[I am]damned glad to see [you...we] had a big fight in the bottom and got whipped like hell."[16] Lieutenant Varnum had also lost his hat and had tied a bandana around his head. He was crying and swearing in frustration and firing haphazardly at the Indians who were now well out of range.[17] It would take time to reestablish military order.

Benteen showed Reno his note from Custer. Reno read it, but it did not dwell on its significance. Varnum noted that when they got to the top of the bluffs, "...we did not average five cartridges to the man..."[18] Benteen was instructed by Reno to share his battalion's ammunition with the remnants of Reno's com-

---

12. DeRudio, in Nichols, *Reno Court,* 323.
13. Taylor, *With,* 47.
14. Martin, interview with Camp, in Hammer, *Camp,* 101.
15. Benteen, in Carroll, *Letters,* 243. This comment may or may not be true or may be exaggerated. An embittered Benteen recorded it years after the fight (January 31, 1896).
16. Godfrey, in Nichols, *Reno Court,* 482.
17. Edgerly, in Nichols, *Reno Court,* 443.
18. Varnum, in Dustin, *Tragedy,*139.

mand. But low on ammunition and with the wounded on the hill and stragglers still making their way up the bluffs from across the river, he would have no choice now but to wait for the packs. In addition, Reno, hatless and with the remnants of Bloody Knife's blood and brains splattered all over him, was clearly flustered, and unable to command effectively.[19]

To his question, "where's Custer?" Benteen received only a faint gesture from Reno, indicating somewhere to the north and a vague response. Benteen mused aloud, "I wonder if this is to be another Maj. Elliott affair?"[20] suggesting that Benteen and other officers suspected that it was he and Reno who may in fact be the ones abandoned. Lieutenant Wallace was of that mind, stating, "There was no uneasiness [about Custer's situation] whatever. I heard a great deal of swearing about General Custer running off and leaving us."[21] Benteen came upon Reno and his routed troopers about a mile from where Custer had sent Martin on his courier mission, so the hapless trumpeter was of no help in locating Custer who had continued to move on northward. For all Benteen knew, Custer was proceeding north to join with Terry and Gibbon.[22] Although Benteen had his suspicion as to Custer moving off to join Terry, it would have to keep. At the moment he had his own fish to fry.

Reno appointed Lieutenant Hare his adjutant. Hare's horse was wounded so he was sent after the packs on the freshest horse

---

19. Graham, *Myth*, 294.
20. Moran, interview with Camp, in Hardoff, *Camp,*102. Private William Moran of the 7th Infantry, detailed to Lieutenant Bradley's scout, recalled that this was reported to be Benteen's response.
21. Wallace, in Nichols, *Reno Court*, 37.
22. Benteen, in Carroll, *Letters*, 187. Benteen supposed that Custer "... had found more indians [sic] than he could conveniently handle with his battalion ... and that he had fallen back to connect with Generals Terry & Gibbon."

that could be found to rush them forward. Hare intercepted the pack train back on the trail; McDougall cut out a pair of ammunition mules and Hare prodded them on to rejoin the beleaguered troops on Reno hill.[23]

Having put Reno in retreat, the Indians turned their attention to Custer and his soldiers downstream and a brief lull in the fighting on the bluffs set in. Waiting for the packs to show up, Captain Weir became uneasy and restless listening to the sounds of gunfire downstream that clearly must have indicated that Custer was now engaged. Unsure as whether Lieutenant Hodgson was missing, wounded or dead, Reno had organized a detail to investigate down by the riverbank where he was last seen, and while they were so disposed, the command pondered the significance of the gunfire.

> ...[We] were satisfied that Custer was fighting the Indians somewhere, and the conviction was expressed that "our command ought to be doing something or Custer would be after Reno with a sharp stick!" We heard two distinct volleys which excited some surprise, and, if I mistake not, brought out the remark from someone that "Custer was giving it to them for all he is worth!"[24]

---

23. Hammer, *Camp*, 69, note 2. Walter Camps interview with Captain Thomas McDougall: "Lieutenant Hare had been on duty with the Detachment of Indian Scouts and after the retreat from the valley fight, Benteen ordered him to ride to the pack train and hurry it up to Reno hill." McDougall thought he was a half-mile behind when Hare rode up. Mills, *Harvest,* 261, says that the pack train was two miles from the bluffs when Hare found it but cites no source. Hare, in his Reno Court testimony says it was Reno who sent him to get the packs, Nichols, *Reno Court,* 289. Benteen also said that it was Reno who dispatched Hare, Carroll, *Letters,* 186.
24. Godfrey, in Graham, *Myth, 142.*

But just where was Custer? Precise details of his final route after Martin was dispatched will never be known, but archaeological data from the battlefield integrated with Indian participants' oral histories provide as good a picture as can be hoped for.[25]

As the village warriors sped south to meet Reno's attack, non-combatant villagers began to migrate north and west. Custer, based on his Washita experience, likely reckoned that by capturing the women, children, and elderly, any warrior opposition would fold. The evidence suggests Custer may have deployed his force into two wings with possible advance details, a common tactic of the day. The left wing, likely comprised of companies E and F, with Captain Yates commanding and companies C, L, and I comprising the right wing, with Captain Keogh commanding.[26] The common belief is that there may have been a probe by the left wing at the ford of the Little Big Horn at the mouth of Medicine Tail Coulee, but if so, the troopers likely did not cross; they were driven back by an Indian defense.

However, the archeological data suggests a new theory: the troopers, realizing that the village was empty and the non-combatants were fleeing northwestward, turned right from Medicine Tail Coulee, left the river and briefly joined the right wing on Calhoun Hill before wheeling around and heading farther downstream in an attempt to head off the escapees. Keogh's wing remained to deal with warriors who were now beginning to disengage from Reno and infiltrate, and in addition, perhaps to provide cover for Benteen's arrival. Yates then retreated to the flank of Cemetery Ridge after most likely concluding that he had insufficient force to

---

25. Fox, Jr., *Archaeology*. The discussion of Custer's maneuvering and final battle is drawn from Fox. See also the data of Scott and Fox, *Insights* and Scott, et al., *Perspectives*.
26. Division of a battalion into wings was a common tactic of the day. Wing commanders were assigned on the basis of seniority.

accomplish a capture of the non-combatants. They waited there for a while but then cautiously moved up toward Custer Ridge to be closer to the right wing. But it was all too late. The Indians, done for the moment with Reno, were now converging on them in large numbers and all hell broke loose.[27]

As the hostile Indians were closing in on Custer for the kill, the situation was still in disorder on Reno hill. Weir approached Lieutenant Edgerly, explaining that he wanted to proceed, and asked him what he would do if Reno and Benteen would not advance toward Custer's presumed position. Edgerly reckoned that he would go and Weir then said he would request permission from Reno or Benteen, suggesting that he was confused as to who was really in command.[28] Weir was attached to Benteen's battalion when Custer split the regiment at the divide, but subsequently on the hill he decided he would seek permission from Reno, indicating he believed, or in fact knew, Reno was technically in command.

When Reno returned from the Hodgson detail Weir spoke with him. There is no detailed account of what transpired but the conversation became heated and an infuriated and unsatisfied Weir stomped off. Weir was waving his arms and gesturing and pointing down river. He apparently decided to go without permission,[29] knowing that Reno was not about to move out without the packs and reserve ammunition being secured. Edgerly, seeing Weir move out with his orderly, mounted the troop and followed toward the direction of the firing downstream, which they

---

27. Fox, *Archaeology*.
28. Edgerly, in Nichols, *Reno Court,* 444. That the conversation even took place is odd, as it smacks of insubordination; there is no circumstance short of being unable to communicate with Reno or Benteen that would have, under Army regulations, allowed Weir to proceed down river on his own initiative without orders.
29. Fox, interview with Camp, in Liddic and Harbaugh, *Camp,* 94-96.

assumed came from Custer. During the lull, Reno and Benteen reorganized; the packs had arrived and the wounded were prepared for transport. When Hare returned from hurrying up the packs, Reno, aware that Weir had departed "...on his own hook..." told him to go to Weir and "...tell him to communicate with General Custer if he could and tell him where we were."[30]

But it was too late. The Indians had vented their wrath; they were finished with Custer and were on their way to take care of the remnants of the 7th on the bluffs. [31] Edgerly and the troop moved down a ravine, probably the one taken by Custer, and were proceeding to the north, while Weir paralleled him on the ridge. Suddenly, Weir gave a hand signal to Edgerly to come to his position; he had sighted a large number of Indians coming his way. Arriving back on the crest, Edgerly saw the command advancing.

Reno was attempting to lead the battalions northward, but the rear units were still on the high bluff behind the strung out intervening companies. The packs were strung-out along the trail, moving slowly. They were followed by Moylan's Company A transporting the wounded and then by the rear guard.[32] But Moylan was unable to maintain the pace and he sent a messenger to Reno to inform him and request assistance. Before Reno could respond, Moylan reached McDougall who released half of his command to assist Moylan's struggling men. Riding ahead he found Reno and told him what was done. Reno "...informed me that it would hardly be necessary for me to move any further in

---

30. Reno, in Nichols, *Reno Court*, 567.
31. In his 4 July letter to Kate, Benteen states that, "...Weir's company was sent out to communicate with Custer, but it was driven back...," Carroll, *Letters*, 156. Edgerly, in Graham, *Myth*, 217 - 220, says that Weir told him afterward he had no permission to proceed, but had decided to advance for a look at the situation before asking Reno for permission.
32. Windolph, in Frazier and Robert Hunt, *Custer*, 99.

that direction as he thought the whole command would have to go back, as from appearances he was under the impression that the whole force of Indians was in front of Captain Weir's command...and firing at us."[33] The lead unit under Weir had gotten no further than about a mile, to what is now known as Weir Point, before they were set upon. From the perch on his eponymous pinnacle Weir, along with Edgerly, commanded a view of the huge village across the river to their left and broad flood plain of Medicine Bow Coulee where it joined the Little Big Horn. Beyond, the rolling hills were partially hidden by dust. "When I went out with the troop...I could see quite a number of Indians galloping back and forth on the battlefield, where we afterwards found the bodies [of Custer and his men], and firing at objects on the ground, but we could not see what the objects were." [34]

Reno and Benteen arrived at Weir point and Benteen placed "...a guidon at the highest point that looked over that country...to present an object to attract the attention of General Custer's command, if it was in sight."[35] Weir's company attempted to proceed further only to encounter rifle fire from the Indians. Weir had his men dismount, form up on the ridge, and return fire. They kept this up for about a half hour and then began a withdrawal.[36] The terrain along their proposed path toward Custer was "black with Indians,"[37] or as Benteen said, "We had not been more than 2 or 3 minutes at that high point before the gorge was filled with Indians rushing towards us..."[38] As they watched the large number of Indians approaching along the bluffs and over the flood plain, the

---

33. Moylan, in Nichols, *Reno Court, 219.*
34. Edgerly, in Graham, *Myth, 219-20.*
35. Benteen, in Nichols, *Reno Court, 423.*
36. Edgerly, in Graham, *Myth, 220.*
37. Varnum, interview with Camp, in Hammer, *Camp, 62.*
38. Benteen, in Nichols, *Reno Court, 409.*

officers generally concluded, with much bitterness, that Custer had abandoned them as he had abandoned Elliott at the Washita.[39]

Benteen, taking the initiative somewhat cautiously, did the only logical thing that could be done under the circumstances. Seeing Weir and his men racing back, Benteen order French to form a skirmish line across the bluffs, send his lead horses to the rear and cover Weir's retreat. But when Weir crossed French's line, French followed in haste. Benteen then ordered Godfrey and his men forward to dismount and do what French should have done.[40] Whatever was up with Custer, for Benteen it was now plain as the war paint on his adversaries' faces, that events had overcome strategy. As Weir and French's troops were being attacked, Godfrey received, via Lieutenant Hare, orders to join the main command. But as he was pulling back he saw "...French's troop come tearing over the bluffs, and soon after Weir's troop followed in hot haste...The Indians almost immediately followed to the top of the bluff, and commenced firing into the retreating troops...." Recognizing the perilous nature of the situation, Godfrey dismounted his men to fight on foot, providing covering fire for the retreating soldiers. The horses were led back to the main command. Godfrey's withering fire halted the Indians temporarily, and he received a second order to pull back to the main command. During the retreat, his men began to show the first signs of panic, which he immediately recognized and quashed.

> Having checked the pursuit we began our retreat, slowly at first, but kept up our firing. After proceeding some distance the men began to group together, and to move a little faster and faster, and our fire slackened. This was pretty good evi-

---

39. Mills, *Harvest*, 264. Gibson wrote his wife that the officers were convinced of Custer's abandoning them shortly after the battle, Fougera, *Cavalry*, 269.
40. Benteen, letter to Goldin, in Carroll, *Letters*, 215-16.

dence that they were getting demoralized. The Indians were being heavily reinforced, and began to come from their cover, but kept up a heavy fire. I halted the line, made the men take their intervals, and again drove the Indians to cover; then once more began the retreat.[41]

The high ground near where the remnants of Reno's battalion had retreated to and which they had just left was the only defensible position so with Godfrey's company providing a heroic rear guard action, the troopers fell back. On the hill, Captain McDougall, a close friend of Benteen's, spoke to him confidentially. If they were not careful, McDougall advised, they could be setting themselves up for another Fort Phil Kearney disaster.[42] Reno was lax in organizing their defenses and being the senior Captain, Benteen had better assume command. Benteen did so. But he was careful; his relationship with Reno was not a warm one and he knew that he had to be cautious in the manner in which he took charge.[43] He looked in on Reno, frequently visiting his position and either suggesting action be taken and sometimes directly

---

41. Godfrey, in Graham, *Myth,* 143. This narrative is a 1908 revision of Godfrey's 1892 article, Godfrey, *Last Battle*. Godfrey, ever the good soldier, knew the importance of maintaining intervals on the line. It has been well established that closing of intervals and bunching up of troops is the first sign of panic among soldiers. For a detailed summary see Fox, *Archaeology*.
42. At Fort Phil Kearny, the Indians used a small party acting as decoys to lure Captain William J. Fetterman and eighty men out of the fort, over a hill, and into a trap where they were annihilated by a large force of Cheyenne who were in hiding. This event is also known as the Fetterman massacre, Utley, *The Indian Frontier*, 105.
43. Benteen wrote to Goldin on 16 January 1892 that "Now, personally, Reno, I know, respected me, but I believe had no great regard for me, from the fact that I once slapped his face in the club room of a post trader's establishment before quite a crowd of officers, telling him he was a 'S.O.B' and if I hadn't given him sufficient, that I would be please to do so; so therefore 'tisn't to be supposed he was at all dying with love for me...," in Carroll, *Letters,* 209.

ordering it.[44] Benteen went to Reno and insisted that the battalions prepare a defensive position on the hill, near where Reno's troops climbed the bluffs; Reno acceded. As the beleaguered soldiers prepared their positions, the Indians began sniping at them from long range and quickly occupied the high ground, soon to be known as Sharpshooter Ridge, north of the their position. Benteen then directed Lieutenant Wallace to place his troop in a line on the right side of what was to be a new defensive alignment. Wallace said, "I have no company, I have only three men." Benteen responded, "Put yourself and your three men there, I will see that you are supported."[45]

As the rest of the troops returned to the defensive position, Benteen strung them around in an arc that ultimately ended up in a horseshoe pattern, with "Wallace on the right, with his brave set of...men...."[46] The defensive perimeter initially formed a semicircle on the northernmost of two gentle knolls separated by a small saddle. A hospital, encircled by the pack mules and horses to provide some limited protection, was established in the intervening swale with Company A under Captain Moylan anchoring the southeast side, facing east with the remnants of Company G immediately to their left They were barricaded behind a patchwork of saddle packs and boxes. Benteen placed his own Company H on the southern hill in a position that afforded his men a full field of fire, in a tight hairpin-like pattern, closed to the south. The rest of the companies were not so well deployed. Either Reno

---

44. McDougall, interview with Camp, in Hammer, *Camp,* 71. McDougall was of the opinion that Benteen did not assert himself earlier because Reno was technically in command of both battalions after Benteen arrived at the hill.
45. Benteen, in Nichols, *Reno Court,* 410. Evidence of how time dulls memory can be found in Benteen's letter of 1 March 1892 to Goldin, wherein he recounts the incident but says that Wallace had only two men, Carroll, *Letters,* 216.
46. Benteen, letter to Goldin, in Carroll, *Letters,* 216.

or the company commanders positioned the troops on the reverse side of the hill, the side away from the river. Placing troops on the far side of the hill put the hill between the defenders and attackers. Inexplicably, these companies were not emplaced on the military crest and this tactical failure probably contributed to the large number of casualties suffered by Benteen's men (three killed and 11 wounded).[47] Benteen's position was on the military crest of the hill: a position just forward of the natural crest that commands the terrain in front out to the maximum range of the weapons employed. Poor placement of the other companies enabled the Indians to flank Benteen's men and get to their rear, the result being that they took more casualties than any other company. He went to his grave scornful of the officers responsible for this lapse in basic tactics and soldiering.[48] One assessment darkly proclaimed, " [T]he other companies laid down on the job, literally as well as figuratively, and depended on [Benteen's Company] to save not only their honor but their scalps as well."[49] As dark fell, the Indian firing abated. All waited for daylight. Despite the lull, the Indians did not completely retire from the field, but kept the troopers encircled while they waited for sunup. Four men who did not escape the timber when Reno abandoned it for the high ground hoped to use the cover of darkness to shield their escape. Lieutenant DeRudio, a trooper from C company, and two scouts, Fred Girard and a half-breed. But as they eased onto the open alluvial plain, they encountered mounted Sioux, and were sent separately scurrying back to the timber where they remained hid-

---

47. Mills, *Harvest,* 265-66.
48. Ibid, 269. Rightfully scornful, according to Mills. Godfrey, in Graham, *Myth,* 144, wrote that "Benteen's troops suffered greater losses than any other, because their rear was exposed to the long-range firing from the hills on the north. The horses and mules suffered greatly, as they were fully exposed to the long range fire from the east."
49. Rector, *Fields,* 72.

den along the river until daylight.[50] They did not safely return to the battalion's lines until the hostilities ceased toward evening of the next day.[51]

Soon after nightfall, Reno walked the line and gave orders upon Edgerly's suggestion to close up the gaps in it.[52] The defensive perimeter was consolidated and Benteen moved his men in closer to the rest of the battalion. Every man not wounded was ordered to the line and when Reno, a whiskey flask in hand, found two civilian packers, B. F. Churchill and John Frett, back with the mules shooting the bull, he became infuriated, asking them what they were up to. The response was not to his liking and he struck Frett, stumbling and spilling some of the whiskey, and telling him if he found him there again he would shoot him. Frett later testified, either truthfully or in retribution, that Reno was drunk when he hit him. Benteen and Edgerly among others testified that Reno was not drunk, Benteen saying that "...there was not whiskey enough in the whole command to make him drunk..." and "...I did not know he had any whiskey or I would have been after some."[53] Benteen tramped the line, checking in with Reno periodically and even resting for 15 or 20 minutes on his bedroll.[54] He and Lieutenant Gibson would prowl among the sentinels, kicking them awake when the exhausted troopers dozed off.[55] And he had his own problems with laggards. During one tour of the line, he found a few mules still carrying ammunition boxes blithely striking out for the river and the Indians. Returning them to the makeshift corral he discovered Lieutenant Mathey, commander of

---

50. Mills, *Harvest,* 269.
51. Varnum, interview with Camp, in Hammer, *Camp,* 62.
52. Edgerly, in Nichols, *Reno Court,* 447.
53. Benteen, in Nichols, *Reno Court,* 478. See footnote 31, Ch. 5.
54. Ibid.
55. Benteen, in Carroll, *Letters,* 173.

the pack train, "gossiping away like an old lady over her tea". He exploded, cussing out Mathey in "broad Saxon", concluding, "I never felt more like damning anyone in my life."[56]

The soldiers could hear throughout the night wild commotion in the Indian village, with "...beating of tom-toms, dancing, whooping, yelling with demoniacal screams, and discharging firearms. We knew they were having a scalp dance."[57] At some point while this was going on, Captain Weir sought out Godfrey. "I want to thank you, Godfrey, for saving my troop." After a pause, Weir continued, "If there should be a conflict of judgment between Reno and Benteen as to what we should do, whose orders would you obey?" Without hesitation, Godfrey replied, "Benteen's."[58]

An ugly story whose veracity is difficult to assess arose surrounding events on Reno Hill as the fragmented regiment dug in and hunkered down for their defense. It seems likely that details of a discussion between Reno and Benteen were taken out of context, confused, misinterpreted or misconstrued. When Benteen finally got around to telling it to Godfrey years later, whatever ambivalence Godfrey held for Reno turned to outright hatred. It was reiterated over the years in officers' clubs and Benteen wrote of it to Goldin.[59] As the story goes, that night on the Hill as they conferred, Reno proposed to Benteen, or offered as a proposition, or perhaps as a discussion point while exploring all options, that they mount all that could ride and attempt an escape to the Powder River camp under cover of darkness. Benteen wanted to know what was to be done with the wounded. "Oh, we'll have to abandon those that can not ride," was Reno's response. "I won't do

---

56. Benteen, letter to Kate, in Mills, *Harvest,* 269.
57. Godfrey, in Graham, *Myth,* 144.
58. Godfrey, letter to J. A. Shoemaker, in Graham, *Myth,* 333-34.
59. Benteen, letter to Goldin, in Carroll, *Letters,* 207.

it," said Benteen, or words to that effect. This is a tale that is the result of considerable spin.[60] Regardless, it certainly intensified Godfrey's hatred of Reno. Whether it was a serious "proposal" or not, it is apparent that there was concern over the safety of the wounded who were in a makeshift hospital in a small saddle along the ridge, surrounded by the mules and horses. However, in his revised narrative of the Custer fight, Godfrey relegated the inci-

---

60. Godfrey, in Mills, *Harvest*, 270. Graham says Benteen's response was, "No, Reno, you can't do that." (Graham, *Myth*, 123). Without attribution, Sklenar states that the whole story of abandoning the wounded that so incensed Godfrey actually originated in idle conversation on Reno Hill between himself (Godfrey) and Weir and Benteen took perverse delight in attributing it to Reno, a fact that was then totally unrecognized and unremembered by Godfrey when Benteen told it to him years later! - "The sad thing is that for most of his life, Godfrey had no comprehension that the story that would so dumbfound and outrage him was one he had helped create. The unworkable idea may have been broached to Reno, and there is some independent evidence that it was, but Reno had plenty of military and personal reasons for rejecting it. As for Benteen, he must have taken perverse delight in dangling that artificial lure in front of so overeager a fish as Godfrey. Some commentators would commend Benteen for standing up to Reno, whereas Benteen himself surely snickered that once again his goose had shit with impunity on the truth." (Sklenar, *Honor*, 314-15.) Shades of Whittaker? Sklenar's treatment of the surviving officers of the Seventh is even more venomous than Whittaker's original attack in 1876. Graham suggests that too much has been made of the abandonment conversation (Graham, *Myth,* 338.), but Mills included it in his biography of Benteen. Nichols, *Reno,* 198, cites a letter to Walter Camp from Private John McGuire who overheard a discussion among several officers including Reno, about breaking camp and escaping under cover of darkness. Reno replied, "I have here a number of wounded men unfit to be moved and I will stay by them until the last man falls." Godfrey believed the story until he died, but historian Fred Dustin thought that the story was preposterous, and could not understand why Godfrey would give it any credence "unless afflicted by senile dementia" (Carroll, *Letters,* 92). It is recounted here as an example of the difficulty in separating fact from fiction surrounding the Custer fight and the ammunition it provides rabid Custerphiles. In 1926 Dustin penned a view that could be written today: the poison of accusations against Reno "...had spread too deeply to be corrected in the minds of the great body of the people whose silly hero-worship of Custer has not ceased to this day..." (Ibid, 133).

dent to a single sentence: "The question of moving was discussed, but the conditions coupled with the proposition caused it to be indignantly rejected."[61]

The ragged battalions would remain under siege through the next day. As the sky began to gray in the east sometime around 0300, two signal shots rang out from the Indians and the fight of 26 June 1876 was on. Pickets that had been sent out under cover of darkness under command of Sergeant Stanislaus Roy scurried back.[62]

Around daybreak, the exhausted Benteen tried to "...'Round up' a few lines of sleep, to make up somewhat for the three night's sleep that I was short of." Undisturbed by Indian fire, he started to get in his "forty winks" before being aroused by a Sergeant with the news that "...Lieut. Gibson of my troop was having a regular monkey and parrot time of it...." The hostiles had slowly moved up to the position on the south perimeter that Benteen had abandoned the previous night. He had to secure his line. With a group of "15 or 16 soldiers and packers" he mustered from packs duty, he had his new charges "carry up sacks of bacon, boxes of hard bread, pack-saddles..." and fortify Gibson's position with hastily built breastworks.[63]

The Indians had completely surrounded the beleaguered defenders of Reno hill, hiding in the tall grass and behind sagebrush. They found good cover in the deeply incised erosional ravines cut in the bluffs and extending down to the river. Benteen, in keeping his command in order, was completely exposed, constantly on the move along his section of the line encouraging his

---

61. Godfrey, in *Myth*, 144.
62. Roy, interview with Camp, in Hammer, *Camp*, 113. Roy recalled that the men who went with him on the night's picket duty were Privates Conner, Gilbert, Bancroft, McClurg, and Harris.
63. Benteen, in Carroll, *Letters*, 173.

men and placing the fire of his troops where it would do the most good. "Men," Benteen would say, "this is a groundhog case; it is live or die with us."[64] At one point the heel of his boot was shot off; unfazed, he looked at it and quietly exclaimed, "Pretty close call – try again."[65] He was objurgated by his men for drawing fire with his exposed nonchalance, to which he replied, "Well they fire about so often anyway."[66]

The men would hunker down in their pits and close to the ground and behind the hastily constructed breastworks while the Indians fired and when a "ki'yi" yell indicating an imminent charge was heard, they "would rise to their knees and fire as hotly as they could to hold the Indians back." A number of soldiers later recalled how oblivious Benteen appeared to enemy fire. Varnum recalled that, "Benteen [was] the only man he ever saw who

---

64. Pvt. Glease, nee Glenn, interview with Camp, in Hammer, *Camp*, 136. According to Glease, Lieutenant Gibson was trying to hide in a rifle pit "...too shallow and was acting so cowardly that he was in the way of men passing back and forth. Benteen got ashamed of him and told the men to run over him if he persisted in lying there." Benteen wrote his wife that rumors were rampant shortly after the fight that Moylan, Gibson and DeRudio "showed the white feather" in the fight of the 25th (Carroll, *Letters,* 149), but he never related the incident Glease refers to, having only faint praise for Gibson. "I know what Gibson did – which was all I told him to do, which wasn't much..." (Ibid, 206). It is not likely that Benteen would have let the story as Glease tells it rest if it were true. He did criticize Gibson in a letter to Kate, saying "I am told that H Co. men are terribly down on Gibson. The men say of G. that he does nothing but curse them in garrison – and when he gets in the field – cannot do anything" This feeling of the troops H Company could explain Glease's story. And in fact, Benteen referred to Gibson in a later manuscript in a familiar way as "Gib, my 1st lieutenant", which doesn't imply much animosity, rather a degree of fondness (Ibid, 173). It is conceivable that time ravaged Glease's memory and he was repeating rumor inasmuch as his interview with Camp occurred in 1908. All in all it is another fine example of the contradictions surrounding the Battle of the Little Big Horn.
65. Martin, interview with Camp, in Hammer, *Camp*,101.
66. Knipe, interview with Camp, in Hammer, *Camp,* 96.

would not dodge when bullets [were] flying – [he] seemed to pay no heed whatever." But things did not look good. "As man after man was killed or wounded it began to look as though defeat was gradually coming on, and even Benteen expressed some doubts about being able to hold out."[67]

Benteen realized that he was in an untenable situation and he immediately made preparations to flush the Indians with a charge. Placing the "Falstaffian crowd" of reinforcements from the packs under Gibson's command, he ordered his Lieutenant "to hold the fort, notwithstanding what might become of us" when he would charge the encroaching Indians. Then, disheveled with his shirttail hanging out, he recalled that "...I walked along the front of my troop and told them that I was getting mad, and I wanted them to charge down the ravines with me when I gave the yell: then each to yell as if provided with a thousand throats." The Indians had crept close enough to the Gibson-Benteen position that they "...were amusing themselves by throwing clods of dirt, arrows by hand, and otherwise..."[68] when, as trumpeter Martin recalled, "We charged out, old Benteen right in front of us."[69] Benteen was in his element:

> ...the throttles of the 'H-sters' were given full play, and we dashed into the unsuspecting savages...[and] to say 'twas a surprise to them, is mild form, for they somersaulted and vaulted as so may trained acrobats, having no order in getting down those ravines, but quickly getting; de'il take the hindmost...To say that I ever had more serene satisfaction at killing a black tailed buck deer, on the bound, with a carbine, than I had in putting one of Uncles Sam's 45s thro' as noble a specimen of the Dakotas as ever fluttered an eagle feather in his scalp

---

67. Varnum, interview with Camp, in Hammer, *Camp*, 62.
68. Benteen, in Carroll, *Letters*, 173-74.
69. Martin, interview with Camp, in Hammer, *Camp*, 105.

lock...there being so many of them around, that one wouldn't be missed...though I'm rather fond of indians than otherwise, but to plump him thro' his spinal, as he was cavorting thro the ravines...that I looked on that dead red with exquisite satisfaction...but I was so tired and they wouldn't let me sleep.[70]

The heat of the day was now upon the hilltop defenders. They chewed grass leaves to exercise their saliva glands and the wounded in particular suffered greatly from thirst. A Private Cowley went insane from thirst and had to be tied up to restrain him. It rained lightly around noon, and some of the men tried to catch water in their ponchos, to little avail. But some of the men realized that with the Indians driven back, this was an opportunity to fetch water and the officers agreed that volunteers could make a dash to the river.[71]

With the Indians hastily hightailing it, and in possession of his previous high ground position, Benteen was able to send Sergeant Fehler and a detail of four volunteers down the hillside flanking a ravine, now devoid of Indians, to an open area that allowed them to apply covering fire to the brush and timber across from its mouth, where it fed into the river. To keep the hostiles from gathering in large numbers, the five plied the brush and timber with withering fire while a "dozen or so volunteers from other companies dashed down its length to gather water." No one was wounded on the first run for water.[72] Lieutenant Hare made his way to Benteen's side in the afternoon to observe the water gathering and see about the men. As he walked around

---

70. Benteen, in Graham, *Myth,* 182. The shirttail observation was made by Glease, interview with Camp, in Hammer, *Camp*,136.
71. Roy, interview with Camp, in Hammer, *Camp,* 114.
72. Benteen, letter to Fields, in Mills, *Harvest,* 273. The soldiers covering the water parties were Sergeant Geiger, and Privates Voit, Mecklin, and Windolph.

with Benteen they were receiving intense fire. Asking Benteen if he wasn't concerned about drawing Indian fire, Benteen replied with a smile, "If they are going to get you they will get you somewhere else if not here."[73]

Sergeant Roy led a subsequent water gathering detail of about a dozen men. At the end of the ravine, the troopers counted off and made a dash over the open 20 yards from the ravine to the river to fill their camp kettles and pots. Although large numbers of Indians were kept from gathering in the cover of the brush on the far bank of the river, the few that were there were not kept from shooting at those filling up containers at the river's edge by the covering detail on the ravine flank. Those Indians on the north side of the Reno's position also fired down on the scrambling water troopers, who dashed from the cover of the ravine to the river, one by one hastily filling their containers before scurrying back to the cover of the ravine walls, where they then transferred the water to canteens. One of Roy's men received a bullet wound that broke his leg. It took about an hour to accomplish the task before they could scamper back up the ravine to the relative safety of their defensive line.[74] Additional parties made forays for water under the protective cover of Benteen's shooters. One was killed and at least two more were wounded. Sergeant Roy opined, "Benteen saved the command, according to my opinion. He was a very brave and nervy man."[75]

After his charge, and now occupying the south hilltop, Benteen realized that he was spread thin. He went to Reno and asked

---

73. Hare, interview with Camp, in Hammer, *Camp,* 67.
74. Roy, interview with Camp, in Hammer, *Camp,* 114-15. Roy stated that the dash from the ravine to the river was about 20 yards. A number of men were hit by Indian fire from those, despite the covering fire, who "skulked along the river". The water party received the Congressional Medal of Honor, Hammer, *Camp,* 114, n. 7.
75. Ibid.

for reinforcement. Reno told him to choose a company, which he did: French's Company M. After considerable delay, M Company moved into place. The repositioning of M Company between Benteen's H and McDougall's B Companies gave the Indians the perception that Reno's position on the north side had been weakened, and they immediately renewed their attack there. [76] Dead horses were dragged up to fortify the breastworks. Benteen returned to Reno and warned him that if something was not done soon, they would be overrun. Reno did not react immediately, prompting Benteen, somewhat impatiently, to say, "You've got to do something here on the north side pretty quick; this won't do, you must drive them back." Reno then ordered preparations be made for a charge and told Benteen to give the word. "All ready now, men. Now's the time. Give them hell. Hip, hip, here we go!" And away they went: Companies B, D, G, and K. One soldier remained in his pit, "crying like a child." Startled, a large group of Indians, preparing a charge themselves, "as Benteen had divined", broke as the soldier's charge started. The troopers advanced nearly a hundred yards before Reno called off the charge and ordered everyone to return to the line. "A most singular fact of this sortie was that not a man who had advanced with the lines was hit; but directly after everyone had gotten into the pits again, the one man who did not go out was shot in the head and killed instantly.[77] At some point during the fighting, Benteen was struck in the thumb by a spent round.

Varnum limped back to a rifle pit occupied by a private of M troop. He was wounded in both legs, one a flesh wound, and the

---

76. Mills, *Harvest,* 273. Benteen was so incensed at the delay that he later refused to endorse a recommendation for the Medal of Honor for M Company's First Sergeant, John Ryan.
77. Godfrey, narrative, in Graham, *Myth,* 145.

other a spent bullet which dented his boot at the ankle that felt "...like a blow of a hammer on my ankle bone, and made me very lame for several days." Feeling blood draining in his boot, Varnum attempted to slide it off with the other foot while lying on his back but his legs waving in the air drew fire and "a bullet struck the dirt...and I dropped my foot." Trying again while lying on his side gave "...the same result" The private chuckled and "I called him a damned chucklehead." Before he could berate the private further, "...a charge of Indians set us at work with our carbines."[78]

Sometime around mid-afternoon the fighting diminished. The charges by the soldiers may have persuaded the Indians that the group on Reno Hill would not be taken as easily as Custer. They lit the prairie grass between the village and the bluffs afire. There was some sniping by Indians and soldiers alike but clearly the situation had eased and it was less dangerous to obtain water. Benteen, nearly exhausted, continued to prowl the defensive line, sucking his sore thumb. Groups of Indians gathered on the hills down river, but their fire was unenthusiastic and diminished over time.[79] At dusk, the Indians pulled up stakes in the village and began the march south to the Big Horn Mountains as the soldiers watched, dumbstruck. The battle of Reno Hill was over but the battalion did not fully believe it. Speculation considered that perhaps the Indians had formulated some grand strategy to renew the battle once the women and children were safely removed. Some thought the break up of the Indian camp was due to General Terry's imminent arrival.

Varnum presented Reno with a plan for him and a sergeant to slip off during the night and contact General Terry. Reno was with Weir when Varnum laid out his plan.

---

78. Varnum, *Scouts,* 93-94.
79. Ibid, 95.

He did not reply for some time and then said he could not afford to lose two good shots and that we would get killed anyway. I said we might as well get killed trying to get relief as to get killed where we were. He said, "Varnum, you are a very uncomfortable companion." I left him.

During the night, the soldiers took their horses and mules down to the river to water them. "It was a pitiful sight to see the poor animals plunge their heads in the water up to their eyes and drink."[80] The officers decided to change their defensive line "as to get away from the stench of dead animals and get nearer water" by moving all the companies downstream of Benteen to the south side of his position. The three men hiding along the river with DeRudio made their way up the bluffs around midnight.[81] They were able to get some sleep finally that night and breakfast the next morning, the first time Varnum, and probably everyone else, had eaten since the morning of the 24 June.[82] The battalion suffered 47 men killed and 53 wounded. Reno ordered the dead men buried and supervised the burial of Benny Hodgson.

Private Morris summed up his and most other trooper's opinion of the battle when he wrote, "Benteen was, unquestionably, the bravest man I ever met. He held the Indians in absolute contempt, and was a walking target from the time he became engaged until the end of the fight at sundown on the 26th. He took absolute charge of one side of the hill, and you may rest assured that he did not bother Reno for permission of any kind."[83] Even those who had an axe to grind could not withhold their admiration for Benteen. "Too much cannot be said in favor

---

80. Roy, interview with Camp, in Hammer, *Camp*, 116.
81. The four were DeRudio, Fred Gerard, a half-breed scout and Lieutenant McIntosh's cook.
82. Varnum, *Scouts*, 95.
83. Pvt. Morris, letter in Brady, *Fighters*, 404.

of Captain Benteen. His prompt movements saved Reno from utter annihilation, and his gallantry cleared the ravines of Indians and opened the way for water for the suffering wounded."[84]

Around 0930 a dust cloud was spotted down the valley "...and from its regular formation we soon made out a Cavalry column." [85] Godfrey and others rode out and met Lieutenant James H. Bradley, Chief Scout for Gibbon's 7th Infantry, and his detail of scouts. "Where is Custer?" was the immediate query. Bradley replied, "I don't know, but I suppose he was killed, as we counted 197 dead bodies. I don't suppose any escaped." Godfrey was "dumfounded."[86] Bradley had conveyed this information to Gibbon who, in his official report to Terry, wrote that Bradley pinned the body count at 194.[87] The discrepancy matters little as the body count would rise substantially.

General Terry was cheered by the troops as he rode up to Reno Hill about 1000.[88] Benteen quickly inquired as to Custer. Terry said, "To the best of my knowledge and belief he lies on this ridge about four miles below here with all of his command killed." An incredulous Benteen responded, "I can hardly believe it. I think he is somewhere down the Big Horn grazing his horses. At the Battle of the Washita he went off and left part of his command, and I think he would do it again." Terry said, "I think you are mistaken, and you will take your company and go down where the dead are lying and investigate for yourself."[89]

---

84. Ryan, narrative, in Graham, *Myth,* 247. Sergeant John M. Ryan was broken to the ranks by Benteen (an action subsequently rescinded by Custer) for stringing up a soldier by his thumbs for a minor infraction. See Ch. 3 and note 75.
85. Varnum, *Scouts,* 95.
86. Godfrey, narrative, in Graham, *Myth,* 146.
87. Gibbon, report, in Overfield, *Little Big Horn,* 85.
88. Knipe, narrative, in Graham, *Myth,* 250.
89. Roe, interview with Camp, in Hammer, *Camp,* 249-50.

Benteen led a contingent of officers and men, including Lieutenant Bradley to the battlefield. They proceeded along Custer's shod trail down a tributary to Medicine Coulee and then dropped down Medicine Tail Coulee to the Little Big Horn. Then they followed Deep Coulee to Battle Ridge. The sight and smell that befell them there was sickening. Many bodies had been grotesquely mutilated and scalped and all had been stripped.[90] They were covered with flies and most were unrecognizable. Two days in the hot sun did not help. A soldier signaled Benteen and when Benteen rode up he recognized Custer. As Benteen stood and studied Custer's body, he quietly said to Bradley, "There he is God damn him, he will never fight any more."[91]

At a second reading, the callousness of that remark takes on a different sound. The 'God damn him' was standard cavalryman's language, often just a figure of speech but capable in this instance of almost any interpretation from a literal wish for God to damn Custer to some completely opposite but unsoldierlike expression such as "poor fellow." This is akin to the sympathetically-meant expression, "the poor s.o.b." However Benteen intended that portion of this remark, the latter part – "he will never fight anymore" – carries a subtle ring of pity or regret.

> Before him was Custer's body, two days dead and stripped not only of clothes but of arrogance, authority and all the traits that had aroused Benteen's animosity. Benteen had seen a lot of dead men in his service career, but the instant of viewing that particular one in the meekness and the total vulnera-

---

90. The Sioux mutilated and disfigured dead enemies in the belief that it prevented them from living the wholesome good life in the hereafter.
91. Colonel Nelson A. Miles, quoted in letter to Graham by R.G. Carter, in Graham, *Myth,* 311. Benteen's comment stirred much controversy, but unless one heard it in context and intonation, it is difficult to interpret.

bility of death and nakedness must have contained an unusual jolt⁹²

This is a common characteristic of warriors. Lieutenant Colonel Daniel Maslowski, US Army, who was shot down in Viet Nam and captured by the Viet Cong, related the death of a comrade in a prisoner-of-war stockade stoically with, "The poor son of a bitch, he died in my arms."⁹³

A substantial body of evidence suggests that Custer, or portions of his command, tried to ford the Little Big Horn at Medicine Tail Coulee. They were driven back and withdrew to Nye-Cartwright Ridge where the remainder of the command probably waited. ⁹⁴ From there at least some elements of the command left and made their way to Custer Ridge. There a group of men from Companies C and L were deployed on a line facing southerly. These troopers faced withering fire from Indian positions south and east. The rest of their comrades in the command moved north, along the ridge. The Indian threat was now deepening from the west and north, and another deployment was made from Custer Ridge (Last Stand Hill) to the head of Deep Ravine. Captain Keogh's Company I was deployed on the east side of the main ridge, possibly in reserve, or possibly to reinforce Lieutenant Calhoun with C and L. So deployed, the troops formed a wide V pattern with the apex to the north, and in that distributed formation, they held their ground. Using the ridges for cover, the Indians laid down a thunderous fire. Calhoun's position fell, and the Indians closed on the remaining deployments. As those deployments were wiped out, they moved up the slope toward Custer's

---

92. Asay, *Gray Head,* 53.
93. See for example, Scott's interviews with downed airmen (Scott, *Shot Down,* 48).
94. Greene, *Enigma.*

position on Last Stand Hill, engulfing the remnants of the command, which was now firing their Colt pistols. As they were overwhelmed, the Indians finished off the wounded and survivors with clubs and hatchets.[95]

All of the bodies had been stripped, totally or to some degree. Squaws severed penises and testicles; the scrotums made fine tobacco pouches. Some bodies were beheaded, throats were slashed and limbs cut off or split open. A few were dragged off (alive?) to the village and burned during the celebratory dancing that night. Bodies were peppered with arrows and stakes were driven into some of them. Tom Custer's horribly mutilated body reflected the Indians' hatred of him. His body bristled with arrows, his heart was cut out, and he was thoroughly scalped. He was identified by a tattoo on his upper right arm. Yates was stripped, scalped and a finger cut off. Smith, stripped to the waist, was found pierced with arrows. Cooke's splendid muttonchops were cut from his face and his thighs were split open. Calhoun was so badly mutilated that he could only be identified by dental examination. Miles Keogh had not been disfigured and his horse, Comanche, was the only living thing found on the battlefield.[96]

Disfigurement of General Custer's body was not reported, likely to spare his devoted widow, Libby. His body was found immediately south or southwest from the present day monument and in fact he was mutilated. He had been shot twice, in the left temple below the ear and in the left side. Both wounds would have been fatal. He was naked, save his socks. Sewing awls had been driven into his ears, "to enable him to hear better,"[97] presumably in the happy hunting ground should he receive any more warnings

---

95. Scott, *Insights*. See also Fox, *Archaeology*. (However it happened, Panzeri, (p. 93) reckons it was all over by 1730.)
96. Schoenberger, *End of Custer,* 210-11.
97. Bighead, in Marquis, cited in Stewart, *Luck,* 472.

from the Indians of the consequences of breaking his word to them. A leg had been split open and an arrow was jammed up his penis.[98]

The distribution of the bodies led Benteen to conclude that there had been little organized resistance, with the possible exception of a defensive perimeter at Last Stand Hill. Rather, the battlefield evidence indicated to him that it was a running fight: "...it was a regular buffalo hunt...."[99] Benteen noted a lack of obvious battle lines in his testimony,

> ...the officers did not die with their companies. Only three officers were found with their companies. That shows that they did not fight by companies. All the officers except Colonel Keogh, Captain Calhoun and Lieutenant Crittenden were on the line with General Custer.[100]

That assessment may have been a little harsh, lines did form but the hapless troopers were driven back by the onslaught, led by Chiefs Gall, who led the attack from the south and east, and Crazy Horse, whose braves swung around and struck from the north and northwest. Panic prevailed in the last stages of the engagement under the relentless pressure of the Indian attack. Physical evidence shows that the soldiers closed their intervals, bunching up in clusters, a sure indicator of panic.[101] Benteen returned to the combined command pale and shaken and said, "we found them, but I did not expect that we would."[102]

On the morning of the 28 June, the men of the 7th went out to bury their dead at the Custer battlefield. With few tools, the

---

98. Carroll, note in Schoenberger, *End of Custer,* 309.
99. Benteen, in Hunt, *Custer,* 189.
100. Benteen, in Nichols, *Reno Court,* 437.
101. Fox, *Archaeology.*
102. Roe, interview with Camp, in Hammer, ed., *Camp,* 250.

dead troopers were buried in shallow graves covered with sandy soil and sagebrush. A little more care was taken with the officers and their graves were marked. Two days were spent cleaning up the mess and burying the dead. Gibbon's men, in the meantime, prepared litters for the wounded. On the night of the 28th the wounded were moved out, headed downstream along the Little Big Horn toward its mouth 15 miles distant and the steamer *Far West*. The litters did not work well, and the detail halted for the night after about four miles.

On the 29th, Terry determined that he needed a map of the scene of the carnage. His engineering officer, Lieutenant Edward McGuire was given the task and Benteen and Company H provided his escort, with Benteen offering commentary on disposition of the dead troops. Their task was completed on the evening of the 29 June; Benteen and McGuire then joined up with Terry and they all moved downstream. The litters had been redone, rigged between tow mules in tandem and worked well enough that Terry ordered everyone to keep moving through the night. The moon went down early, around midnight, making it difficult to maintain the trail and it began to rain. The going was grueling and the wounded suffered greatly. They reached the steamer in the wee hours of the morning, just before dawn, on the 30 June and the wounded were laid on the deck. Captain Grant Marsh maneuvered the *Far West* down the Big Horn to the Yellowstone, where there was a delay in continuing downstream, while the Terry command along with the 7th was ferried to the north side of the Yellowstone, to Gibbon's "Fort Pease." The steamer finally launched for Bismarck on 3 July while Terry and the 7th Cavalry remained camped at Fort Pease to digest the recent events and ponder the rest of the Sioux campaign of 1876.[103]

---

103. Willert, *March*.

Benteen wrote in 1892 about an event that occurred while at Camp Pease on the Yellowstone,

> ...I was really ill with a malarious dysentery. However, I was well enough, too, to tell Col. Weir before a dozen or so officers that he was a d___d liar, and this was occasioned by some remarks he made about Custer and Reno, and the fight at Little Big Horn....Weir said that meant "blood". "Well," said I, "there are two pistols in my holsters on saddle (near him); take your choice of them; they are both loaded, and we will spill the blood right here!" The crowd went off, Weir with them, and the next time I met him he shoved out this hand to me to shake! Aha! I scarcely knew what to make of it, but at same time had his accurate measure. At the organization of 7th Cavalry, Weir had been my first lieutenant.[104]

Others claim that Benteen was suffering from a bout with a bottle of whiskey rather than a self-described case of "malarious dysentery," but whatever may have aggravated the situation, there were bad feelings between Weir and Benteen.[105]

Reno wrote his official report immediately after the battle and singled out only Benteen for special mention by name. The battalion's officers were angered and never forgave Reno for what they considered to be a major slap in their collective face and an impediment to their career advancement. As far as Benteen's opinions were concerned, "...had I anything to say in the matter, I should have recommended for brevets, first, Hare, then Varnum, and lastly, Godfrey, yes Wallace too, before Hare, then I think I should have stopped."[106]

---

104. Benteen, letter to Goldin, in Carroll, *Letters,* 219.
105. Mills, *Harvest,* 283.
106. Benteen, letter to Goldin, in Carroll, *Letters,* 230.

The Army patrolled up and down the Yellowstone, in some instances by steamboat, in an attempt to monitor, and prevent if possible, Indians from crossing it and heading north. By 24 August, Benteen and the 7th were at Camp Supply at the Powder River confluence. Benteen was mulling unenthusiastically over an offer of a recruiting assignment in New York. The 24th was his and Hare's birthday and DeRudio's was just two days previous. The three threw themselves a grand party. Benteen wrote his wife that, "This campaign is 'played'."

Custer, through arrogance or compelled by a perceived need to redeem himself in President Grant's eyes, made gross errors of judgment that led to his undoing: he ignored or disbelieved the intelligence of large numbers of hostiles brought to him by his scouts, he divided his troops in the face of these superior numbers, he failed to fully communicate his battle plan to his subordinates, he attacked a numerically superior force absent the element of surprise, may have poorly deployed his men when under attack, and possibly disobeyed his orders by engaging the enemy before reinforcements were in place.

It is generally recognized that military intelligence *per se* does not result in victory. "[D]ecision in war is always the result of a fight...." Despite the breaking of the Enigma code by the British and firsthand foreknowledge of the impending German parachute invasion of Crete in 1941, the outnumbered German airborne invaders took the island because of bad military decisions made by the British commander independent of that intelligence.[107] Custer's apparent disregard of his field intelligence in and of itself might not have done him in; rather, in Benteen's considered opinion, it more than likely was Custer's poor execution on the battle-

---

107. Keegan, *Intelligence*.

field that did so. His survey of the battle site led him to conclude that Custer's battalion had not defended well, writing,

> ...it is my firm belief, and always has been, that Custer's command didn't do any "1st-class" fighting there and if possible were worse handled even than Reno's batt'n. 300 men well fought should have made a better showing.[108]

On recruiting assignment, Benteen reached General Terry's headquarters in St. Paul about the time the 7th Cavalry marched into Fort Lincoln. Convinced that he did not want to be a recruiter, he received a release from the recruiting assignment from Colonel Sturgis. Meanwhile the officers of the 7th met at the Fort Lincoln Officers' Club for a blowout. Everyone got rooting, tooting drunk and Reno, subject of all kinds of rumors and innuendo regarding his behavior at Little Big Horn, started fighting. He tried to throw an Infantry officer out of the club, and was "wrestled to the ground by Lieutenant Varnum." Reno bellowed for pistols, threatening to kill Varnum. When Lieutenant William Robinson, newly posted to the regiment, intervened, Reno shoved him, screaming derisively, "Who the hell are you?"[109] Despite Benteen's opinion that the campaign was "played", the fighting 7th was still at it.

---

108. Benteen, letter to Goldin, in Carroll, *Letters,* 305.
109. Mills, *Harvest,* 285-86.

TERRENCE J. DONOVAN

CHAPTER 7

DILIGENCE OR DALLIANCE

By mid-July, before the column returned from the field, rumors had already surfaced in the Powder River supply camp as a direct consequence of the disbelief that Custer could have been so soundly whipped by Indians. As time went by, it was Reno who would incur the wrath of Custerphiles. And largely because of his well-known dislike for Custer, Benteen also was not spared, and a particularly grievous charge surfaced that he dallied on the trail, ignoring Custer's direct order "to come and be quick" and thereby was a key contributor to his commander's downfall. This accusation lingers yet and it would embitter Benteen to his dying day.

Benteen's route on the left oblique was not documented, and attempts at reconstructing it tended to generalize the trail as a dashed line on a map,[1] or sometimes as a series of arrows, arcing in semicircular fashion clockwise from the divide where the

---

1. See, for example, Hutton, *Reader*, 232 and Miller, *Fall*, 72.

command split until it intercepted Custer's trail along Reno Creek. Lack of a precise track presented too large a temptation for some who concluded that Benteen must have dallied out there somewhere, thereby abetting in no small way Custer's demise. There was also some considerable stretching, ignoring, and inventing of fact. Well before the shattered remnants of the 7th Cavalry returned home to Fort Lincoln, ugly rumors of cowardice, malfeasance, and misfeasance had become rampant. On 17 July Benteen wrote Kate from Camp Supply on the Powder River:

> ...Lieut. Walker of the 17th [Infantry] showed me a portion of a letter from his wife, in which she stated that they had a rumor down there that Moylan, Gibson & deRudio showed the white feather in fight of the 25th: the same rumor prevailed thro' the camp on Powder River....[2]

Many of these rumors became embodied in the Little Big Horn literature, if not as fact, at least as points of discussion. Interestingly, the most vociferous purveyors of rumor and unsubstantiated allegations were not participants of the battle. One of the first to attack Reno publicly was General Thomas L. Rosser, who had been quartered in the same dormitory with Custer at West Point. A Virginian, Rosser resigned from the Academy at the beginning of the Civil War to join the Confederacy. As a Major General, he fought against Custer in a number of cavalry battles of the Shenandoah campaign.[3] After the war, he became a successful Engineer with the Northern Pacific Railroad in St. Paul, Minnesota, which gave him an opportunity to renew his friendship with Custer during the Stanley Expedition of 1873.[4] In defense of an

---

2. Benteen, letter to Kate, in Willert, *March,* 143.
3. Utley, *Controversy,* 46.
4. The Stanley Expedition was comprised of a party of Northern Pacific Railroad engineers and surveyors with an Army escort under the command of Colonel David S. Stanley, which pushed west from Fort Rice. See Utley, *Lance,* 112-15.

editorial attack of Custer in the St. Paul *Pioneer-Press and Tribune*, Rosser responded with a letter to the paper accusing Reno of cowardice and of abandoning his commanding officer in the field. Reno, incensed, wrote a summary of the events as he saw them and demanded that Rosser make it right. Rosser refused and the fight was on.[5] The allegations became further codified in Frederick Whittaker's *Complete Life of Major General George Armstrong Custer*, published shortly after the Little Big Horn debacle in 1876, and in a series of letters to newspapers and correspondents in which Whittaker charged Reno and Benteen with cowardice and dereliction of duty.[6] Their well-known dislike for Custer had easily made them suspect.

Whittaker was infatuated with Custer's widow, Libbie. A British pulp writer living in the United States, he had published in September 1876 a reasonably balanced account of the defeat in *Galaxy Magazine*, in which he argued that although Custer was brave enough, he more than met his match with superior numbers of Indians.[7] Then he met Libbie. She had set upon a life-long mission to create what would become the Custer Myth. Who contacted whom first is unknown, but under her spell and as her champion, Whittaker wrote Custer's biography, relying on the General's *My Life on the Plains*, and unpublished correspondence and other materials furnished by Libbie.[8] Now whatever impartiality he might have originally had disappeared, and blame was placed squarely on Custer's battalion commanders, Reno and Benteen.[9] It is possible that Captain Weir may have had a role in singling out Benteen and Reno. He had been very close to the

---

5. Utley, *Controversy*, 47.
6. Whittaker, *Custer*.
7. Ibid.
8. Ibid, 212.
9. Leckie, *Elizabeth*, 208-10.

Custers and was a true Custerphile who disliked both Reno and Benteen, with whom he had run-ins. He visited Libbie sometime after the battlefield disaster, after she had moved east. They began a correspondence, and Weir confided that he had information that he was reluctant to put in writing but would pass on in private.[10] He is a likely source of information for Whittaker, perhaps playing innocently into his hands, or perhaps indirectly through Libbie, but one cannot be sure. When pressed by Whittaker to sign an affidavit condemning Reno's cowardice, he refused.[11] It has also been suggested and is equally likely that the unscrupulous Whittaker enlisted Weir's aid as a "silent partner" after Weir's death on 9 December 1876.[12]

Not all believed Whittaker's fables. And in fact, he came to conclude after talking with Trumpeter John Martin privately at the Reno Court of Inquiry, that he had done Benteen a great wrong.[13] It mattered little that Whittaker concluded he had grievously harmed Benteen; the die was cast and Benteen would live with the calumny until he died. And he was an easy target for amplification of the allegations, for he had apparent motive; he thoroughly despised Custer and because of the abuse he took over it, his feelings grew to outright hatred as time passed.

A number of individuals lashed out at Whittaker,[14] but enough believed him to cause grief to Reno and Benteen for the rest of their lives. A running battle in the press and elsewhere was

---

10. Mills, *Harvest,* 287.
11. Utley, *Controversy,* 53.
12. Price, letter to Philadelphia *Times,* March 13, 1879, in Graham, *Myth,* 330.
13. Utley, *Controversy,* 59.
14. Graham, *Myth,* 329-32. It was to (Robert Newton) Price, a former classmate of Lt. Benny Hodgson at West Point, that Benteen had given the "Come on. Be quick." note as a keepsake. According to Mills, *Harvest,* 286, Price had been an officer in the 10th Cavalry and was allowed to resign from the Army in 1869 after killing two privates in a quarrel.

launched. Whittaker's allegations sowed seeds of suspicion that continue to be harvested into this century.[15] Custer fell on 25 June 1876 but Libbie, Rosser, Whittaker and many of the Boy General's admirers believed, and wanted others to believe, that he must have been pushed. And it was all the more galling to Custer's supporters that a number of 7th Cavalry officers, including those known to despise him thoroughly, survived to tell the world that Custer's actions that day sealed his own fate and that of those under his immediate command. Surely, thought his admirers, others had to be responsible for the debacle.

On 24 August 1917, Walter Camp marked the place on the divide between Davis and Reno Creeks where the 7th crossed into the Little Big Horn drainage with a circular brass placard. The placard was set at the request of the Montana State Historical Society. This spot where Custer crossed the divide had been independently identified by the Custer scouts Curly, on 4 August 1909, and George Herendeen, on 27 July 1910.[16] A few hundred yards or so beyond the marker, on 25 June 1876, Benteen and his battalion, on orders from Custer, had separated from the main column and headed westerly on a 45 degree oblique to scout Custer's left flank. The time was about 1210.

In 1987, Roger Darling published a remarkable map of Benteen's probable route. Darling used the written recollections of the various participants, rates-of-march, and distance computations along with terrain analysis to map out the route. Custer's column and the pack train were observed by Benteen's men from time to time on Reno Creek, allowing unique identification of the

---

15. See, for example, du Bois, *Lion.* A television documentary aired as recently as 8 January 1998, on the Arts and Entertainment Channel, provocatively entitled *Betrayal at Little Big Horn*, accused Reno and Benteen of willfully refusing to leave the Reno-Benteen battlefield to go to Custer's aid.
16. Hardoff, *Camp,* 25-26.

vantage points along the "bluffs" and high terrain from where these observations must have been made.[17] His reconstruction of the scout includes estimated clock times for the battalion's arrival at key geographic points along the route.

The terrain that the troopers traversed was difficult, deceptively so. The men of the 7th were soldiers, not geologists or topographers, and they described its features loosely in terms such as "bluffs" and "rough." "Rough" may not be physiographically precise, imparting only a vague notion of the true nature of the lay of the land, but it is a good starting point. "The view from the point where the regiment was organized into battalions did not discover the difficult nature of the country, but as we advanced farther, it became more and more difficult."[18] The alluvium of many of the dry ravines was deeply incised and their vertical walls exceeded ten feet in places. Despite the rough nature of the country, the battalion was able to pick its way through, but with difficulty, and the terrain invariably had had an impact on the rate of travel. Most of Benteen's critics failed to appreciate the difference in the nature of the terrain covered by Benteen and that traversed by Custer in their rushed marches to the Little Big Horn.[19] Gray, for example, constructed a number of detailed time-distance plots for the various participants, [20] concluding that Benteen had not only tarried, presumably along with all of the officers and men of

---

17. Darling, *Scout*.
18. Godfrey, *Last Battle*. Windolph, in Hunt, *Custer,* 80, stated: "It was rough, rolling country we were going over, and it was hard on the horses.".
19. See, for example, Stewart, *Luck*, 379.
20. Ibid, 261-62, note. Gray had access to Darling's map in pre-publication form but apparently did not rely on it, concluding that it supported his analysis

the battalion as well, but also blatantly lied about it to cover up.[21] Maybe so, maybe no.

Custer had climbed the Crow's Nest that morning shortly after 0830 h and viewed the panorama laid out before him.[22] He wanted to see for himself evidence of the Indian village reported by the scouts. The Indian scouts pointed out the Sioux encampment, which he was unable to see. He probably didn't see it because the Indian scouts had seen smoke from the village in the clear post-dawn light and now, as the day heated up, the summer haze obscured his view.[23] Although scout Mitch Bouyer assured him that the hostile camp was there, Custer was skeptical. But, regardless, he would have gained a firm fix on the lay of the land. He now knew from his perch that the Little Big Horn River was a good dozen or more miles away, even if he couldn't see the Indian village or the entire river valley. He also could ascertain from his vantage point that the "line of bluffs" most likely to afford a view of the Little Big Horn River valley and the lower reaches of Reno Creek and any Indians they might harbor, was about four or five miles away, forming the eastern interfluvial boundary of the South Fork of Reno Creek. But there was also the possibility that the intervening ridges flanking the south side of Reno Creek might also have permitted a limited view. After he climbed down from the lookout, Varnum and the Indian scouts had observed a "dark mass", which they knew was a band of Indians with their equipment and lodges. It turns out that this was a smaller village of about sixty lodges that had been camped on the flood plain of

---

21. Gray, *Campaign*. A fact that makes a cover-up difficult to accept is that Captain Weir was a company commander in Benteen's battalion. He and Benteen did not get on well and Weir was a staunch member of the 7th Cavalry's insider Custer clique. By extension, Edgerly and Godfrey, who were lieutenants at the time but who went on to become generals, would have been *de facto* co-conspirators, a highly unlikely scenario.
22. Upton, *Adventure,* 113, note. "Custer did not go to the Crow's Nest but to a spot nearby where the view of the valley was similar."
23. Stewart, *Luck,* 275.

Reno Creek a few miles up from its mouth. The Indians were breaking camp to join up with the larger village along the Little Big Horn, which was hidden behind the bluffs along the river. That information, along with the information from a scouting party that the Indians had been discovered, was passed on to Custer.[24] Later, as he trotted down Reno Creek, his perspective of the topography changed and he issued amendments to his original orders to Benteen.

At the divide, after chastising Benteen, who was in the lead on the march up Davis Creek, for setting too rapid a gait, Custer and Cooke palavered privately for a while, furiously scribbling on a scratch pad. When they broke, Custer then divided the regiment into Battalions and sent Benteen off on his scout. Benteen's orders from Custer were given orally and witnessed only by officers who would perish with Custer.[25] Nor were those orders passed on directly to his company commanders. Accounts as to exactly what the orders were have varied over time, as have estimates of the distances involved, but Custer apparently did instruct Benteen

> ...to send well-mounted officers with about six men, who would ride rapidly to a line of bluffs about five miles to our left and front with instructions to report to me, if anything of Indians could be seen from that point. I was to follow the movements of this detachment as rapidly as possible. Lt. Gibson was the officer selected....[26]

In Benteen's opinion, the orders sending him on a reconnaissance were downright foolhardy, but Custer likely was carrying out, at least in action if not in spirit, General Terry's instruction to

---

24. Ibid, 276. Stewart cites numerous sources in piecing together the events surrounding the Crow's Nest observations.
25. Mills, *Harvest*, 252.
26. Benteen, in Overfield, II, *Little Big Horn*, 39.

keep feeling to his left. Private Windolph had ridden up to request permission to swap horses with another trooper just as the officers were conferring and overheard some of the conversation. Benteen voiced his concern: "Hadn't we better keep the regiment together, General? If this is a big a camp as they say, we'll need every man we have."

"You have your orders", was Custer's curt reply.[27]

On the trail, Benteen rode "...maybe a hundred yards or so in front of the battalion, while Lieutenant Gibson now rode a quarter mile or so on ahead of him."[28]

He started out from the divide at a brisk walk and then a trot,[29] and shortly thereafter Trumpeter Henry Voss rode up with new orders, that if nothing was found on the first ridgeline, he should proceed to the second, to pitch in, and notify Custer at once. Some fifteen minutes or so later, Sergeant Major William Sharrow arrived with additional orders from Custer: if Benteen saw nothing at the second line of bluffs, then he should go on until he came to a valley, "... to pitch in and notify him [Custer] at once, being also included." Ambiguities arise: was he to report if

---

27. Windolph, in Hunt, *Custer*, 76. Benteen testified that, "My orders were to proceed out into a line of bluffs about 4 or 5 miles away, to pitch into anything I came across, and to send back word to General Custer at once if I came across anything. I had gone about a mile when I received instructions through the chief trumpeter of the regiment; if I found nothing before reaching the first line of bluffs, to go on to a second line with the same instructions. I had gone, I suppose, a mile further when I received orders through the sergeant-major of the regiment that if I saw nothing from the second line of bluffs, to go on into the valley, and if there was nothing in the valley, to go on to the next valley. ...I was to send an officer and about six men in advance of my battalion and to ride rapidly. The officer I selected was my first lieutenant and six men from my own command to head my battalion." Benteen, in Nichols, *Reno Court,* 403.
28. Windolph, in Hunt, *Custer,* 80. For at least some of the time, Benteen rode ahead, (Nichols, *Reno Court,* 403.
29. Windolph, Hunt, *Custer,* 80. Sgt. Windolph says Gibson rode ahead at a gallop.

Indians were encountered, or "pitch in" to anything encountered and report, or report regardless of whether anything was encountered? The orders were ambiguous enough that Benteen apparently concluded, rightly or wrongly, that in the absence of a positive sighting an immediate report was not required.[30] Benteen testified,

> We started out by twos but we had to go by file through defiles and up around rugged hills that were too steep to ascend and we had to circle around them. ...We were at a trot from the time we left General Custer's column to the time we watered the horses at the morass.

Actually, Benteen's horse was a fast walker and "...it is impossible for a column of cavalry to keep up with him without being at a trot." So, "It was not necessary to give the command 'trot' because they were all at the trot at the time to keep up with me." It is also clear from reading Benteen's various accounts that the valley in question was the valley of the Little Big Horn River and not any tributary.[31]

Part of the confusion in the record about the nature of Benteen's scout stems from a lack of precise geographic terminology by him and by the troops in the field and part from either purposeful deception, sloppy reporting, or conscious or subconscious rationalization. Benteen's critics have been unmerciful in accusing him of everything from lying to malfeasance to a gross cover-up. But anyone who has been to Reno Creek (including General Custer), would know that the most likely spot for a reasonably unobstructed view of the Little Big Horn valley is in fact from the line of bluffs bounding the South Fork of Reno Creek about four

---

30. Graham, *Myth,* 179-80.
31. Benteen, in Nichols, ed., *Reno Court* 432- 33.

miles distant from the point at which Benteen began his scout, and not from the intervening ridges between there and the divide.[32] It is unrealistic and unscientific to infer that a seasoned officer of Custer's caliber and experience could not read the topography. From the Crow's Nest, it appeared as if some of the intervening ridges might afford a clear view of the Little Big Horn valley, but a traverse down Reno Creek demonstrates that not until one reaches the bluffs bounding the east side of the South Fork is such a view possible. Consequently, Custer amended his orders to Benteen twice as he proceeded down Reno Creek and evaluated the terrain. Gibson tried to get a peek from the intervening ridges but since neither he nor Benteen could see the valley, they continued on to the distant line of bluffs along the South Fork of Reno Creek as ordered.

Subsequent embellishments and distortions of just what Custer's orders to Benteen are thought to be "...an excrescence gathered through the years for the purpose of maligning or defending some of the actors in the ensuing tragedy."[33] Benteen was the one most often maligned. In the context of Darling's map, this may be too harsh a judgment. It was difficult to piece together a consistent description of Benteen's route from his testimony, letters, and narratives related over time. Benteen's references to the rugged nature of the country and his "highly fluid distance estimates"[34] led to widespread suspicion that he was covering up his poking along on the trail. But in his own eyes, it was a useless and

---

32. For consistency here, except when quoting the participants, the terminology "line of bluffs" is used for the high steep-sided bluffs bounding the east side of South Fork of Reno Creek, from which Gibson observed the valley of the Little Big Horn. Intervening ridgelines along Benteen's scouting route, which he also referred to as lines of bluffs, are simply referred to as "ridges" or "ridgelines."
33. Stewart, *Luck* 319.
34. Darling, *Scout*, 72, note.

senseless mission that directly contributed to Custer's annihilation. "...But through the whole oblique to left, the impression went with me that all of that hard detour was for naught, as the ground was too awfully rugged for sane Indians to choose to go that way to hunt a camp – or, for that matter, to hunt anything else but game."[35]

His disdain for his mission comes through time and again, as well as his attempt to justify terminating his scouting mission when he did:

> I knew that I had to come to some decision speedily, when I had given up the idea of further hunting for a valley and being thoroughly impregnated with the belief that the trail Custer was on would yield quite a sufficiency of Indians; ... so the question with me was, shall I 'valley hunt' any more, or shall I hasten with these three troops to where I feel sure of getting all the fighting they can want, and maybe help someone out of a hole there?[36]

As he had done after the Battle of the Washita and would do again during the upcoming Fort Duschene fiasco, Benteen vented his disdain for his commanders by deriding Custer's generalship and Crook's quartermastering in snide letters to newspapers. He repeatedly put the scout to the left in the worst possible light. He

---

35. In his account published in Brininstool, *Troopers,* 76, Benteen waxed poetic: "To say the country terrain was rough is but putting it mildly – expletives could be worked in front of 'rough' that would be more truly descriptful, and by no means exaggerative of the lay of the land. But on we went with high intent from embankment to embankment. ...Forward again once more, but no valley nor sign of valley was to be seen."
36. Ibid, 76-77. Benteen's reference to "valley hunting" implies that he was ordered to prevent any Indians from escaping southward through a Reno Creek tributary. The South Fork of Reno Creek is the only feasible route of escape other than the Little Big Horn Valley itself.

was chiding Custer's ghost. His embellished descriptions of the fruitless reconnaissance were laden with sarcasm, harshly criticizing Custer's strategy and implying that if his battalion hadn't been off on some wild goose chase, the outcome of the day might have been different. In his official report, Benteen wrote that he proceeded to those bluffs five miles distant, saw nothing, and continued "about fully ten miles."[37] This is clearly a falsehood, an error, or an exaggeration. In a letter to his wife a week letter, composed on 2 July he referred to his task as "...to go left for the purpose of hunting for the valley of the river –indian [sic] camp – or anything I could find." And, "I found nothing, and after marching 10 miles or so...determined to return to Custer's trail."[38] Again, a misstatement of the distance or maybe it seemed like ten miles at the time.

He trotted on, ultimately crossing two ridgelines and their intervening valleys before arriving at the line of bluffs east of South Fork.[39] As ordered, "Gibson and party went to [the] tops of several hills and reported no Indians...."[40] Benteen and the battalion did not proceed all the way to the bluffs, waiting instead in the valley east of the South Fork, while Gibson climbed the bluffs to survey the Little Big Horn valley with his field glasses.[41] The companies held there until Gibson rejoined them and reported that he had at last viewed the Little Big Horn valley and, although his view to the north was obstructed by river bluffs at a bend in the river, the valley to the south was clear of Indians. As far as Benteen was concerned, his mission was accomplished; he

---

37. Benteen, in Overfield, *Little Big Horn*, 39.
38. Benteen, letter to Kate, in Graham, *Myth*, 187.
39. The valley is nameless on U.S.G.S. maps. Gray, *Campaign*.
40. Edgerly, interview with Camp, in Hammer, *Camp,* 54.
41. Mills, *Harvest,* 253. Benteen had loaned Gibson his French field glasses. If Benteen climbed to the top of the bluffs with Gibson, he would have seen the relatively expansive valley of the South Fork. That might have satisfied him that he had indeed completed his mission of "valley hunting."

headed for Reno Creek to join up with Custer. Godfrey stated that, "...our gait was pretty rapid. My company was in the rear and I had quite often to give the command 'trot' to keep up with the rest of the command."[42]

Given his fluid estimates and exaggerations in Benteen's official report, the five-mile estimate to the line of bluffs has caused considerable consternation among historians of the Custer fight, some accusing Benteen of stretching the distance from the first ridgeline from one to five miles to cover up dalliance on the trail.[43] Custer would not have sent the two couriers with amended orders if this were the case. Custer was well aware from his march down Reno Creek that the ridges along Benteen's route to the line of bluffs at South Fork that he would ultimately reach, could not afford a good view of lower Reno Creek and the Little Big Horn valley. It is the imprecise terminology used by the participants that creates the confusion. It is also difficult to believe that an experienced Cavalry officer would be so far off with a distance estimate. But what is likely in this case is that Benteen was accurately estimating the distance from the divide to the final line of bluffs where Gibson was able to view the valley of the Little Big Horn, and not the "first line of bluffs" i.e., ridgeline, he encountered on his scout, only a mile or so from the start of his scout. Custer himself also must have been referring to five-mile distant bluffs when he issued his modified orders sent via courier to the senior captain, for Benteen again testified, "My orders were to proceed out *into a line of bluffs about 4 or 5 miles away* ... [t]he ground was very rugged and we had to go through defiles and around *high bluffs to get to the point to which I had been sent.*" [Emphasis added.][44] This is

---

42. Godfrey, in Nichols, *Reno Court,* 479. Edgerly, Ibid., ed., 44,. testified that "[o]ur march was a rapid one...."
43. See, for example, Gray, *Campaign*, 259.
44. Benteen, in Nichols, *Reno Court,* 403-04.

clearly what Gibson had in mind when he wrote his wife on 4 July after the battle: "Benteen's battalion was sent to the left about 5 miles to see if the Indians were trying to escape up the valley of the Little Big Horn, after which we were to hurry and rejoin the command as soon as possible."[45] Godfrey thought the distance to the bluffs where the battalion turned to the main trail was about "three or four miles."[46] Edgerly believed that it was five or six miles.[47]

On 8 August 1876, Benteen corrected himself by substantially reducing his erroneous estimate in his official report, eliminating any mention of traveling beyond the bluffs that were five miles away, "I was sent with my battalion to the left to a line of bluffs about five miles off, with instructions to look for Indians and see what was to be seen, and if I saw nothing there to go on, and when I had satisfied myself it was useless to go further in that direction, to join the main trail."[48] The critical item in Benteen's mind that he wished to address was probably to identify the point at which he considered he had fulfilled his orders, and sensing a big fight, sought to rejoin the regiment.

> My idea was there was more for me to do on the trail, that there was fighting going on or would be going on the trail, and that I had better go back and help them. I thought I had gone far enough and that I would be needed on the trail.[49]

Others agree:

---

45. Gibson, letter to Katherine Gibson, in Fougera, *Cavalry*, 268.
46. Godfrey, in Nichols, *Reno Court*, 479.
47. Mills, *Harvest*, 255.
48. Benteen, in Graham, *Myth*, 227 Graham includes communication of Benteen and Reno in the New York *Herald*, published August 8, 1876. Note also that there is no mention of any requirement to report negative results to Custer.
49. Benteen, in Nichols, *Reno Court*.

...[Benteen's] battalion apparently went over the first ridge to the left after leaving Custer's trail and into a small valley down which they rode. About a mile and a half off the trail they crossed an insignificant branch of the Little Big Horn River and *rode toward the bluffs which they had been ordered to explore.* [Emphasis added.]" [50]

As it happens, that distance is about four miles on Darling's map.[51] In later years, Benteen volunteered that he was in at least technical violation of his orders. This was undoubtedly a fabrication put forth to serve some unknown purpose or justification, for "[i]n fact Benteen probably did exactly what Custer wanted and expected him to do, and there was no sense in his saying that he felt he had violated his orders."[52]

Benteen was technically correct in writing that he saw no sign of the valley, but of course, Gibson did see it from the vantage of the bluffs bounding South Fork, and Benteen obfuscates the issue with his imprecise topographic terminology over the years which confuses and interchanges the "line of bluffs" to which he was sent with the intervening "ridges." Benteen wrote later in life that ten men were sent in advance.[53] Earlier he wrote that the number was "about" six.[54] Since the actual number is insignificant in the grand scheme of things, the difference probably reflects a genuine faulty memory in this case. At the "line of bluffs" to which he had been sent five miles distant, Gibson not only had a view of South

---

50. Stewart, *Luck*, 379.
51. Although the distance as drawn by Darling, *Scout,* is actually about four miles, the reference to five miles is retained to avoid confusion about the historical record.
52. Stewart, *Luck*, 381.
53. Benteen, unpublished ms cited in, Graham, *Myth.*
54. Benteen, in Overfield, *Little Big Horn,* 39.

Fork valley but Little Big Horn valley as well, and could see no sign of Indians in either. The battalion then turned to the main trail.

When Benteen veered left over the high ground at the start of his scout, the battalion could see Custer heading down Reno Creek at a gallop or fast trot; the pack train followed at a walk. Benteen struck the main trail a mile or so ahead of the pack train. Custer had already passed that point, as evidenced by the regiment's shod tracks. So despite the widely varying and sometimes fanciful estimates of time and distance traveled by Benteen and his detachment, Benteen could not have diverted from Reno Creek so far or for so long as to place himself more than four or five miles behind Custer. Had he traveled at a slower pace than he did, he would not have hit the trail ahead of the packs.

But interpretation is subject to the interpreter's own biases and open to dispute,[55] and the very real danger is that of putting words in the mouth of the subject, so to speak. The question remains: Did Benteen tarry on the trail and attempt to cover it up by lying about the nature and length of his route? Retracing the routes, as reconstructed by Darling, on horseback, by foot, and by flying over them in a light airplane, provides considerable insight into the geography of Benteen's scout and Custer's simultaneous charge down Reno Creek. From that exercise, it is apparent that the differences in topography must have affected both the rates at which the columns proceeded and the relative wear and tear on the horses. Not all of Benteen's various descriptions of the route were due to prevarication or poor memory. Others agreed that the trail was indeed difficult. Private Windolph commented that,

---

55. Compare the descriptions of Benteen's scout from the divide to the morass as given by Willert and Sklenar (Willert, *Diary,* 266-69, 95-96 and Sklenar, *Honor,* 220-24.)

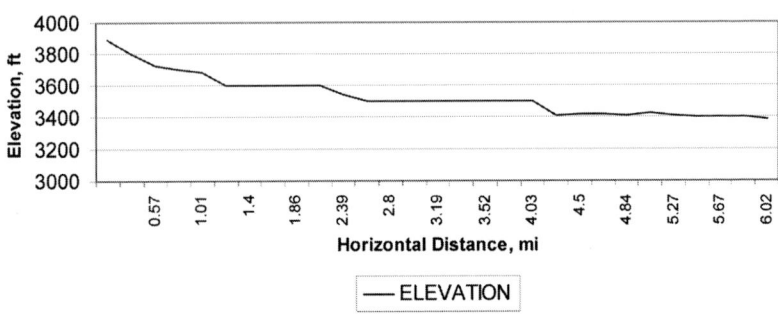

Figure 7.1. Profile of Custer's route from the point of separation of the battalions near the divide to the confluence of Darling's Valley 3 and Reno Creek

> I suppose we must have been going up and down those rugged hills for the best part of two hours before we turned back on the Custer trail. I think we covered somewhere around seven or eight miles. That doesn't sound very much, until taking into consideration how hard-going it was.[56]

And, "The fatigue of crossing ridges and valleys heavily distressed our horses, many falling behind."[57]

Figures 7.1, 7.2 and 7.3 are computer-generated cross-sections drawn from a digital topographic database along the routes followed by Custer and Benteen. The routes depicted are from their separation point just west of Camp's marker to the point where Benteen rejoined the main trail; Custer's route is shown going down Reno Creek and Benteen's on his oblique scout to the left. Darling concluded that the

---

56. Hunt, *Custer*, 80.
57. Darling, *Scout*, 68 note. Godfrey, in Graham, *Myth*, 295.

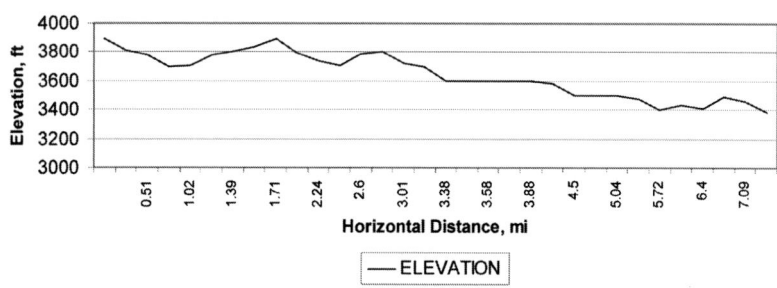

Figure 7.2. Profile of Benteen's route from the point of separation of the battalions near the divide to the confluence of Darling's Valley 3 and Reno Creek

... scout participants, at least from the information now available on the record, do not have anything to apologize for. The scout was well executed. It moved along at a relatively fast pace; was carried out without unnecessary deviations en route; it achieved the purpose for which it was launched. If

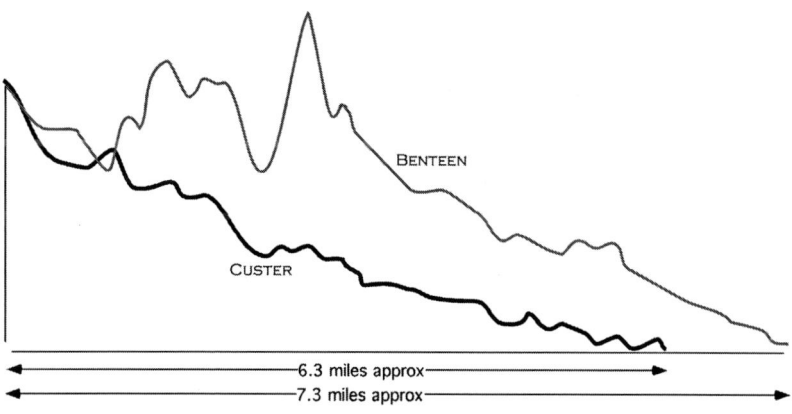

Figure 7.3. The two profiles have been combined and their vertical scale equally exagerated to show more effectively the drastic differences between the two routes.

there was a major flaw, it was not reporting the scout results to Custer as soon as they were obtained.[58]

But was Benteen expected to rush a report to Custer that he had seen nothing? Probably not. Benteen, in his official report, wrote, "...if in my judgment there was nothing to be seen of Indians, Valleys, &c., in the direction I was going, to return with the battalion to the trail the command was following."[59] And in a later narrative he wrote he was "...to pitch into any Indians I could see, and *in such case,* to notify [Custer] at once." [Emphasis added.][60] There is no mention of any instruction to report the absence of Indians in any discussion of Benteen's orders.

Accepting Darling's itinerary to be as good an estimate as can be made with the present state of knowledge, it is possible to compare statistically the rate of Benteen's advance with that of the main column proceeding down Reno Creek. But with time estimates garnered from various sources such as unsynchronized watch readings, estimates of time from distances traveled, recollections of participants, average speed of trotting horses and plodding mules, etc., it is impossible to assign absolute statistical error. In the case at hand, some arbitrary error must be attached to the time values. Consider Gray and Darling's estimates for Benteen's return to the main trail after his scout to the left. Gray calculated that Benteen arrived there at 1432; Darling calculated 1416. If one assumes, for example, that the time estimates have an error of least ±10% per hour, then Gray's 1432 would represent any time between 1426 and 1438, or 1432 ±6 minutes. Similarly, Darling's value could range from 1410 to 1422, or 1416 ±6 minutes. But

---

58. Darling, *Scout*, 54.
59. Benteen, in Overfield, *Little Big Horn*, 39-40.
60. Benteen, in Carroll, *Letters,* 182.

now only four minutes separate Gray's lower bound from Darling's upper bound.

Six minutes' variation is not particularly great, but the possibility of a 12-minute spread due to worst-case error-compounding between successive time estimates emphasizes that there is indeed uncertainty in the values. The 10% error in this example is arbitrary and perhaps not conservative, but it is a somewhat convenient choice because it allows the reporting of time in hours and decimal hours (6 min = 0.1h).

To account for time uncertainty, the times of Gray and Darling have been converted to decimal hours. To avoid any possible confusion between A.M. and P.M., all times are referenced to the 24 hour clock. The rules of rounding are also applied; the following conventions have been adopted: all time estimates are rounded to the nearest tenth hour. Midrange values are rounded to the nearest even tenth. Thus 4:20 P.M. is rounded to 16.3 h and 4:21 P.M. is rounded to 16.4 h. Where the data of Gray and Darling require no rounding, their values are retained and converted to decimal hours.[61] This procedure assigns a maximum error of ±5% (±3 min) at any specific time reference by Gray or Darling, and a maximum error of ±10 percent (6 min) due to error compounding between any two adjacent points or successive time references on

---

61. Jonathan Betts, in the foreword to Woodward, *Time,* states, "Anyone seriously attempting to design a clock for accurate timekeeping must first ask himself what we really *mean* by accurate timekeeping. The horological intellectual recognizes that this actually means a clock, which is more easily *predictable* in its behaviour. By definition, the time told by each and every working clock is a perfectly accurate response to the natural influences upon it. What we call 'errors' in timekeeping are merely those influences upon a clock which we haven't compensated for in its design, or which we haven't accounted for in interpreting what the clock says." The same concepts can be extrapolated to humans and their time estimates, or as noted by Quinnet, *Darwin's Bass,* "The measurement of time is something new, even for humans. Time never needed keeping until man invented time keepers."

a given itinerary. Thus rounding down at the start and rounding up at the finish of an itinerary leg results in a positive error of 6 min. Rounding up at the start and down at the finish of a leg results in a negative error of 6 min. If that error were compounded throughout the approximately four hours' duration of the march, a resulting ±10 percent error would amount to about 24 minutes.

Distances between points at the battlefield and its environs, at least in part, are known. The locations of the divide between the Rosebud and Little Big Horn valley and where Custer crossed it are known, as are Reno Hill, Custer Ridge and the spot where Reno retreated across the river. Detailed analyses by several researchers have located (but with less certainty) the probable sites of the Lone Tepee and the morass, etc., but the principles of uncertainty as outlined above still apply. Some of these estimates could easily be off by a quarter mile, perhaps more. Consequently, all time-distance arguments must be viewed in the context of measurement error. Unfortunately, no rational assignment of error can be made, so all distance estimates and calculations are rounded to the nearest tenth mile with the same rounding convention as that used for time. These conventions, although imperfect, attempt to address the uncertainty in the reported times and distances and thereby reduce the temptation to put too fine an interpretation on events which are imprecisely chronicled and places which are imprecisely located. Given these arguments, the fundamental itineraries developed by Gray and Darling remain unchallenged; they are merely modified to reflect a best estimate at a level of uncertainty.

Two upper and lower bounds and a best estimate of actual time and distance can now be constructed. This first bound is a theoretical one, limiting the earliest and latest possible time that any of the columns could have arrived at any given point if no halts were called. The fastest continuous rate any column could have achieved is 7.5 mph, the standard Cavalry rate for a gallop. The slowest continuous rate that was likely to be achieved was 3 mph, the standard Cavalry rate for a walk. Thus, the earliest Custer could have arrived at the North Fork of Reno Creek, about 11.2 miles distant from the separation point near the divide, is 13.7 h. At a continuous walk he would have arrived there at 15.9 h. Benteen could have reached the same point at a gallop, about 12.6 miles distant by his route, just minutes behind Custer at 13.9 h. At a walk without halts, Benteen would have arrived at North Fork at 16.4 h. Of course, it is well documented that both battalions arrived there sometime in between those bounds. But these hypothetical clock times serve as framework boundary limits within which the historical events must have occurred, and indicate that Benteen theoretically should have been between 0.2 h and 0.5 h behind Custer if neither halted along their respective routes and both proceeded at a gallop or a walk or some rate between.

To examine the most probable itineraries of the Benteen and Custer battalions, the basic data of Darling and Gray are employed with these additions and modifications: first, a halt of one tenth hour (6 minutes) each was assumed to have occurred at Darling's Plateau A and Ridge B in order for Benteen and Gibson to reconnoiter and confer. Second, because of the steeper relief of the line of bluffs from which Gibson could observe the Little Big Horn and because Gibson climbed it to scout the floodplain while the battalion essentially stood by in the adjacent valley to await his report and for him to join up, a halt of two-tenths of an hour is conservatively imposed. Third, Benteen's actual arrival at the main trail is interpolated from Darling's data. Fourth, a pause of three-tenths of an hour is estimated for Benteen to water his men and horses at the morass.[62] Fifth, no substantial time delay is assumed for the meeting with Trumpeter Martin. Finally, Camp's locations of the Lone Tepee and morass as published by Donahue are used.[63]

Table 7.1 tabulates the Custer and Benteen itineraries. More realistic upper and lower boundary values than those derived from the theoretical maximum and minimum rates outlined above can be assigned by taking into account the published itineraries and by assigning reasonable error estimates to clock time estimates as outlined above. If one assumes, for example, a compound timing error in the Custer-Benteen itineraries of, say, ±10% per elapsed hour, then Custer could have arrived at the North Fork of Reno Creek at 14.6 h on the negative error side and 15.4 h on the positive error side. Similarly, Benteen would have arrived there at 15.8 h and 16.7 h. The data of Table 7.1 are plotted on Figures 7.4 and 7.5 for Custer and Benteen respectively, with the ±10 percent error bars shown. Because these points are based on prior knowledge of the estimated actual rates, the elapsed times with the error bars can be used to provide upper and lower boundary values. The bounds may not be probable, but they are possible. Taking the worst compound error case, e.g., Custer's earliest possible time of arrival and Benteen's time of arrival and *vice versa*, Benteen would have lagged Custer by 0.4 h to 2.1 h. If the itinerary estimates of Table 7.1 are in fact reasonable, it appears that Benteen arrived at the North Fork of Reno Creek at about 16.2 h, or 1.3 h

---

62. Gray, *Campaign,* 263-64 states that participants reckoned that the halt lasted anywhere from 15 to 30 minutes. He settled on a value of 20 minutes (0.3 h) for the halt, which is used here.
63. Michael Donahue, *Battlefield,* 7-8. Walter Camp documented with a photograph and marked the location of the morass on a sketch map, essentially at the confluence of the South Fork with Reno Creek. This is slightly downstream from where Darling places it.

after Custer and only two tenths of an hour earlier than he would have if he and his battalion walked all the way! Did they?

Gray estimates that Custer arrived at the Lone Tepee at 14.3 h (14:15) and Darling places him there at about 14.0 h (14:03). Gray places the Lone Tepee at the 8-mile point and Darling locates it at about 8.4 miles from the divide. Darling's analysis stopped at the Lone Tepee, so the itineraries of the Custer and Benteen columns from where Benteen joined the main trail are taken from Gray. Digital reconstruction of the routes as shown on Figures 7.2 and 7.3 indicates that the distances both battalions traveled to the point where Benteen rejoined the main trail differ somewhat from the estimates of Darling and Gray. The values of 6.3 miles for Custer and 7.3 miles for Benteen as derived from that analysis are used here, and the remaining time-distances are adjusted accordingly. This discrepancy may result from using different start points, i.e., the divide *vs.* the point of separation of the battalions. Gray estimated that Custer was 36 minutes (0.6 h) en route to the North Fork from the Lone Tepee but the Lone Tepee as located here was a bit farther down the trail from the start, which would shorten the time by about a tenth hour. This would put Custer at North Fork at about 14.9 h and Reno at the ford on the Little Big Horn close to the same time (about 15.0 h).

How much time Custer's halt consumed at the Lone Tepee is unknown, but some considerable time must have been spent there in order for him to confer with Cooke and others, to receive Varnum's report, and for Girard to make his observations from the knoll. Gray's 36 minutes (0.6 hr) for Custer to get from the Lone Tepee to North Fork is probably as good an estimate as any, and it suggests that, conservatively, at least 0.1 h was spent at the Lone Tepee. Benteen had not yet struck the main trail, and he could not have been closer than two-and-a-quarter miles away and more than likely was farther behind on the trail than that. And, like Reno, he too was ignorant of Custer's intentions.

Time-distance curves of the Custer and Benteen battalions' itineraries are shown on Figure 7.6. Several qualitative assessments can immediately be made by inspection. Until he reached the first

Table 7.1 Custer and Benteen Itineraries

Custer Time/Distance	Elapsed (hr)	Clock (hr)	Distance (mi)
Depart Divide	0	1210	0.0
Mouth of Benteen Cynl	1.5	1345	6.0
Lone Teepee (arrive)	2.1	1420	8.4
Lone Teepee (depart)	2.2	1425	8.4
N. Fork, Reno Ck	2.7	1455	11.2
N. Fork, Reno Ck (depart)	2.9	1505	11.2
Benteen Time/Distance			
Depart Divide	0	1210	0
Ridge A (arrive)	0.5	1240	2.0
Ridge A (depart)	0.6	1245	2.0
Ridge B (arrive)	0.8	1300	2.9
Ridge B (depart)	0.9	1305	2.9
Base, Ridge C (arrive)	1.1	1315	3.5
Base, Ridge C (depart)	1.3	1330	3.5
Darling's Point D	2.3	1420	7.1
Mouth of Benteen Cyn	2.4	1425	7.4
Morass (arrive)	2.6	1435	8.3
Morass (depart)	2.9	1455	8.3
Lone Teepee (arrive)	3.2	1515	9.8
Lone Teepee (depart)[1]	3.2	1515	9.8
Meet Kanipe	3.6	1540	10.7
Meet Martin, halt	3.9	1600	11.6
Continue	4.0	1605	11.6
N. Fork, Reno Ck	4.1	1610	12.6
Reno Hill	4.3	1625	13.9

1. Benteen halted at the Lone Teepee, but he was leading the battalion and was several hundred yards ahead of it. He examined it quickly and as the battalion approached, moved on without calling a general halt.

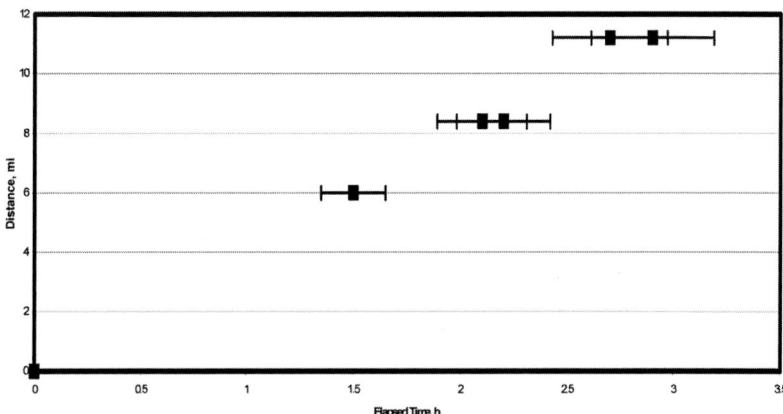

Figure 7.4. Custer time-distance plot with ten percent compound time error bars and bounds drawn.

Figure 7.5. Benteen Time-Distance plot with 10 percent compound time error bars and bounds drawn.

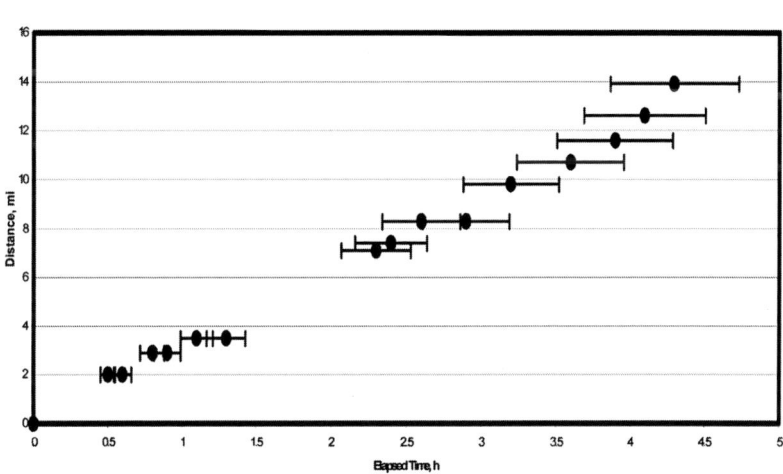

ridge, Benteen proceeded at a rate essentially equal to Custer's. After completing his reconnaissance overlooking the South Fork and moving on to join the main trail and march to the morass, his rate was again approximately equal to Custer's, as evidenced by the near-parallel slopes of the time-distance curves. Any difference can be attributed to terrain. With a fast-walking horse and the wide range in the quality of typical cavalry horseflesh, Benteen may have even slowed down some to keep his men from stringing-out on the trail, given their thirsty mounts.

Benteen struck the main trail along Reno Creek at about 14.4 hours, turned downstream and shortly thereafter, stopped at a "morass" to water his men and horses. A lingering criticism concerning possible dalliance hinges on Benteen's decision to water there. Why didn't he wait and water farther down the trail below the Lone Tepee as did Custer and Reno?[64] Sunday, 25 June 1876, was a hot day, a scorcher, and the regimental stock hadn't had water since the night before. Custer reached the North Fork and watered his horses at 14.9 hours. Reno reached the ford on the Little Big Horn River at about 15.0 hours, and although there was no formal halt, his column paused to water horses and fill canteens while crossing the river. They halted on the West side to organize for the attack and continued to water. As many as fifteen minutes may have been spent at the river.[65] Benteen came upon the morass at 14.6 hours and watered. So, all of the battalions watered within about 24 minutes of each other. The close correlation should not be considered a coincidence; horses, mules, and men thirst because of dehydration which is dependent upon exertion rate, ambient temperature, and elapsed time since their last

---

64. Gray, *Campaign*, 265.
65. Ibid, 272,.Stewart, *Luck*, 331, Willert, *Diary*, 273. Hare, interview with Camp, in Hammer, *Camp*, 65.

quench, among other things, but not because of geographic position. Just how thirsty they were is evident from the behavior of the pack mules trailing Custer's path down Reno Creek, which literally stampeded into the morass when they sensed its proximity, despite the best efforts of the mule skinners and escort to restrain them. Benteen's horses suffered equally or more so from their trek over rough terrain. Reno and Custer knew that a fight was imminent; Benteen did not know how imminent but suspected he might be engaged at some point during the afternoon; all three commanders prudently chose to water their horses when need and opportunity intersected. After about 20 minutes (0.3 h) Benteen resumed his trek to the Little Big Horn, at first being careful not to outdistance himself from the packs.

Meanwhile, Custer sent Martin to fetch Benteen with the infamous "Be Quick" note. But where was Benteen? Unless Custer's verbal orders to Benteen were more specific than what has been reported, Custer had no way of knowing with any certainty where Benteen and his battalion might be until Boston

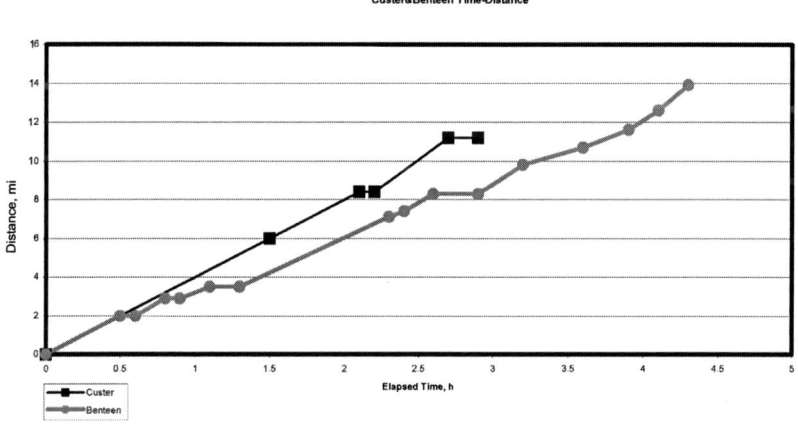

Figure 7.6. Custer and Benteen Time-Distance Plots.

Custer rejoined him and could report his having passed Benteen on the main trail. For all Custer knew, Benteen could in fact have followed his orders to the extreme and gone on the oblique to the valley of the Little Big Horn. From his vantage point on the bluffs he may have observed the dust back along the main trail and guessed that Benteen by now had returned to it or perhaps the dust could be from the pack train alone.[66] He could have been sending Trumpeter Martin on a forlorn journey or relying solely on "Custer's luck." Had Benteen not returned to the trail when he did, but instead continued on his oblique scout, would Trumpeter Martin ever have found him?

As far as Benteen and other officers of his battalion were concerned, their regimental commander had sent them on a "wild goose chase...valley hunting *ad infinitum*"[67] and generally "wandering among hills...."[68] As it turned out, Benteen "...decided to take advantage of the discretion allowed by his order that if in his judgment there was nothing to be seen of Indians, valleys, and so on ...."[69] he would return to the Reno Creek trail of his own volition. Custer's luck prevailed for the moment. But it would be the last bit of luck he would ever have. And given that it is statistically unlikely that Benteen dallied on the trail, then any of his alleged sins of omission or commission must have occurred after he rejoined the main trail.

After getting the "Come Quick" order, Benteen faced a new dilemma. How could he hurry to join Custer and yet bring the

---

66. Stewart, *Luck*, 340. Stewart argues that dust rising from the back trail was evidence that Benteen had rejoined it, but unless two dust columns were visible, Custer could not have known whether it was Benteen or the pack train.
67. Kulhman, *Legend,* 88.
68. Godfrey, in Stewart, *Luck*, 380.
69. Ibid, 380. Gibson wrote a letter to Godfrey, dated August 8, 1908, in which he said that he had a view of the Little Big Horn valley 'for a long distance' and when this was reported to Benteen, he changed course to join the trail.

packs? And there was confusion among the battalion officers. With regard to the packs instruction, Lt. Edgerly stated that "[t]he remark was made by someone, either by Captain Weir or myself, that he [Custer] could not possibly want us to go for the packs as Captain McDougall was there and would bring them up." Edgerly also thought that Benteen believed that Custer himself might have been confused about the disposition of his command. Of meeting Kanipe on the trail, Edgerly testified that,

> A sergeant of C Company came back from General Custer's command and gave General Custer's compliments to Captain Benteen and he wanted him to bring up the packs. Captain Benteen said he thought he had made a mistake, that Captain McDougall was in charge of the pack train and showed him the place and he went.[70]

In any event, Benteen soon resolved the issue in his own mind. Since the Indians were "skedaddling," as reported by Trumpeter Martin, "there was less necessity for me going back for the packs."[71]

Martin recalled that after passing on the note from Custer, Benteen rode

> ...quite a distance in front of the troops, with his orderly trumpeter, at a fast trot. The nearest officer to him was Captain Weir, who was at the head of his troop, about two or three hundred yards back....The pack train was not very far behind them. It was in sight, maybe a mile away, and the mules were

---

70. Edgerly, in Nichols, *Reno Court*, 440-41. Brininstool, *Troopers*, 77-78. Benteen wrote, "A mile or so further on [from the Lone Tepee], I met a Sergt. Kanipe coming from the adjutant of the regiment with order - written *for the commander of the pack-train."* (Original emphasis).
71. Benteen, in Nichols, *Reno Court, 404.*

coming along, some of them walking, some trotting, and others running."

But now assured by his own scout that no Indians were behind or could flank the pack train, he moved out and let the packs keep up as best they could. "We moved on faster than the packs could go, and soon they were out of sight, except that we could see their dust."[72] That increase in gait is apparent from Figure 7.6.

If Benteen did not unduly tarry on the trail, as this analysis suggests, then the only other opportunity he had to willfully delay was in joining Reno as his command retreated to the high bluffs on the east side of the Little Big Horn River. He encountered Reno "...broken, disorganized, routed." He still did not know where Custer was, but with five troops surely he could take care of himself. It was Reno's command that was *"in extremis"*, shattered and in immediate danger of being wiped out.[73] Reno's ammunition was shot, literally. Reno's men had expended it "...wildly, prodigally, and uselessly during the fight in the valley below."[74]

It is fairly clear that when he encountered Reno in disarray, he effectively received new orders from Reno himself, "For God's sake, Benteen, halt your command and help me. I've lost half my men."[75] Benteen had no choice; although Reno's plea was cast as a request, it was in effect a military verbal order. Benteen was a Captain, Reno a Major, and military protocol required that Benteen obey the last order given him by a superior officer.[76] Article I,

---

72. Martin, in Graham, *Myth*, 291.
73. Ibid, 294.
74. Ibid.
75. Martin, Ibid, 291.
76. Rickey, in Fox, *Archaeology,* 370-71, note.

Paragraph 1 of the Revised Regulations of the Army of the United States of 1861 is clear:

> All inferiors are required to obey strictly, and to execute with alacrity and good faith, the lawful orders of the superiors appointed over them.

This paragraph was included verbatim in the Regulations of 1881.[77] So for the twenty-year span that brackets the Battle of the Little Big Horn, the regulations on discipline clearly required Benteen to follow Reno's lawful orders.[78] Lieutenant Godfrey testified, "After about 12 O'clock that day [June, 25th] I was under command of Captain Benteen and in the afternoon sometime we joined the command of Major Reno and *served under his command thereafter.*" (Emphasis added) Edgerly made a similar statement.[79] Benteen was in a pickle. His written order from Custer commanded him *to bring the packs* and technically Reno's "request" to halt and help could not countermand that specific order. But in fact it is almost irrelevant, whether Benteen felt obligated to halt and assist Reno as instructed or *wait for the packs* as instructed by Custer: *in either event he had to wait.*[80]

Benteen undoubtedly was in no mood for philosophical reflection, but in fact, was presented with a classical problem in uncertainty, which his critics have tended to ignore. The Law of Information asserts that knowledge of the present and past is

---

77. "Regulations of the Army of the United States and General Orders in Force," (1881); "Revised Regulations of the Army of the United States," (1861).
78. Graham, *Myth*. Graham, an attorney and Army Judge Advocate, understood this completely.
79. Godfrey, in Nichols, *Reno Court*, 478. Edgerly, in Nichols, *Reno Court*, 438. This testimony by Godfrey and Edgerly clearly indicates that Benteen's battalion fell under Reno's command on Reno Hill.
80. See discussion in Willert, *Diary*, 364.

highly imperfect – one simply cannot know everything about a given situation. And *Spencer's Laws of Data*, adapted to Benteen's situation, can be summarized as: Anyone can make a decision, given enough facts. A good commander can make a decision without enough facts. A perfect commander can operate in perfect ignorance.

How much did Benteen know and how much could he be expected to know about what was going on beyond that next ridge? Furthermore, critics have pretty well ignored the constraints on, and the interactions among, Benteen's choices and the consequences of charging off on jaded horses to find Custer. Custer's whereabouts were still unknown and abandoning the wounded and leaving the balance of the packs with their escort to fend for themselves with an unknown, but presumably large, number of howling hostiles all about the countryside was not a feasible option.

What changes in the battle situation as it evolved and what interaction of those changes impacted his thinking? As the events on and around Reno hill unfolded, fluid changes in the tactical situation created contingencies, which in turn influenced biases and decisions. Can any tactic or strategy achieve *exactly* its desired effect?[81] And any analytical inquiry must distinguish between *what can be asserted* and *what can be supported*. Benteen's (and to some extent, Reno's) detractors have tended to be pretty loose on this issue and to ignore, or actually violate, the aforementioned princi-

---

81. An illustrative example of the Law of Information can be found in the bombing of Pearl Harbor on 7 December 1941. Although masterfully planned and executed by Admiral Yamamoto, the attack did not achieve its objective of destroying the U. S. Pacific Fleet at anchor because Yamamoto did not know that the aircraft carriers were not moored, but were at sea, a fact that ultimately cost Japan the war. A corollary might be what I call the Rule of Uncertainty: Unforeseen events often dictate unforeseen outcomes.

ples of uncertainty. Unknown, of course, is what external influences actually did affect Benteen's thinking and decision-making processes.[82]

Benteen was in a bind and he had to get control of the situation. Reno, who was officially in command, if not factually, stated in testimony that

> It did not occur to me that Custer with 225 men need anyone quickly; his force could hold off quite a number of Indians if properly disposed. …It [the "Come Quick"' note] did not make any great impression on me at the time, because *I was absorbed in getting those packs together, and did not intend to move until I had done so.*"[83] (Emphasis added.)

When Benteen arrived at Reno Hill, Custer was probably already engaged, even though Benteen had no way of knowing it. Should Benteen have abandoned Reno to pursue Custer's trail? Not in Lieutenant Gibson's on-the-spot considered opinion: "It was impossible as we could neither abandon our wounded men, nor the packs of the command."[84] It would be folly to run off in search of Custer without any knowledge as to where he might be, with only half his ammunition ration (after sharing with Reno).[85] He knew the packs were behind and he would have to wait for them to join up in order to provide for their protection. In addi-

---

82. Of course, the biggest externality that Benteen and his command faced was a not small number of riled, unpredictable hostiles bent on doing them in.
83. Nichols, *Reno Court, 581.*
84. Gibson, letter to wife, in Fougera, *Cavalry,* 269.
85. Just how much ammunition Reno expended is in dispute. Godfrey, in his diary, wrote that they were anxiously awaiting the packs for their ammunition. Later, according to Stewart, *Luck* 394, he suspected that lack of ammunition may have been an excuse for Reno to procrastinate. Wallace emphatically stated they had used up much of their ammunition in the valley. Nichols, *Reno Court,* 23, 50-51.

tion to Reno's wounded, who needed tending, stragglers were still coming across the river and up the bluffs looking for safe haven and possibly for covering fire. Benteen had to assume command of the defense at Reno hill for some unspecified period of time, at least until Reno regained his poise.[86] Although Reno may or may not have exhibited cowardice in the valley, he most certainly had lost his composure. He was rational but excited, under stress, and probably unable to lead a military operation for the time being. He "...was perfectly cool, though by no means heroic...."[87] Faint praise indeed.

Reno and Benteen both have been harshly criticized for the delay following Reno's retreat to the bluffs.[88] The critics apparently not only share Custer's lack of concern for fallen troops: to hell with the wounded, but further expected Reno and Benteen to leave the pack train to fend for itself in a countryside swarming with hostile Indians, and to ride pall-mall, low on ammunition, to rescue a battalion whose whereabouts was uncertain. A central question that has never been fully addressed is: did Benteen so despise Custer that he was willing to sacrifice five companies of his regiment to see him done in? In view of the fact that he refused to abandon the wounded at Reno Hill, it seems unlikely that he would knowingly and indifferently let the other half of his regiment go to slaughter.

---

86. Mechling, interview with Camp, in Hardoff, *Camp*, 78. That Benteen was effectively in command was generally agreed among the officers and men on Reno Hill. Mills, *Harvest*, 273-74, quotes from multiple sources: First Sergeant John Ryan stated, "Too much cannot be said in favor of Captain Benteen. His prompt movements saved Reno from utter annihilation, and his gallantry cleared the ravines of Indians." Lt. Varnum: "Benteen was really the only officer looking out for the whole command and he handled things well and fought very gallantly." Sergeant Roy: "Benteen saved the command, according to my opinion. He was a very brave and nervy man."
87. Edgerly, in Graham, *Story*, 148.
88. Mills, *Harvest*, 263.

Sidebar

In the parlance of probability and statistics, a *null hypothesis* H_0, can be proposed that the rates of Custer and Benteen were the same, i.e., the pooled data comes from the same distribution:
H_0: C(t) and B(t) are equal; ie, the rates of Custer, C(t), and Benteen, B(t), are from the same or a similar distribution.
There also exists an *alternative hypothesis*: the two rates are statistically significantly different:
H_1: C(t) and B(t) are not equal; the rates of Custer, C(t), and Benteen, B(t), are different.
The probability of wrongly rejecting the null hypothesis H_0 in favor of the alternative hypothesis H_1, is the *significance level*.

Once on the main trail, Benteen followed Custer's trail, until the North Fork of Reno Creek. Thereafter their routes diverged. Each battalion proceeded at a rate that has been estimated. Therefore it is useful to compare the rates of travel of the two battalions to a common point. The comparison here is for Custer's rate for the first eleven miles (almost to the North Fork) and Benteen's rate for the first twelve miles (almost to the North Fork.) On face value, the overall rates appear to be quite different, but is there a statistical difference? If the calculations show that the rates of the two battalions are unlikely to be different as a *result of chance*, then any difference between the two rates can be said to be statistically insignificant. And, if the calculations show that the rates are similar and are unlikely to be drawn from the same distribution due to chance, then it is probable that the rates are drawn from the same distribution and the result is statistically significant.

What then constitutes likely, unlikely, or very unlikely? Probability levels can be assigned to these descriptive terms and, as might be expected, statisticians have established "standard" probability or critical levels. If an observed similarity is likely to occur by chance with a frequency of more than once in 20 times (more than 5%), it is not accepted as being significantly similar. A probability of greater than 5% is regarded as inadequate to accept a hypothesis that the data come from the same or a similar distribution. Now, if the observed similarity is likely to occur by chance once in 20 times, this is considered to be unlikely due to chance. The odds are 19 to 1 in support of the null hypothesis. A similarity at this probability level is termed *significant*.

If the observed similarity is expected to occur by chance only once in 100 times (a probability of 1%), the odds are now 99 to 1 in favor of the null hypothesis and it is *very unlikely* that any similarity is due to chance. In other words, the probability of wrongly rejecting the null hypothesis is 1%. An event at this probability level is termed *highly significant*.

The *Kolmogrov-Smirnov or K-S two sample test*[*] compares two sample distributions and yields a statistic **D**, which permits an assessment as to the probability that the two samples were drawn from the same or similar distributions. Thus the null hypothesis that **C(t) = B(t)** will be rejected if **D** exceeds a calculated probability value (derived from statistical tables[†]) corresponding to a selected level of significance of 0.05 on the grounds that if the null hypothesis *were* true, such a large value of **D** is unlikely or improbable.

The estimated rates of Custer and Benteen in Table 7.1 are recast to determine distance as a function of elapsed time. From these data, the elapsed time for each mile traversed can be calculated in order to pool the samples into a single array (Table 7.2). The two empirical distribution functions are calculated as:

$$C_i(t), B_i(t) = \# \leq t \text{ in sample}/n_i$$

The K-S two-sample test statistic is:

$$D_i = \max|C(t) - B(t)|$$

A value of **D** less than the critical value of 0.568 supports H_0. The maximum value of **D** as calculated in Table 7.2 is 0.333, indicat-

---

[*] The *K-S One and Two Sample Tests* are nonparametric statistical tests. Nonparametric statistics is a collective term describing methods of hypothesis testing and estimation that can be applied to a wide variety of practical problems. Nonparametric statistics are distribution-free methods, meaning that the inferences are based on a test statistic whose sampling distribution is independent of the distribution of the population from which the sample is drawn; i.e., they do not require specific distribution assumptions, such as normality, as required in classical statistics. The only assumption is that the samples come from continuous populations. References abound, for example, Bartoszynski, Robert and Niewiadomska-Bugaj, *Probability,* Gibbons, *Statistics* and Siegal and Castellan, *Statistics.*

[†] For example, Beyer, *Tables.*

ing that the null hypothesis should not be rejected and therefore the rates of Custer and Benteen are statistically similar.[‡]

Table 7.2. Kolmogorov-Smirnov test for Benteen/Custer itineraries

Pooled elapsed time (hr)	C(t)	B(t)	D [C(t)-B(t)]	n1*n2*D
0.2*	1/11	0	1/11	12
0.2	1/11	1/12	0.008	1
0.5*	2/11	1/12	0.098	13
0.5	2.11	2/12	0.015	2
0.8*	3/11	2/12	0.106	14
0.9	3/11	3/12	0.023	3
1.0*	4/11	3/12	0.114	15
1.2*	5/11	3/12	0.205	27
1.3	5/11	4/12	0.121	16
1.5*	6/11	4/12	0.212	28
1.6	7/11	5/12	0.220	29
1.8*	7/11	5/12	0.220	29
1.9	7/11	6/12	0.136	18
2.0*	8/11	6/12	0.227	30
2.2*	9/11	6/12	0.318	42
2.3	9/11	7/12	0.235	31
2.4*	10/11	7/12	0.326	43
2.5	10/11	8/12	0.242	32
2.7*	11/11	8/12	0.333	44
2.9	11/11	9/12	0.250	33
3.4	11/11	10/12	0.167	22
3.7	11/11	11/12	0.083	11
3.9	11/11	12/12	0.000	0

n1,n2= 11   12
*Custer data
Custer=C(t), Benteen=B(t)
Null hypothesis H0: C(t)=B(t)
  H1: C(t) =/= B(t)
Confidence level = 0.05   1.36 sq rt n1+ n2/n1*n2=0.568
Critical value=0.568 > D=0.333 therefore do not reject null hypothesis

---

[‡]. This analysis was done on a desktop computer using *MathCad®* and an *Excel®* spreadsheet.

Although the delay in getting everyone moving caused Reno and Benteen much grief in the years to come, too much has been made of it; Moylan explained it clearly in his testimony: from the time he crossed the river and ascended the bluffs, it took "...half or three quarters of an hour..." for the pack train to arrive, and some interminable period thereafter to gather up the packs, distribute the ammunition to the troops, and arrange for transport of the wounded, many of whom were not ambulatory. "Soon after the pack train came up the order was given for the men to be supplied with ammunition...and to prepare themselves at once to move forward."[89] Moylan ordered that the blankets be stripped from some of the horses to be used as litters, "...it taking nearly all the men I had left to carry these wounded men...and it took four men to carry each blanket."[90] The unseated horses were led. Benteen himself, in a letter to his wife on 4 July, was so straightforward that it is difficult to construe that there was some purposeful or premeditated delay: "When I joined Reno's command, we halted for the packs to come up, & then moved along the line to bluffs toward the direction Custer was supposed to have gone in...."[91] But by that time it was too late. Custer and all his men were done in.

Benteen was under a written order to bring the packs, which he knew were not far behind, and until his arrival at the bluffs, were secure. He showed Custer's order to Reno when they first joined on the bluffs. The two battalions were then technically or directly under Reno's command, and it was Reno's duty either to assume responsibility for the order to bring the packs or to enable Benteen to execute the order. His insistence on not moving out

---

89. Moylan, in Nichols, *Reno Court,* 218.
90. Ibid. Graham says it took six men to carry each wounded man, Graham, *Story,* 65.
91. Benteen, letter to Kate, in Carroll, *Letters,* 156.

until the packs arrived was not only proper execution of his duty, but good military judgment. Leaving the packs to fend for themselves with minimal guard in the face of all the hostiles roaming the countryside would have been a recipe for further disaster.

TERRENCE J. DONOVAN

CHAPTER 8

END OF THE LINE

The court-martial of Frederick William Benteen was convened on 7 February 1887. Much had transpired in the nearly eleven intervening years since the Little Big Horn fight. He was not happy with his assignment as Commander of the 9th Cavalry, comprised of Negro troops, but he recognized that it was a necessary career move to gain his majority. Nonetheless, "It was not proper to remain with a race of troops I could take no interest in and this on account of their low down rascally character."[1] The disastrous events that transpired at Fort DuChesne would force a separation from this unwanted assignment but with unwanted consequences. The deck was stacked against him from the start, in substantial part because of his own character and behavior. General Crook did a fine job in packing the Benteen court. Ten officers were appointed but only nine appeared; one was ill at Fort Douglas.

---

1. Foster, *9th cavalry,* 6

The court-martial board first met briefly on 7 Feb 1887 at Fort DuChesne. On 8 Feb during the challenge phase, Benteen challenged in writing the composition of the entire board on the grounds that the members would be prejudicial to a fair trial. In his testimony he outlined his side of the story and carefully disavowed any knowledge as to the authorship of the Kansas City *Times* letter that had so infuriated General Crook. But he shrewdly knew that the proceedings would be reviewed by higher authority and he wanted something meaty for the reviewers to chew on, so he introduced, for the record, the *Times* flowery condemnation of Crook. It was accepted, but his written testament was not. He then challenged the board members individually, but succeeded in getting only one removed for prejudice. The charges were then read: drunk on duty, with six specifications, and conduct unbecoming an officer and gentleman. Specifically, he "…did…conduct himself in a scandalous manner in the post trader's store – using obscene and profane language; taking off his clothes, to quarrel with citizens, and exposing his person. This to the dishonor and disrepute of the military service at Fort DuChesne, Utah, on or about the eleventh day of November, 1886." Benteen pleaded not guilty to all charges and specifications.[2]

Eleven witnesses for the prosecution were called by Captain Allan Jackson, the Judge Advocate. Benteen's counsel, his adjutant, Lieutenant Harry Bailey (the same Bailey of the tent-pissing episode), called ten. Benteen often took over his own defense and at times the proceedings were contentious. However, before all his witnesses had appeared and after more than two weeks of trial, Benteen unexpectedly rested his case. He submitted a long, written exhibit for the record summarizing his case and the evidence

---

2. Mills, *Harvest*, 360-61.

and detailing his military career – again for the benefit of the proceedings' reviewers.

In his summation, Judge Advocate Jackson argued that Benteen's ungentlemanly behavior and drunkenness dulled his otherwise illustrious Army service. On 25 Feb 1887, the court agreed and found Benteen guilty of three of the specifications of drunkenness and conduct unbecoming an officer and gentleman. He was sentenced "to be dismissed from the United States Service."[3]

His strategy of including a detailed summary of his military service in the court record certainly did not bring him any additional grief. On 9 April, the findings were endorsed by General Sheridan and forwarded to President Grover Cleveland with a recommendation for remission of the sentence for "reasons given in the record of his services", with which Sheridan had first-hand knowledge. President Cleveland approved the court's result but reduced the sentence of dismissal to one of suspension from active duty for one year at half pay for "…his long and honorable service and the reputation he has earned for bravery and soldierly qualities."[4]

Reno fared less well. In a fruitless attempt to squelch rumor and innuendo about his conduct at the Little Big Horn. Reno had demanded a Court of Inquiry, which was held in Chicago from January 13 to February 11, 1879.[5] After hearing a number of eyewitness accounts with scant praise but little condemnation of Reno, the court concluded in an "insipid exoneration"[6] that no further action be taken against him. But he was damned by that faint praise. His drinking became more problematic and the animosity of his colleagues intensified. All the officers, except Ben-

---

3. Court record, in Ibid, 363-64. See also Huetter, *Duchene*.
4. Carroll, in Mills, *Harvest*, 364.
5. Nichols, *Reno Court*.
6. Utley, *Cavalier*, 7.

teen, ostracized Reno while they were posted to Fort Meade, Dakota Territory in 1879.[7] He brawled and carried on in what was generally regarded as an ungentlemanly manner until he was brought up on charges of conduct unbecoming an officer and gentleman. The court-martial found him guilty of conduct prejudicial to the good order and discipline of the service, a conviction that would not necessarily have resulted in his dismissal from the Army. However, while confined to Post during the proceedings against him, he was caught peeping through a window at the comely twenty-one-year-old daughter of Colonel Sturgis, the commanding officer of the 7th. That did him in, and on 16 March 1880 President Rutherford B. Hayes signed off on the sentence of dismissal, despite General Sherman's recommendation that the sentence be commuted to one year's suspension. He moved to Washington, D.C. in a vain attempt to regain his rank. He died of cancer, broken and disgraced, in a hospital there on 30 March 1889.

After hearing that his sentence had been mitigated to a suspension, Benteen petitioned the Army that he be allowed to serve the suspension at his farm near Atlanta. The request was granted, and the Benteens returned to the homestead to manage their affairs. Kate and son Freddie urged Benteen to support Freddie's application for an Army commission, but he stalled (and continued to stall for a good ten years until Freddie was too old to be commissioned). After serving his sentence, Benteen reported in at Headquarters, Department of the Platte, in Omaha on 17 April 1888 and immediately went about politicking to get an assignment that would ensure his separation from his enemies in the Army. He particularly wanted to avoid serving under direct command of Hatch or Crook, who had in the meantime been promoted to

---

7. Terrell and Walton, *Trumpet,* 300.

Major General and shunted off to the Division of Missouri headquarters in Chicago. He was only partly successful. He succeeded in getting assigned to Fort Niobrara, Nebraska, commanded by Colonel August V. Kautz, a cohort of Hatch and President of Benteen's court-martial board. Throwing in the towel and in deference to his own poor health, Benteen applied for Medical Retirement. After some delay, he met with a Medical Retiring Board at Fort Leavenworth, which concluded that he was "incapacitated for active service because of defective vision, frequent micturition caused by either spinal lesion or inflammation of the prostate gland and neuralgia; all of which are incident to the service." On 7 July 1888 Benteen became a civilian.[8]

Benteen returned to the Atlanta farm in Fulton County and settled in. His father had overseen the farm in much of his absence. Old Charley built a house on Casanova Street, which was subsequently destroyed in a fire; Benteen Elementary School now occupies the property. Charley died on the farm on 3 March 1885.[9]

Benteen slipped into easy retirement, not rich but comfortable. But he was eaten up inside over the accusations by outsiders and Custerphiles that he was responsible for the Custer disaster, despite the fact that those views were not shared by his colleagues or the Army hierarchy. In Atlanta he had time to develop a correspondence with the famous photographer, D. F. Barry. Importantly for the historical record, he entered into a correspondence with a former enlisted man at the Little Big Horn, who was now a colonel in the Wisconsin National Guard, a self-taught lawyer, somewhat of a charlatan, as well as Chairman of the State Republican Party: Theodore W. Golden. Through this correspondence

---

8. Mills, *Harvest,* 365-67.
9. Julian, *General Benteen,* 29.

Benteen could privately vent his spleen.[10] He was persuaded that Custer was thoroughly out-generalled and out-fought by his enemy. He was never dissuaded from his conviction, first voiced back in 1867, that Custer was a rotten poker player. Custer gambled and lost. Benteen's analysis was nonetheless straightforward:

> Tell me please, was there any generalship displayed in so scattering the regiment that only the merest of chance, intervention of Providence – or what you will – saved the whole 12 troops from being "wiped out"? That is all I blame Custer for – the scattering, as it were, (two portions of his command, anyway) to the – well, four winds, before he knew anything about the exact or approximate position of the Indian village or the Indians."[11]

But in his writing about the granite marker at Custer's grave at West Point, the bitterness comes through. "It is about as well – or perhaps better – that the world should look back upon Custer as a martyr [rather] than the full fledged, braying donkey that he was."[12]

Benteen's embitterment was not only derived from his intense dislike of Custer, which had evolved over years, but from personal tragedy as well. In December of 1868, the Benteens lost an infant daughter at Fort Harker one week after birth. While on the Stanley (Yellowstone) Expedition in 1873, Benteen received word that baby daughter Fannie was gravely ill at Fort Rice, Dakota Territory. Custer refused Benteen's request for leave and the baby died without her father's presence. In the winter of 1875, baby Theodore was put to rest at Fort Rice.[13] In all, four young

---
10. Carroll, *Letters*.
11. Ibid, 213-14.
12. Benteen, letter to Barry, in Mills, *Harvest,* 342.
13. Leonard, *Nemesis.*

children would be buried on the windswept western frontier. Only Freddie, who obviously became the apple of his father's eye, would survive. Benteen may have become outwardly resigned to his children's deaths but carried with him the suspicion that he himself might have been the carrier of their fatal meningitis.[14] How these emotionally painful events may have affected his outlook and interpersonal relationships is impossible to tell, but they certainly must have lessened whatever inherent affability the man might have possessed. Regardless, his hatred for Custer evolved over time and there is scant evidence that it had yet fully flowered by June 1876.[15]

His opinion of other officers changed over time as well. Throughout his active service he was fond of Godfrey and got along well with him. But after Benteen retired, Godfrey had befriended Libby Custer and had written articles favorable to her late husband, incurring Benteen's disdain. Others suffered the same fate.

In 1890 the U.S Senate, after a considerable lapse, approved awarding brevets for bravery in the Indian wars.[16] Benteen's name was among those submitted by the Army. In 1894 Benteen accepted a brevet to Brigadier General for "gallant service in action against Indians of the Little Big Horn, Montana, June 25 and 26, 1876, and in action against Indians at Canyon Creek, Montana, September 13, 1877."[17] He was the only officer of the

---

14. Mills, *Harvest*, 212.
15. Asay, *Gray Head*, 32.
16. "Brevet ranks were authorized for the Regular Army in the Articles of War of 1806; they were authorized for the US Volunteers on March 3, 1863. Partly as a result of dissatisfaction with the end-of-war brevet giveaway, brevet promotions were discontinued in 1869; although officers who had been given brevets before that date continued to use them. They were reinstated for the Spanish-American war and continued in use until after World War I." (Webb, *Brevet Union Generals*).
17. Citation, in Julian, *General Benteen*, 29.

7th so recognized for his actions against the Sioux. This was a striking indication that the higher echelons of the Army found no fault with his conduct at the Little Big Horn. Comments about his actions at Canyon Creek by his cohorts echoed those made following the Little Big Horn fight.

Benteen maintained the farm but moved to a home he built in Atlanta, at 395 Pavilion Street, S.E. He would often spend the weekends on the farm while Kate remained in town so she could socialize. He died of a stroke on 22 June 1898. He was interred at Westview Cemetery, but in November 1902, his body was transferred to Arlington National Cemetery. Kate followed him there in 1906. Freddie, although now at age thirty-two was too old to be eligible for a commission, was in fact given an appointment as a second lieutenant by President McKinley, who stated, "I'm going to give you a commission on the basis of your father's record."[18] He went on to a distinguished career, seeing action in Cuba during the Spanish-American war.

Many of the subalterns who served under Benteen throughout his career and went on to become general officers modeled their comportment and leadership style after him. General Hugh L. Scott, who would rise to become Chief of Staff of the Army, was a notable example. He later wrote that as a young lieutenant, fresh out of West Point,

> I found my model early in Captain Benteen, the idol of the Seventh Cavalry on the Upper Missouri in 1877, who governed mainly by suggestion; in all the years I knew him I never once heard him raise his voice to enforce his purpose. He would sit by the open fire at night, his bright pleasant face framed by his snow-white hair, beaming with kindness and humor, and often I watched his every movement to find out

---

18. Bentley, in Mills, *Harvest,* 374.

the secret of his quiet, steady government, that I might go and govern likewise....If he found that this kindly manner were misunderstood, then his iron hand would close down quickly, but that was seldom necessary, and then only with newcomers and never twice with the same person. Benteen's policy, which I adopted in 1877, has paid me large dividends.[19]

Regardless, bad luck and character flaws conspired to curse Benteen during and after his lifetime: he was his own worst enemy in being unable to keep his pen at rest or his mouth shut and just as importantly, most of his admirers and defenders died early, while his enemies, detractors, and Custerphiles lived on and were able to perpetuate the case against him to this day.[20] But one knowledgeable admirer concluded,

> Benteen was Custer's bitter and outspoken enemy. Not even death served to change his attitude; to the day of his own passing he never abated his hatred. But his known character and the habit of his entire life refutes the imputation that at any time or in any circumstances he failed in his duty as an officer and a soldier. He fought as he had lived, fearless, uncompromising, and grimly stern. Benteen was one of the best soldiers the United States Army has ever possessed.[21]

So the summary has to be: Did Benteen tarry on the trail? Probably not. And is this the last of the story? Probably not.

---

19. Scott, *Memories*.
20. Don Rickey, 1999, Oral communication.
21. Graham, *Story*, 105-06.

TERRENCE J. DONOVAN

APPENDIX A - BENTEEN'S ANONYMOUS LETTER TO THE MISSOURI DEMOCRAT

8 February 1869
(Reprinted by the *New York Times*, 14 February 1869)

Fort Cobb, I.T. Dec. 22, 1868
My Dear Friend:

I wrote to you from Camp Supply, which place was left on the 7th, arriving at this post on the evening of the 18th. On the 11th we camped within a few miles of our "battle of the Washita", and Gens. Sheridan and Custer, with a detail of one hundred men, mounted, as escort, went out with the view of searching for the bodies of our nineteen missing comrades, including Maj. Elliott.

The bodies were found in a small circle, stripped as naked as when born, and frozen stiff. Their heads had been battered in, and some of them had had the Adam's apple cut out of their throats; some had their hands and feet cut off, and nearly all were mangled in a way delicacy forbids me to mention. They lay scarcely two miles from the scene of the fight, and all we know of the manner they were killed we have learned from Indian sources. It seems that Maj. Elliott's party was pursuing a well-mounted party of Cheyennes in the direction of the Grand Village, where nearly all the tribes were encamped, and were surrounded by the reinforcements coming to the rescue of the pursued, before the Major was aware of their position. They were out of sight and hearing of the Seventh Cavalry, which had remained at and around the captured village, about two miles away. As soon as Maj. Elliott found that he was surrounded he caused his men to dismount, and did some execution among the Indians, which added to the mortification they must have felt at the loss of the village and herds of their friends and allies, and enraged them so that they determined upon the destruction of the entire little band.

Who can describe the feeling of that brave band, as with anxious beating hearts, they strained their yearning eyes in the direction whence help would come? What must have been the despair that, when all hopes of succor died out, nerved their stout arms to do or die? Round and round rush the red fiends, smaller and smaller shrinks the circle, but the aim of that devoted, gallant knot of heroes is steadier than ever, and the death howl of the murderous redskin is more frequent. But on they come in masses grim, with glittering lance and one long, loud, exulting whoop, as if the gates of hell had opened and loosened the whole infernal host. A well-directed volley from their trusty carbines makes some of the miscreants reel and fall, but their death-rattles are drowned in the greater din. Soon every voice in that little band is still as death; but the hellish work of the savages is scarcely begun, and their ingenuities are taxed to invent barbarities to practice on the bodies of the fallen brave, the relation of which is scarcely necessary to the completion of this tale.

And now, to learn why the anxiously-looked-for succor did not come, let us view the scene in the captured village, scarce two short miles away. Light skirmishing is going on all around. Savages on flying steeds, with shields and feathers gay, are circling everywhere, riding like devils incarnate. The troops are on all sides of the village, looking on and seizing every opportunity of picking off those daring riders with their carbines. But does no one think of the welfare of Maj. Elliott and party? It seems not. But yes! A squadron of cavalry is in motion. They trot; they gallop. Now they charge! The cowardly redskins flee the coming shock and scatter here and there among the hills [to] scurry away. But it is the true line - will the cavalry keep it? No! no! They turn! Ah, 'tis only to intercept the wily foe. See! a gray troop goes on in the direction again. One more short mile and they will be saved. Oh, for a mother's prayers! Will not some good angel prompt them? They charge the mound - a few scattering shots, and the murderous pirates of the Plains go unhurt away. There is no hope for that brave little band, the death doom is theirs, for the cavalry halt and rest their panting steeds.

And now return with me to the village. Officers and soldiers are watching, resting, eating and sleeping. In an hour or so they will be refreshed, and then scour the hills and plains for their missing comrades. The commander occupies himself taking an inventory of the captured property which he had promised the officers shall be distributed among the enlisted men of the command if they falter or halt not in the charge.

The day is drawing to a close and but little has been done save the work of the first hour. A great deal remains to be done. That which cannot be taken away must be destroyed. Eight hundred ponies are put to death. Our Chief exhibits his close sharpshooting and terrifies the crowd of frightened, captured squaws and papooses by dropping the straggling ponies in death near them. Ah! he is a clever marksman. Not even do the poor dogs of the Indians escape his eye and aim as they drop or limp howling away. But are not those our men on guard on the other side of the creek? Will he not hit them? "My troop is on guard, General, just over there," says an officer. "Well, bullets will not go through and around hills, and you see there is a hill between us," was the reply, and the exhibition goes on. No one will come that way intentionally - certainly not. Now commences the slaughter of the ponies. Volley on volley is poured into them by too hasty men, and they, limping, get away only to meet death from a surer hand. The work progresses! The plunder having been culled over, is hastily piled; the wigwams are pulled down and thrown on it, and soon the whole of it is one blazing mass. Occasionally a startling report is heard and a steamlike volume of smoke ascends as the fire reaches a powder bag, and thus the glorious deeds of valor done in the morning are celebrated by the flaming bonfire of the afternoon. The last pony is killed. The huge fire dies out; our wounded and dead comrades - heroes of a bloody day - are carefully laid on ready ambulances, and as the brave band of the Seventh Cavalry strikes up the air, "Ain't I Glad I've Got Out of the Wilderness", we slowly pick our way across the creek over which we charged so gallantly in the early morn. Take care! do not trample on the dead bodies of that woman and child lying there! In a short time we shall be far from the scene of our daring dash, and night will have thrown her dark mantle over the scene. But surely some search will be made for our missing comrades. No, they are forgotten. Over them and the poor ponies the wolves will hold high carnival, and their howling will be their only requiem. Slowly trudging, we return to our train some twenty miles away, and with bold, exulting hearts, learn from one another how many dead Indians have been seen.

Two weeks elapse - a larger force returns that way. A search is made and the bodies are found strewn around that little circle, frozen stiff and hard. Who shall write their eulogy?

This, my dear friend, is the story of the "battle of the Washita", poorly told.

TERRENCE J. DONOVAN

APPENDIX B - BENTEEN'S OFFICIAL REPORT

BENTEEN'S OFFICIAL REPORT, July 4, 1876
taken from the
ANNUAL REPORT OF THE SECRETARY OF WAR, 1876
Pages 479 - 480
FORTY-FOURTH CONGRESS, FIRST SESSION
HOUSE EXECUTIVE DOCUMENT
No. 1
SERIAL VOLUME 1742

HISTORICAL NOTE

The following is the text of the report written by Capt. Frederick W. Benteen July 4, 1876, nine days after the Battle of the Little Big Horn. The report was attached as Appendix 3Bb to the annual report of General Alfred H. Terry, Commander of the Department of Dakota for the year 1876 as contained in the Annual Report of the Secretary of War for 1876.

This report was prepared at the request of Maj. Marcus A. Reno to be attached to a report which he completed the next for General Alfred Terry.

---

3 Bb. --- REPORT OF CAPT. F. W. BENTEEN.
Camp Seventh Cavalry, July 4, 1876
Sir:

In obedience to verbal instructions received from you, I have the honor to report the operations of my battalion, consisting of Companies D, H, and K, on the 25th ultimo.

The directions I received from Lieutenant-Colonel Custer were, to move with my command to the left, to send well-mounted officers with about six men who should ride rapidly to a line of bluffs about five miles to our left and front, with instructions to report at once to me if anything of Indians could be seen from that point. I was to follow the movement of this detachment as rapidly as possible. Lieutenant Gibson was the officer selected, and I followed closely with the battalion at times getting in advance of the detachment. The bluffs designated were gained, but nothing seen but other bluffs quite as large and precipitous as were before me. I kept on to those and the country was the same, there being no valley of any kind that I could see on any side, I had then gone about fully ten miles; the ground was terribly hard on horses, so I determined to carry out the other instructions, which were, that if in my judgment there was nothing to be seen of Indians, valleys, &c., in the direction I was going, to return with the battalion to the trail the command was following. I accordingly did so, reaching the trail just in advance of the pack-train. I pushed rapidly on, soon getting out of sight of the advance of the train, until reaching a morass, I halted to water the animals, who had been without water since about 8 p.m. of the day before. This watering did not occasion the loss of fifteen minutes, and when I was moving out the advance of the train commenced watering from that morass. I went at a slow trot until I came to a burning lodge with the dead body of an Indian in it on a scaffold. We did not halt. About a mile farther on I met a sergeant of the regiment with orders from Lieutenant-Colonel Custer to the officer in charge of the rear - guard and train to bring it to the front with as great rapidity as was possible. Another mile on I met Trumpeter Morton (sic), of my own company, with a written order from First Lieut. W. W. Cook to me which read:

"Benteen, come on,
Big village. Be quick. Bring pacs.
W. W. Cook
P. Bring pac's."

I could then see no movement of any kind in any direction; a horse on the hill, riderless, being the only living thing I could see in my front. I inquired of the trumpeter what had been done, and he informed [me] that the Indians had "skedaddled," abandoning the village. Another mile and a half brought me in sight of the stream and plain in which were some of our dismounted men fighting, and Indians charging and recharging them in great numbers. The plain seemed to be alive with them. I then noticed our men in large numbers running for the bluffs on right bank of stream. I concluded at once that those had been repulsed, and was of the opinion that if I crossed the ford with my battalion, that I should have had it treated in like manner; for from long experience with cavalry, I judge there were 900 veteran Indians right there at that time, against which the large element of recruits in my battalion would stand no earthly chance as mounted men. I then moved up to the bluffs and reported my command to Maj. M. A. Reno. I did not return for the pack-train because I deemed it perfectly safe where it was, and we could defend it, had it been threatened, from our position on the bluff; and another thing, it savored too much of coffee-cooling to return when I was sure a fight was progressing in the front, and deeming the train as safe without me.

    Very respectively,
F. W. BENTEEN,
 Captain Seventh Cavalry
    Lieut. Geo. D. Wallace,
     Adjutant Seventh Cavalry

APPENDIX C - BENTEEN'S LETTER TO THE KANSAS CITY TIMES

3 January 1887
Fort Leavenworth

The recent assignment of Colonel Edward Hatch, 9th Cavalry, to the command at Fort DuChesne, Utah, has been the cause of more or less gossip among the officers and men at this post. All kinds of rumors have been circulating as to this mismanagement in the location of the post and the administration of its affairs by those in authority. It was also reported that the supply departments of the Department of the Platte were the cause of much suffering among the troops stationed thereat. Matters kept going from bad to worse until it was finally determined to send an inspector to the post, investigate the conditions of affairs and report results. This culminated in directing Colonel Hatch to report to General Crook for instructions and his departure for Duchesne where he is now in command.

A few days ago a member of the 9th Cavalry belonging to one of the troops stationed at DuChesne arrived here, having been discharged from the service by expiration of term. While in conversation with him, the Times correspondent, who noticed that he was quite an intelligent man, proceeded to ask him for such information about affairs at DuChesne as he was able to give. The result below proves that he is either well posted or able to tell a pretty good story. If what he avers is true the matter should certainly be thoroughly investigated by the proper authorities and the blame placed where it properly belongs.

"The United States government," said this discharged soldier, "is noted for the bungling manner in which its agents transact the business placed in their charge, but I honestly believe that in the establishment of that post the army has outdone itself in that respect. From the time the orders were received at Forts McKinney and Sidney, up to the time of my departure from DuChesne red tape has ruled supreme and with an iron hand, while the indifference of department headquarters and incompetency of the department staff has exceeded anything heretofore heard of."

"When did you start for the point where the post is situated?"

"August 2 the order was received at McKinney and we were obliged to pack up and be on the road by August 4. The packing of all the property was poorly done, causing the loss of hundreds of dollars dollars worth of public and private property. The troops had not time to weigh a single package and couldn't properly mark any of them as we didn't know where we were going. But we got off on time, and after a pleasant march reached Rock Creek where we expected to halt a day for a breathing spell and get into a little better shape."

"Did you?"

"No sir. We there found an order awaiting us to come on at once to Fort Bridger. An agent of the quartermasters department was at Rock Creek to load the command. He put us aboard the cars in such a way, mixing up the companies and headquarters, that we wasn't straightened when I left there two weeks ago. The transportation furnished us by the Union Pacific railroad was the worst I have seen in the service, and I have been in it a good many years. For two large companies of cavalry, its officers and their wives, this road furnished three small, dingy and filthy emigrant cars. Old, and so dirty we had to clean them out before we could enter them at all. But this railroad is noted for being the meanest road to everybody in the United States, and this meanness seems to have permeated the whole corps of officials.

"On reaching Curtis Station we were rushed off that same night eleven miles to Fort Bridger where we expected to have a chance to rest. But no! Here we met the department commander who started us out for DuChesne before we could supply ourselves with the necessaries. We did draw rations, but were short of everything else, even forage, not having sufficient wagons. The companies of the 21st Infantry from Fort Sidney had started three days ahead of us, and we were told we must overtake them, and this over a mountain trail where infantry can make better time than cavalry. One day orders were received from the department commander to divide the cavalry and send one company ahead faster, as trouble was expected. Had there been trouble with the Indians, there would not have been a man left to tell the story. The department commander pushed ahead so rapidly in his ambulance, overtaking the infantry and making them march 50 miles the last day into DuChesne, 32 of it without water. These troops were so exhausted when camp was reached that had there been an attack the Indians would have killed every man of them without firing a shot. One day behind the infantry came one cavalry company and still a day behind this came Major Benteen and one company of cavalry and this over a mountain road and through canyons where these small detachments could have been literally eaten up by the Indians had they so chosen. Indians and citizens laughed at such a march and asked us if we had lost our senses.

"The department commander reached the site of the present post one afternoon, raised his hand and said, 'Here's Fort DuChesne,' and by sunrise next morning was well on his way back to Fort Bridger, obeying in this thorough manner his orders to locate a new post. It evidently mattered not to him how uncomfortable the site might be. He well knew he would not have to be stationed there, so, like most army posts we found ourselves located in the most dreary spot in the whole section of that desert country. Had the post been established fourteen miles up the river to the foot of the mountains, a beautiful site would have been obtained. The post, as now located, is on the Uinta River, a large stream of water so warm in summer that fish are not found in it during that season. The formation of the country is such that the camp gets the benefit of all the wind when it blows, which it does constantly in the fall, picking up the alkali dust, as fine as flour, covering everything with it. The sand is so fine that it sifts through the tent canvas so that the troops get it not only thoroughly ground into their skin, but have to eat no small amount of it with their meals. From the rosy promises made us at fort Bridger by the department commander and his staff, we supposed that when we reached the spot where the post is now located, supplies would be promptly shipped us so we could begin making ourselves comfortable. The march from Fort McKinney had been so hurried that we left that post as light as possible - one suit of clothes and a blanket to a man, and barely tentage sufficient to cover the command, and a portion of this had to be left at Bridger for want of transportation. But we tried to be happy, thinking that thirty days at the outside would see us supplied. Day after day went by, and nothing came.

We were evidently forgotten. The officers made the necessary requisitions at Bridger again as soon after getting to Fort DuChesne as possible. Pleading, begging and sharp letters were written by the post commander, demanding that his troops be supplied, but to no purpose. The days were long and hot thermometers reaching ninety-six in the shade, while the nights were so cool that ice formed in our tents in the water buckets, making a change of sixty degrees in twenty-four hours. Men suffered for want of sufficient bedding, while the hard work we were compelled to perform soon wore out the one suit of clothes and we looked more like ragamuffins than soldiers of such a government as ours and even up to the time when I left - less than two weeks, with snow on the ground - the company property was not all received, nor had the quartermaster's department clothing sufficient to issue to the troops.

"But if the garrison couldn't be supplied, we had something to laugh at. The first teams that arrived had on shelter tent poles, an article that is never used. The next teams brought street lamps. Then came a train loaded with doors and window frames, but not a nail a pick or axes or helve, and we were compelled to wait for these things for months. Good mules were sent us, but not a shoe had the post quartermaster been able to get for them. He has done the best he could, but had to work them night and day till the feet of some of them were worn to the quick and liable to die from that cause alone. When I left the blacksmiths were at work cutting up wagon tires and iron bunks to get iron to make shoes and save the mules. Their horses are barefoot and unable to take to the field at all. Not a veterinary instrument or pound of medicine has been received at the post.

"After months of delay, contracts were let. All the stoves at the post are coal burners, so the only fuel contracted for is wood, and rotten cottonwood at that to save $2 a cord when the extra $2 would have purchased cedar. There is no earthly reason why the quartermaster's department should not have contracted for coal, there being plenty of it in that section. Even the post office department has gone back on the garrison and no mail route that can be depended on; the government being too poor to pay what it is worth to bring it in from Price's Station, their nearest railroad station. It is left to the Union Pacific railroad to send it in from Green River, 200 miles over a bad road and by an unreliable courier who makes the trip or not, just as he pleases. There is plenty of fine timber about forty miles from there, but the only sawmills the government has sent them [are] old and worn out ones, not worth the price of getting them into that country. One of them has already blown up, killing one man and injuring two others. The other is at a standstill, it too having broken down. The troops are still in tents. Had the quartermaster's department done its duty the men would have been in quarters by the end of October.

"As you may know, such a state of affairs could not last long without complaints being made by someone. A scapegoat for all this had to be found. Major Hall, 22d Infantry, the acting inspector general of the department was sent out to inspect and investigate. He came there and stayed a few days, made no investigation whatever, that is he did not ask a single question of an officer or man, as far as the garrison has been able to find out. He returned to Omaha and, it is said, made a most disgraceful report against the commanding officer. He may have obtained his information from Mormon citizens on the road back, and anyone who has anything to do with Mormons knows them to be the biggest liars in the country, and to have their ill will is really a recommendation for an honest man.

"Were I in Major Benteen's place I would not rest until the whole matter was thoroughly investigated, not by any whitewashing board but by an officer who is not dependent upon favors from department headquarters.

"What I have related," concluded the soldier, "covers the whole matter and if it will be the cause of stirring up a hornet's nest I feel that a duty has been performed toward my suffering comrades at Fort DuChesne."

TERRENCE J. DONOVAN

APPENDIX D
BENTEEN'S RETIREMENT MEDICAL EXAMINATION REPORT

Submitted 23 April 1888

I have examined this officer on the 19th, 20th and 21st instant, his pulse, respiration and temperature being as follows:

Pulse	Respiration	Temperature	Dates
90	23	99-4/5	19th
93	20	100	20th
88	22	100	21st

During this time he has suffered from neuralgia - affecting the eye, temple, back of the ear on left side, on 19th - and over the forehead, the temple, and neck on the left side on night of 20th, and 21st, in both instances attributable by him to walking or driving out, viz: to walking out at night late on sixteenth, and to driving in an open buggy in afternoon of 20th instant. The pain was finally alleviated by local application of chloral solution. The attacks did not confine him to his room. States, he is subject to neuralgia in the stomach and bowels, the last attach occurred at Fort DuChesne, Utah, in August 1887; that they are sometimes so painful as to produce nausea; that they require morphia to allay the pain and the application of an India rubber bag containing hot water externally to seat of pain, copious draughts of hot water internally and fasting for two or three days. He will be 54 years of age in August; entered the Army September 1, 1861, and has never been on sick leave.

The sounds of the heart are heard over considerable area, bruit with the first sound. He has never had any palpitation of the heart. His vision for distant objects is defective, and for reading he requires glasses. No.12 magnifying lenses. Tested by Snellen's Test-Type, vision of right eye is 2; left eye 3. Corrected by eyeglasses he could read No.1 Diamond; No. 2 Pearl; No. 4 minion; No. 6 Bourgeois; No. 8 Small Pica. I did not detect any lesion by Ophthalmoscope.

He believes his vision was injured by glare of snow in the campaign of winter of 1868-69 in the Indian Territory, he having loaned his protective goggles to Dr. Lippincott.

An examination of his urine showed specific gravity 1022; color pale, normal; reaction acid, normal; containing mucus, attributable to vesical or urethral irritation. He ordinarily urinates frequently (every hour or so) when opportunity offers, and frequently at night. He voided three and one-half (3 ¾) fluid ounces of urine in my presence, the stream not intermittent, nor twisted; medium sized.

Frequent micturition at night (say 8 times if not lessened by medicine) causes loss of rest.

Riding on horseback causes pain and frequent micturition. He has never been unable to pass urine voluntarily, nor needed the introduction of a catheter for that purpose. Digital examination - per rectum - is painful to him.

States that he was treated by Dr. Morse K. Taylor at Fort Sill, I. T., in 1884-5 for rheumatism, which troubled him in the shoulders; that at Fort McKinney, Dr Turrill treated him between March 19th and June 22nd, 1886, for neuralgia of the stomach and bowels, and also of the head, but at different periods; that Dr. Frank H. Hamilton, of New York, treated him in 1882, for acute gastritis; that he had an attack of rheumatism in Atlanta, Georgia, six or eight weeks ago, located in both knees and the shoulders. For this he treated himself.

His teeth are defective.

Major Benteen states his application for retirement was made an account of defective eye-sight; pain in the seat and constant desire to urinate at short intervals; principally on account of pain experienced in riding; he never rides when he can avoid it; every drill in garrison producing pain; he believes that he is very susceptible to neuralgia. In drilling at garrison he has opportunities - during halts - for voiding urine, and this he has done - so that he did not have to apply to the medical officer; when on duty away from garrison he was not required to ride on horseback. Ordinarily the insertion of the nozzle of an enemy syringe occasions pain; he cannot ride on horseback for 15 or 20 minutes without having a call to get off and urinate.

He is of opinion that he could not stand a continuous ride - say 15 miles - of any urgency without great pain. He could ride in a buggy with much less inconvenience.

Dr. Turrill has treated him for neuralgia of the head, face, and eyes on some occasions; at other periods for neuralgia of the stomach, and at other periods for neuralgia of the bowels. He first noticed pain on riding horseback in 1876 before any attack (he believes) of neuralgia of the stomach. Has had attacks of neuralgia of the head (beginning in the eyes) ever since his eyes were affected in 1868 - a campaign in the snow. After loaning his goggles to Dr. Lippincott, he blackened the eyelids above and below, with powder moistened with saliva. The glare affected the vision of the horses and men. He was on campaign from March 1877 to January 3d, 1878, rounding up the Nez Perces in Montana, Dakota and Wyoming. He attributes his rheumatism to exposure; neuralgia to this, and glare of the snow; the irritation of the bladder to hard riding. He first suffered excessive pain in riding January 3d; 1878, the day he reached his post, Fort Rice, Dakota. Since that, when convenient, has ridden in a buck-board or buggy, with his men, when on ordinary march.

He has not been under regular systematic treatment, nor complained except when his condition required - his duty has been performed notwithstanding discomfort or pain. He has a cicatrix on right hip posteriorly - the gluteal region - received in an affair with horse-thieves (when he was a civilian residing in Georgia) in May 1866. The bullet has never been extracted. He has a movable tumor or swelling in the pectoral region of this size [shown by a bean sized drawing in the right margin] on a line with the nipples, to right medial sternal region. This is painful on pressure but of no immediate inconvenience. He states that he applied to be sent to a post to perform such duties as he was able to do.

He has an assemblage of symptoms more or less connected with neuralgia, rheumatic diathesis, and irritability of the bladder.

There has been no continuous, attentive observation and treatment adequate to fix the responsibility on any particular disease or organ. This should precede his appearance before the

Retiring Board, might alleviate some symptoms, and could be done at the post to which he may be ordered. He is unfit for full duty as a cavalry officer - mounted duty. There are garrison duties he could perform; such as he has heretofore done; Inspection, Board of Survey, etc., not requiring prolonged physical exertion.

Respectfully submitted,
T. A. McParlin,
Colonel and Surgeon, U.S. Army
Medical Director
Headquarters Dept. of the Platte,
Medical Director's Office
Omaha, Neb; April 23, 1888

TERRENCE J. DONOVAN

APPENDIX E
AUTHOR'S NOTE ON NUMERICAL PRECISION AND UNCERTAINTY

The time-motion analysis of Gray and the reconstruction of Benteen's route by Darling are creatively conceived but I believe they lead to a misconception: they imply a precision that is unjustified by the basic data. If one says the time is "4:00", what does that really represent? It depends, of course, on the precision with which the time was measured: clock or watch, precision chronometer, atomic clock, estimation from distance traveled, or an estimate from one's internal biological clock, for example. Further, if a measuring device is used, is the device calibrated, or has it drifted from some reference mark? And if one says "about 4:00", what precision can be assigned?

To say that the geological Cretaceous Period ended 65 million years ago plus or minus 10 minutes is obviously a ludicrous statement. Almost intuitively we assume that date has an uncertainly of plus or minus a few million years. When a value or measurement is not known precisely, the amount of uncertainty is called "error". In a scientific context, error represents "uncertainty" and not sloppiness or a mistake. There are acceptable conventions in dealing with uncertainty. Important here is the concept of maximum and minimum range of measured values, whether they are time or distance. If a quantity is said to have a value of 5, by convention it is understood that the value could be anywhere between 4.5 and 5.5. But if the value is said to be 5.0, then it is understood that it lies between 4.95 and 5.05. Consider the ambiguity of a number such as 500.

Does it represent a value lying between 450 and 550 or 499.5 and 500.5? There are technical methods for writing this number to remove or reduce the ambiguity, depending upon the precision desired.

If a measured distance is reported as 950 $\pm$19 ft then the 19 ft value is referred to as the absolute error. On a graph the measured value is plotted with the range of uncertainty shown as line called an error bar. Another way of reporting this is 950 ft $\pm$ 2%. The rules for compounding measurements by addition (or multiplication) are founded on the assumption that the worse possible coincidence of errors will occur. Thus 950 $\pm$ 19 ft + 350 $\pm$ 7 ft = 1300 $\pm$ 26 ft. This approximation to uncertainty is based on maximum pessimism i.e., worse case. Commonly, however, there is a cancellation of errors in compounding measurements because on a random basis some of the original measurements will have values that are too high and others will have values that are too low. But in any event, the assignment of uncertainty or error limits depends on the measuring instrument, the object, the judgment of the investigator, and the precision requirements.

With time estimates garnered from various sources such as watch readings, estimates of time from distances traveled, recollections of witnesses, average speed of trotting horses, etc., it is impossible to assign absolute error. In the case at hand then, some arbitrary absolute or percentage error must be attached to the time values. If one assumes, for example, that the time values of Gray have an error of least ± 10%, then 4:00 would represent any time between 3:54 and 4:06, or 4:00 ± 6 minutes. Six minutes is not a particularly large margin, but the possibility of a 12 minute spread from worse case error compounding between successive time estimates emphasizes that there is indeed uncertainty in the values. The 10% error in this example is arbitrary and perhaps even unconservative, but it is a somewhat convenient choice because it allows the reporting of time in hours and decimal hours (6 min = 0.1h). Repeating the discussion on pages 213-214, to account for time uncertainty, I elect to convert the times of Gray and Darling to decimal hours. To avoid any possible confusion between A.M. and P.M., all times are referenced to the 24 h clock. The rules of rounding can also be applied and I adopt the following conventions: All time estimates are rounded to the nearest tenth hour. Mid-range values are rounded to the nearest even tenth. Thus 4:20 P.M. is rounded to 16.3 h and 4:21 P.M. is rounded to 16.4 h.

This procedure assigns a maximum error of ± 5% (3 min) at any specific time reference of Gray or Darling, and a maximum error of ± 10% (6 min) due to error compounding between any two adjacent points or successive time references on a given itinerary. Thus rounding down at the start and up at the finish of an itinerary leg results in positive error of 6 min and rounding up at the start and down at the finish of a leg results in negative error of 6 min. Where the data of Gray and Darling require no rounding, their values are retained and converted to decimal hours.

Distances between points at the battlefield and its environs, at least in part, are known. We know where the divide between the Rosebud and Little Big Horn valleys is, and where Custer crossed it. We know where Reno-Benteen hill and Custer Ridge are and where Reno retreated across the river. Detailed analysis by several researchers has located (but with less certainty) the probable sites of the lone tepee and the morass, etc., but the principles of uncertainty as outlined above still apply. Some of these estimates could easily be off by a quarter mile, perhaps more. Consequently, all time-distance arguments must be viewed in the context of measurement error. Unfortunately, no rational assignment of error can be made so I round all distance estimates and calculations to the nearest decimal mile with the same rounding convention as that used for time. My own analysis of Benteen's scout to the left differs insignificantly from that of Darling, which also correlates well with Gray's, so I use his published itinerary for Benteen's route (until joining the main trail) and Gray's itinerary for the main column and pack train and the continuation of Benteen's march after he joined the main trail.

These conventions, although imperfect, attempt to address the uncertainty in the reported times and distances and thereby reduce the temptation to put too fine an interpretation on events which are imprecisely chronicled. Given these arguments, the fundamental itineraries developed by Gray and Darling remain unchanged; they are merely modified to reflect my best guess at a level of uncertainty.

BIBLIOGRAPHY

"Massacred." Tribune, July 6 1876, 1.

"Regulations of the Army of the United States and General Orders in Force." 9, 1881.

"Revised Regulations of the Army of the United States.'" 9, 1861.

Ambrose, Stephen E. Crazy Horse and Custer: Meridian, 1986.

Anon. The Story of the Battle of the Washita [Web Site]. National Park Service, 1999 [cited 05/16/02 2002]. Available from www.nps.gov/waba/story/htm.

Asay, Karol. Gray Head and Long Hair: The Benteen-Custer Relationship. New York: The Mad Printers of Mattituck, 1983.

Bankes, James. "Wild Bill Hickok." Wild West, August 1996, 50.

Barnett, Louise. Touched by Fire. The Life, Death, and Mythic Afterlife of George Armstrong Custer. New York: Henry Holt and Company, 1996.

Bartoszynski, Robert and Niewiadomska-Bugaj, Magdelana. Probability and Statistical Inference. New York: John Wiley and Sons, 1996.

Beal, M. D. I Will Fight No More Forever - Chief Joesph and the Nez Perce War. New York: Ballantine Books, 1991.

Benteen, F. W. "Report to Reno (Via Wallace)." In The Little Big Horn, 1876: The Official Communications, Documents and Reports with Rosters of the Officers and Troops of the Campaign, edited by L. J. Overfield, II, 39-41. Lincoln: University of Nebraska Press, 1876.

Beyer, W. H., ed. CRC Standard Probability and Statistics Tables and Formulae. Boca Raton: CRC Press, 1991.

Brady, C. T. Indian Fights and Fighters. Lincoln: University of Nebraska Press, 1971.

Brininstool, E. A. Troopers with Custer. Harrisburg: Stackpole, 1952.

Carroll, J. M., ed. The Benteen-Goldin Letters on Custer and His Last Battle. Lincoln: University of Nebraska Press, 1991.

---, ed. Cavalry Scraps: The Writings of Frederick W. Benteen: Guidon Press, 1979.

---, ed. They Rode with Custer. Mattituck, N.Y.: J.M. Carrol & Co., 1993.

Connell, Evan S. Son of the Morning Star - Custer and the Little Bighorn. New York: Harper and Row, 1985.

Cooper, Marilyn. Kidder Massacre [Web Site]. Sherman County Historical Society, n.d. [cited 05/02/02 2002]. Available from www.goodlandnet.com/history/kidder.htm.

Darling, Roger. Benteen's Scout-to-the-Left. El Segundo: Upton and Sons, 1987.

---. Custer's Seventh Cavalry Comes to Dakota. El Segundo: Upton and Sons, 1989.

---. A Sad and Terrible Blunder, Geneals Terry and Custer at the Little Big Horn: New Discoveries. Vienna, VA: Potomac-Western Press, 1992.

DeWolf, James M. "The Diary and Letters of Dr. James Dewolf." North Dakota History 25, no. Nos. 2 and 3 (1958).

Dippie, Brian W. "Custer: The Indian Fighter." In The Custer Reader, edited by P. A. Hutton, 103-15. Lincoln: University of Nebraska Press, 1992.

Donahue, Michael. "On the Battlefield." Greasy Grass Magazine, May 1998, 2-17.

du Bois, C. G. Kick the Dead Lion. El Segundo: Upton and Sons, 1987.

Dustin, Fred. The Custer Tragedy. El Segundo: Upton and Sons, 1987.

Eales, A. B. Army Wives on the American Frontier. Boulder: Johnson Books, 1996.

Evans, D. C. Custer's Last Fight. Vol. I, Battle of the Little Big Horn. El Segundo, CA: Upton and Sons, 1999.

Faust, P. L., ed. Historical Times Illustrated Encyclopedia of the Civil War. Harper Perennial ed. New York: Harper Perennial, 1991.

Finerty, J. F. War-Path and Bivouac. Lincoln: University of Nebraska, 1966.

Foster, Robert. 9th Cavalry in Utah [Website]. 9th Memorial Cavalry - Buffalo Soldiers, n.d [cited May 13 2004]. Available from http://www.9thcavalry.com/utah.htm.

Fougera, K. G. With Custer's Cavalry. Lincoln: University of Nebraska Press, 1986.

Fox, R. A., Jr. Archaeology, History, and Custer's Last Battle: The Little Big Horn Reexamined. Norman: University of Oklahoma Press, 1993.

Frazer. Forts of the West. Norman: University of Oklahoma Press, 1965.

Frost, Lawrence A. The Court-Martial of General George Armstrong Custer. Norman: University of Oklahoma, 1987.

---. General Custer's Libbie. Seattle: Superior Publishing Company, 1976.

Gibbons, J. D. "Nonparametric Statistics." In Handbook of Statistical Methods for Engineers and Scientists, edited by H. M. Wadsworth, 11.1-11.26. New York: McGraw-Hill, 1990.

Godfrey, Edward S. "Custer's Last Battle." Century Magazine, January, 1892 1892, 43.

---. "Some Reminiscences, Including the Washita Battle, November 27, 1868." In The Custer Reader, edited by P. A. Hutton, 159-79. Lincoln: Univesity of Nebraska Press, 1992.

Graham, W. A. "Come On! Be Quick! Bring Packs!" In The Custer Myth, 287-300. Lincoln: University of Nebraska Press, 1923.

---. The Story of the Little Big Horn. Mechancisburg, PA: Stackpole Books, 1994.

Graham, W. W. The Custer Myth, a Source Book of Custeriana. Lincoln: University of Nebraska Press, 1986.

Gray, J. S. Custer's Last Campaign, Mitch Boyer and the Little Big Horn Reconstructed. Lincoln: University of Nebraska Press, 1991.

Greene, Jerome A. Evidence and the Custer Enigma: A Reconstructon of Indian-Military History. Reno, NV: Outbooks, 1979.

Guernsey, H. G. and Alden, H. M. Harper's Pictorial History of the Civil War. Facsimile ed. Fairfax: The Fairfax Press, 1977.

Hammer, Kenneth, ed. Custer in 76: Walter Camp's Notes on the Custer Fight. Norman: University of Oklahoma Press, 1990.

Hardoff, R. G., ed. Camp, Custer, and the Little Big Horn. El Segundo: Upton and Sons, 1997.
Hart, Herbert M. Frontier Forts of the West. Seattle: Superior Publishing Company, 1967.
Hoig, Stan. The Battle of the Washita. Garden City, N.Y.: Doubleday, 1976.
Huetter, R. A. "A History of Fort Duchene, Utah, and the Role of Its First Commanding Officer, Frederick W. Benteen." unpublished M.A., Brigham Young, 1990.
Hunt, Frazier and Robert. I Fought with Custer: The Story of Sergeant Windolph, Las Survivor of the Battle of the Little Big Horn. Lincoln: University of Nebraska Press, 1987.
Hutton, P. A., ed. The Custer Reader. Lincoln: University of Nebraska Press, 1992.
---. Phil Sheridan and His Army. Lincoln: University of Nebraska Press, 1985.
Jackson, Donald. Custer's Gold. Bison Book Edition ed. lincoln: University of Nebraska Press, 1972.
Julian, A. P. "Brevet Brigadier General Frederick W. Benteen." Atlanta Historical Bulletin XI (1966): 19-31.
Keegan, John. Intelligence in War. New York: Alfred A. Knopf, 2003.
Keenan, Jerry, ed. Encyclopedia of American Indian Wars, 1492-1890. Santa Barbara: ABC-CLIO, 1997.
Kinsley, D.A. Custer - a Soldier's Story. New York: Promontory Press, 1988.
Kulhman, Charles. Legend into History. Combined edition with Did Custer Disobey Orders at the Battle of the Little Big Horn? ed. Harrisburg: Stackpole, 1994.
Leckie, S. A. Elizabeth Bacon Custer and the Making of a Myth. Norman: University of Oklahoma Press, 1993.

Leonard, S. M. Frederick W. Benteen: Custer's Nemesis [Website]. www.americanhistory.about.com, 2001 [cited May 13 2004]. Available from http://americanhistory.about.com/library/prm/blcuster1.

Lewis, Lloyd. Sherman. New York: Smithmark Publishers, 1994.

Liddic, B. R. and Harbaugh, Paul, ed. Custer and Company: Walter Camp's Notes on the Custer Fight. Lincoln: University of Nebraska Press, 1995.

Marquis, T. B. Keep the Last Bullet for Yourself. New York: Two Continents Publishing Group and Reference Publications, 1976.

McChristian, D. C. The U.S. Army in the West, 1870-1880. Norman: University of Oklahoma Press, 1995.

Merington, Marguerite, ed. The Custer Story - the Life and Intimate Letters of General George A. Custer and His Wife Elizabeth. New York: Devin-Adair, 1950.

Michno, Gregory. The Mystery of E Troop. Missoula: Mountain Press Publishing Co., 1994.

Miles, N. A. Personal Recollections and Observations of General Nelson A. Miles. New York: Da Capo Press, 1969.

Millbrook, M. D. "The West Breaks in General Custer." In The Custer Reader, edited by P. A. Hutton, 116-58. Lincoln: University of Nebraska Press, 1992.

Miller, D. H. Custer's Fall: The Indian Side of the Story. Lincoln: University of Nebraska Press, 1985.

Miller, M. E. Hollow Victory: The White River Expedition of 1879 and the Battle of Milk Creek. Boulder: University of Colorado, 1997.

Mills, C. K. Harvest of Barren Regrets: The Army Career of Frederick William Benteen, 1834-1898. Glendale, CA: Arthur H. Clark, 1985.

Monaghan, Jay. Custer: The Life of General George Armstrong Custer. Lincoln: University of Nebraska Press, 1959.

Morris, William E. "Was Major Reno a Coward?" In That Fatal Day: Eight More with Custer, edited by J.W. and Davis Wengert, E. E., 25- 30. Howell, MI: Powder River Press, 1889-1898?

Nichols, R. H. In Custer's Shadow: Major Marcus Reno. Ft. Collins: The Old Army Press, 1999.

---, ed. Reno Court of Inquiry. Hardin, MT: Custer Battlefield Historical and Museum Association, 1996.

Nightengale, Robert. Little Big Horn: Far West Publishers, 1996.

O'Connor, Richard. Sheridan, the Inevitable. New York: Knoecky and Knoecky, 1993.

Overfield, L. J., II, ed. The Little Big Horn, 1876: The Official Communications, Documents and Reports. Lincoln: University of Nebraska, 1990.

Panzeri, Peter. Little Big Horn 1876: Custer's Last Stand. Edited by Lee Johnson, Campaign. Oxford: Osprey Publishing, 1995.

Quaife, M. M., ed. George Armstrong Custer, My Life on the Plains. Lincoln: University of Nebraska Press, 1966.

Quinnet, Paul. Darwin's Bass: The Evolutionary Psychology of Fishing Man. Kansas City: Andrews McMeel Publishing, 1998.

Rector, William G. "Fields of Fire: The Reno-Benteen Defense Perimeter." Montana: the Magazine of Western History 1966, 65-72.

Reedstrom, E. L. Bugles, Banners and War Bonnets. New York: Bonanza Books, 1978.

Rickey, Don Jr. Forty Miles a Day on Beans and Hay. Norman: University of Oklahoma Press, 1963.

---., 1999.

Sandoz, Mari. The Battle of the Little Big Horn. Lincoln: University of Nebraska, 1978.

Schindler, Harold. Benteen in Utah: Hero of the Little Bighorn, Brigham Young's Grandson Are Picture-Perfect Pair on Fort Douglas Porch; Benteen: Fallen Hero in Utah [Website]. www.historytogo.utah.gov (Salt Lake Tribune), 1997 [cited May 13 2004]. Available from http:///historytogo.utah.gov/72097benten.html.

Schoenberger, Dale T. End of Custer. Blaine, WA: Hancock House, 1995.

Scott, D. D., and Fox, R. A., Jr.,. Archaeological Insights into the Custer Battle. Norman: University of Oklahoma Press, 1987.

Scott, D. D., Fox, R. A., Jr., Connor, M. A., and Harmon, Dick. Archaeological Perspectives on the Battle of the Little Bighorn. Norman: University of Oklahoma Press, 1989.

Scott, H. L. Some Memories of a Soldier. Translated by Memories. New York: The Century Publishing Co., 1928.

Scott, Phil. "I Got Shot Down" Tales of Misery and Survival. Smithsonian Air and Space, May 2004 2004, 42-49.

Siegal, Sidney and Castellan, N. J., Jr. Nonparametric Statistics for the Behavioral Sciences. New York: McGraw-Hill, 1988.

Sklenar, Larry. To Hell with Honor. Norman: University of Oklahoma Press, 2000.

Stewart, E. I. Custer's Luck. Norman: University of Oklahoma Press, 1955.

Taylor, William O. With Custer on the Little Bighorn. New York: Viking Penguin, 1996.

Terrell, J. U. and Walton, George. Faint the Trumpet Sounds: The Life and Trail of Major Reno. New York: David McKay, 1966.

Tulapurkar, Shripad. "Review of 'How Many People Can the Earth Support?'" Science (1996).

Upton, Richard, ed. The Custer Adventure. el Segundo: Upton and Sons, 1990.

Urwin, Gregory J. W. Custer Victorious - the Civil War Battles of General Goerge Armstrong Custer. Lincoln: University of Nebraska Press, 1990.

Urwin, Gregory J. W. and Fagan, Roberta E., ed. Custer and His Times: Book Three, Custer and His Times. Conway, AR: University of Central Arkansas Press, 1987.

Utley, R. M. Cavalier in Buckskin. Norman: University of Oklahoma Press, 1988.

---. Custer and the Great Controversy. Pasadena: Westernlore Press, 1980.

---. Custer Battlefield National Monument, Montana. Washington, D.C.: National Park Service, 1969.

---. The Indian Frontier of the American West, 1846-1890. Albuquerque: University of New Mexico Press, 1984.

---. The Lance and the Shield. New York: Ballantine Books, 1994.

---, ed. Life in Custer's Cavalry: Diaries and Letters of Albert and Jennie Barnitz, 1867-1868. Lincoln: University of Nebraska Press, 1987.

Van de Water, F. F. Glory-Hunter: A Life of General Custer. Lincoln: University of Press, 1988.

Varga, Jon. "The Davis Tutt-Wild Bill Hickok Showdown Had Dramatic Buildup and Face-to-Face Action." Wild West 1996, 22-26, 82-85.

Varnum, Charles A. Custer's Chief of Scouts. Edited by J. M. Carroll. Lincoln: University of Nebraska, 1987.

Vestal, Stanley. Sitting Bull. Norman: University of Oklahoma Press, 1989.

Wagner, G. E. Old Neutriment. Lincoln: University of Nebraska, 1989.

Webb, Kerry. Brevet Union Generals of the Civil War www.alia.org.au, 2002 [cited May 13 2004]. Available from http://www.alia.org.au/~kwebb/Brevets/.

Wert, Jeffry D. Custer. The Controversial Life of George Armstrong Custer. New York: Simon and Schuster, 1996.

Whittaker, Frederick. A Complete Life of General George A. Custer. 2 vols. Lincoln: University of Nebraska Press, 1993.

---. "General George Armstrong Custer." Galaxy Magazine, September 1876, 362-71.

Willert, James. Little Big Horn Diary: A Chronicle of the 1876 Indian War. New ed. Vol. 6, Custer Trails Series. El Segundo: Upton and Sons, 1997.

---. March of the Columns: Chronicle of the 1876 Indian War, June 27 - September 16, 1876. Vol. 4, Custer Trails Series. El Segundo: Upton and Sons, 1994.

Woodward, Philip. My Own Right Time: An Exploration of Clockwork Design. New York: Oxford University Press, 1995.

About the author

Terrence J. Donovan is an experimental test pilot and research scientist. His professional interests are in the areas of airborne geophysics, remote sensing, intelligence and reconnaissance, and aircraft certification.